# THE ADAPTABLE FEAST

## SATISFYING MEALS FOR THE VEGETARIANS, VEGANS, AND OMNIVORES AT YOUR TABLE

*Ivy Manning*

Photography by Gregor Torrence

SASQUATCH BOOKS
SEATTLE

*This book is dedicated to Gregor, who challenges me to create mixed-diet meals every day, and to Alice B. Toklas, my eager recipe taster and the smartest dog in the world. May she be feasting in her next life.*

Printed in China

Published by Sasquatch Books

Distributed by PGW/Perseus

15 14 13 12 11 10 09    9 8 7 6 5 4 3 2 1

Cover photographs: Gregor Torrence
Cover design: Rosebud Eustace
Interior design and composition: Rosebud Eustace
Interior photographs: Gregor Torrence

Library of Congress Cataloging-in-Publication Data

Manning, Ivy.
  The adaptable feast : satisfying meals for the vegetarians, vegans, and omnivores at your table / Ivy Manning ; photography by Gregor Torrence.
      p. cm.
  Includes bibliographical references and index.
  ISBN-13: 978-1-57061-583-2
  ISBN-10: 1-57061-583-7
  1. Cookery. 2. Vegetarian cookery. 3. Cookery, International. I. Title.
  TX714.M3393 2009
  641.5'636—dc22
                              2009018963

Sasquatch Books
119 South Main Street, Suite 400
Seattle, WA 98104
(206) 467-4300
www.sasquatchbooks.com
custserv@sasquatchbooks.com

# TABLE OF CONTENTS

# ACKNOWLEDGMENTS

The amount of work it took to reinvent recipes for the mixed-diet format and edit them to create clean, understandable sets of instructions was a Herculean task. I'd like to thank my editor Gary Luke for trusting in my idea and project editor Rachelle Longé for being patient, funny, and very organized. Thanks also to Andy Manning and all of the other mixed-diet cooks who were eager to try my recipes and give me honest feedback. And finally, a heartfelt thank-you to my husband, Gregor Torrence, who has stuck to his vegetarian guns all this time.

# GETTING STARTED IN A MIXED-DIET KITCHEN

Ethical omnivore, vegetarian, "flexitarian," pescatarian, vegan. Our vocabulary is quickly evolving to describe the way Americans are changing their eating habits for reasons of health, ethics, and the environment. With all these dietary variations, it's common for families to have vegetarians or vegans in their ranks while the rest of the family eats meat. So how do you cook for everyone in a mixed-diet family without making two separate meals every night or shortchanging vegetarians or vegans by serving them nothing but tofu dogs or side dishes?

I have learned from personal experience just how challenging these questions can be. When I met my vegetarian husband, friends said it would never work. "You are far too good at cooking meat," they scoffed. "You'll have him eating your barbecued ribs in no time, or you'll go your separate ways." I must admit that in the beginning of our relationship, I urged Mr. Tofu to cave to my meat-eating ways. Eventually I realized that I needed to respect his dietary choices, so I switched to cooking vegetarian food for both of us, but I often missed eating meat. Finally, I began tinkering with dishes I had been cooking for years, making some of each dish vegetarian while still adding meat to my portion.

It's been five years now, and Mr. Tofu and I are married (against some friends' bets), and cooking mixed-diet meals is now second nature to me. My husband appreciates that I no longer plead with him to try a bit of chicken, and I love that I can have my old familiar favorites with a bit of sustainably raised meat in them. Plus, I've become more open-minded and have learned to love tofu, seitan, and other vegetarian proteins. We're living proof that harmony can happen; it just takes an open mind and an adventurous spirit in the kitchen to make it work.

*The Adaptable Feast* will show you how to cook for omnivores, vegetarians, and vegans on every occasion, whether it's a weeknight quick fix for your immediate family, cocktail nibbles for a group, or a special-occasion holiday meal when you want everyone to feel welcome, no matter their dining preference. This book will show you how to cook one meal by preparing a portion with tasty protein-rich meat alternatives like tofu, seitan, or beans and the rest with sustainably raised meat or seafood. With more than eighty-five recipes ranging from familiar favorites like Red Chile Enchiladas with Chicken or

Tempeh (page 118) to exciting Asian fare like Pad Thai with Shrimp or Tofu (page 150), this book will show you how to cook delicious, nutritionally balanced meals for the whole family without dirtying every pan in the kitchen or discounting anyone's diet.

Whether you are a curious omnivore who would like to test the vegetarian or vegan waters without jumping in completely, or you are the designated cook in a mixed-diet family who is tired of doing double duty, this book will launch you into a world where meat eaters, vegetarians, and vegans can sit together and share scrumptious meals in harmony.

## A PLEA FOR RESPONSIBLE OMNIVORISM

What we choose to eat has environmental, social, and economic impact. If you choose to eat meat, I urge you to be mindful of where it comes from. Animals that are raised in inhumane factory farms are not only subjected to undeserved cruelty but are also less safe and less savory to eat. Please seek out beef and lamb from animals that are grass fed, genuinely free range and organic poultry, and pigs that are raised humanely. Buy sustainable fish that are caught only from fisheries deemed healthy. (See Recommended Reading and Media for informative Web sites that can help you make smart choices when buying meat and fish.) It's not only vegetarians and vegans who should be mindful of what they eat; it's every-vore.

# THE ADAPTABLE FEAST METHOD

The recipes in this book follow the same conventions found in standard recipes, with one difference. At some point in the instructions while you are chopping, stirring, and prepping each meal, you'll come across a step or steps marked **VEGETARIAN**. The instructions that follow (set in bold type) will be specifically for the vegetarian or vegan portion of the recipe so you will know when you are cooking that something should remain meat-free. At times this section can be as simple as setting aside a vegetarian portion of the recipe at the end of cooking before adding meat to the remaining dish, as with recipes like Fried Green Tomatoes (and Sometimes Bacon) with Smokey Blue Cheese (page 25). In other recipes the meal is made up of individual servings, like the Antipasto Calzones (page 67), so while most of the servings are made with Italian sausage (for instance), the rest is made with a tasty vegetarian protein alternative. In other recipes, the basis of the dish is the same for both omnivores and vegetarians or vegans, but it is separated into two portions before incorporating the proteins. In the recipe for Shepherd's Pie (page 129), for example, a vegetable-based stew is divided into two baking dishes. Soy crumbles are added to one dish and ground lamb is added to the other.

If there happens to be a vegan in your ranks, never fear! Over half of the vegetarian recipe variations in this book also happen to be vegan. The vegan recipes are clearly marked with a **V** beside the recipe title. Additionally, wherever possible, I have included a Vegan Variation note at the end of a recipe where a few changes to the existing instructions can make the vegetarian portion of the recipe suitable for vegans.

The Adaptable Feast method may seem a bit foreign at first, but after you try a few recipes, I am sure you will find it almost as simple as cooking single-diet meals, and with time you'll be able to apply the same adaptable principles to your own recipes.

## TRANSITIONING TO MIXED-DIET COOKING

Beyond the tempting recipes, I've also included sections to help you transition all your cooking to the mixed-diet format. The Alternative Protein Primer (see page xvii) demystifies the world of meat alternatives so you can confidently add everything from edamame to tempeh to your cooking. A section on umami (see page xii) explains how to use ingredients naturally high in glutamates to make meals taste more satisfying, meat or no. The Special Occasions chapter provides do-ahead vegetarian alternatives for those who won't be partaking of the Thanksgiving turkey, Christmas roast, or St. Patrick's Day corned beef, and the Basics chapter helps with tricky substitutions for common meat-based ingredients like chicken stock and fish sauce.

## CHANGING THE QUANTITIES

Because most mixed-diet families tend to be weighted toward omnivores, these recipes serve one to two vegetarians or vegans and three to four omnivore adults. (I specify servings before each recipe.) If more flexible eaters want to try a vegetarian dish or you are feeding more vegetarians, you can double the vegetarian ingredients in most recipes to make additional meat-free portions. When you double a portion of the recipe, however, use common sense. A chart with teaspoon-tablespoon-cup conversions can help you change the quantities, but with strong spices like cayenne, rosemary, and sage, you may need to add them to taste instead of doubling them.

## KEEP UTENSILS SEPARATE

When you're sautéing, stirring, and setting the table all at the same time, it can be tricky to remember which spoon was used to stir the beef broth and which was for the vegetarian soup. To keep things straight, I have one utensil holder full of wooden spoons and colorful spatulas that I use exclusively for vegetarian cooking. In another holder I keep a set of metal spoons that I use only for meaty food. In addition to the utensils, I keep my cutting boards separate. So there is never a question about cross-contamination, I do all my vegetable prep on wooden cutting boards, and I cut meat and seafood on a dishwasher-safe plastic cutting board with a grippy bottom. Some vegetarians and vegans insist that food be cooked in pans that have never seen a speck of meat. If that is the case in your home, I suggest you buy a set of good-quality pots and pans and use the smaller ones (the small saucepot and sauté pan, for instance) only for vegetarian cooking.

# THE MIXED-DIET PANTRY

Though most of the dishes I make now are virtually the same as they were in my pre–Mr. Tofu days, I have added a few items beyond tofu and seitan to my pantry to make cooking mixed-diet meals tastier. I recommend having the following on hand:

**BOUILLON CUBES AND DEMI-GLACE BASE:** Vegetable stock is usually a good substitute for chicken or beef stock. However, some recipes, like French Onion Soup (page 31), don't taste right to most omnivores unless they have a meaty flavor. In such cases, I add a good-quality bouillon cube or veal demi-glace base to the omnivores' portions to add the rich, savory character omnivores expect in certain dishes. I like the widely available Knorr chicken and beef bouillon cubes and Better Than Gourmet demi-glace bases (see Resources). If you add bouillon cubes to a dish, season to taste with salt at the end of cooking to account for the cubes' ample sodium content.

**CANNED BEANS:** Though I'd love to tell you that I am always organized enough to soak dried beans overnight and simmer them from scratch, it just isn't the case. I always have several cans of garbanzo, cannellini, pinto, and black beans on hand to add to recipes when protein and flavor are needed. Though the brand I use varies depending on the bean, I read labels carefully and make sure to buy beans that are not loaded with sodium. Always rinse and drain canned beans well to remove the thick, salty liquid they are packed in.

**DRIED MUSHROOMS AND MUSHROOM POWDER:** Mushrooms add depth and a rounded umami flavor to dishes, and they are especially good at making vegetarian foods taste rich and "meaty." I find dried mushrooms especially useful because they keep well in the cupboard and need only to be reconstituted before being added to stir-fries, soups, and sauces. I buy dried shiitakes in large packages from Asian markets—the quality is always better and the price is much lower than in gourmet shops. I also love dried porcini mushrooms; they have a sweet, earthy flavor that adds great depth to risotto, soups, and stews. If you have a spice grinder (a coffee-bean grinder used just for spices), try grinding dried porcini mushrooms into a powder and use it as you would bouillon cubes to add savory flavor to sauces and soups.

**LENTILS DU PUY:** These small dark green-gray lentils, sometimes labeled French lentils, hold their shape when cooked, are tender in about 20 minutes, and serve as a great stand-in for ground meat in most stews, chilis, and casseroles. They can be found in bulk in natural food stores or online (see Resources).

**PARMIGIANO-REGGIANO CHEESE:** Several recipes call for Parmigiano-Reggiano cheese. When I say Parmigiano-Reggiano, I mean the imported hard Italian cheese, not the waxy, domestic, shredded cheese or the horrible sandy stuff that comes in a green can. Parmigiano-Reggiano is not cheap, but it has an intense flavor so you don't have to use much to really taste it. Find it at most grocery stores and cheese shops in wedges or in tubs already grated. You can also order it online from gourmet cheese companies (see Resources).

**VEGETABLE AND MUSHROOM STOCKS:** Chicken stock is used in most kitchens as the neutral base for countless sauces, gravies, and soups. Since chicken stock is obviously out of bounds for vegetarians, I've learned to cook with vegetable stock instead. I find most canned varieties to be very strongly flavored (and salty), so I make my own (see the Basics chapter for recipes). Homemade stocks are quick to make, don't use much space in the freezer, and add a distinctive homemade flavor. When I don't have homemade vegetable stock on hand, I use Imagine brand No-Chicken Stock or Pacific Foods Mushroom Stock because they both have a clean, neutral flavor and neither needs to be diluted.

Another great staple is vegetarian "no-chicken" bouillon powder—an all-natural bouillon that uses richly flavored yeast extract to make a light, flavorful golden stock. I use the Harvest Vegetarian Bouillon Mix chicken flavor, which you can find at Asian markets and in the bulk foods section of health food stores.

## MMM, UMAMI

If you've ever enjoyed the hearty, delicious flavor of a pasta sauce rich with Parmigiano-Reggiano cheese, or a mouthwatering ripe tomato salad, or the "meaty" savor of a dish rich in shiitake mushrooms, you've gotten up close and personal with umami. It may sound exotic, but it is actually the fifth taste receptor on our tongues—right next to the receptors that tell us if something is salty, sour, sweet, or bitter.

In 1908 a curious chemist from Tokyo named Kikunae Ikeda wanted to isolate the cause of the distinct, delicious flavor of dashi, the basic stock familiar to Americans as the base for miso soup. After painstaking work, he isolated the naturally occurring glutamates (an amino acid) in the kombu kelp used to make dashi as the source of the distinct flavor sensation he called umami—roughly translated as "delicious essence." The chemist went on to develop the highly concentrated food additive monosodium glutamate (MSG), which is now a popular flavor enhancer in Asian dishes and a sometimes-reviled food additive in the United States.★

Ikeda's umami theory remained just a theory until 2000, when researchers at Miami University discovered the specific taste receptors on our tongues that perceive umami, making it officially our fifth basic taste sensation.

The list of foods naturally high in glutamates and three other nucleotides that contribute to umami flavor includes a wide range of fermented foods and foods high in protein like roasted meat, ham, shellfish, meat stocks, fish sauce, and even breast milk.

Fortunately, there is also a wealth of vegetarian sources for natural umami flavor—tomatoes, mushrooms, potatoes, aged cheeses, fermented soy products like soy sauce and miso, fermented black bean sauce, truffles, sea vegetables (think nori seaweed), and dried shiitake mushrooms, to name a few.

Using ingredients high in natural glutamates is especially helpful if you are a vegetarian or are transitioning to a mostly plant-based diet: it adds a rich, satiating quality to dishes, so you are less likely to miss the meat. The following chart, showing some of the most valuable players on the umami team and their relative quantities of umami-boosting glutamates, will help you on your way to umami-rich cooking. For more information see the Bibliography.

---

★ The debate over MSG still rages. Though the U.S. Food and Drug Administration has not been able to find any long-term negative effects from consuming the additive MSG and has declared it safe, there are those who swear they suffer adverse affects after consuming it. If you feel you are MSG-sensitive, read food labels and avoid products that contain it. The foods discussed in the chart on page xiv contain natural levels of glutamates and are perfectly safe, whereas MSG is a highly concentrated additive, which may account for the sensitivity some have to the product.

## *Glutamates in Foods*

| DAIRY AND OTHER SOURCES | (MILLIGRAMS PER 100 GRAMS) |
|---|---|
| PARMIGIANO-REGGIANO CHEESE | 1200–1600 |
| SOY SAUCE | 782–1090 |

| MEAT, POULTRY, AND SEAFOOD | |
|---|---|
| BEEF | 107 |
| CHICKEN | 1.5–44 |
| CURED HAM | 337 |
| FISH SAUCE | 950 |
| PORK | 2.5–40 |
| SARDINES | 280 |
| SHRIMP | 43 |

| VEGETABLES | |
|---|---|
| PEAS | 200 |
| POTATOES | 102 |
| RIPE TOMATOES | 246 |
| SHIITAKE MUSHROOMS | 71 |
| SOYBEANS | 66 |
| TRUFFLES | 8.5 |

# GETTING ENOUGH PROTEIN IN MIXED-DIET MENUS

If you are cooking for vegetarians or vegans and worry about providing them with sufficient protein, you are not alone. Recent nutritional fads have misled the public into believing that we can never get too much protein. However, protein deficiency is very rare in developed nations. In fact, in America the health problems associated with getting too much protein are much more common than health problems from protein deficiencies. Medical studies published in leading clinical journals have linked high-protein high-cholesterol meat-based diets with serious health problems like heart disease, osteoporosis, and even cancer.

Protein *is* important. We are quite literally made of protein: our skin, hair, muscles, hemoglobin, and the antibodies in our immune systems are made mostly of protein. Protein is essential for muscle development and repair, cognitive function, and many other actions our bodies perform daily. Of the twenty amino acids that make up protein, our bodies can synthesize eleven, but nine we must get from food.

The nine indispensable amino acids are found in meat, fish, eggs, dairy, and a few plant-based sources like quinoa and soybeans. Vegetables, legumes, and nuts also contain amino acids but are considered incomplete because they do not contain all the amino acids we need from food in a single source. That said, consuming a varied daily diet made up of beans *and* rice or grains *and* nuts will ensure that vegetarians get the full range of amino acids. In other words, vegetarians cannot live on tofu dogs alone.

So how much protein should we be getting? As with seemingly all nutritional issues, controversy abounds. The official figures from the RNI (Reference Nutrient Intake, formerly titled Recommended Daily Allowance) recommend that the average adult consume .37 grams of protein per pound of body weight per day, or about 15 percent of overall calories. To calculate the grams, take your healthy (ideal) weight and multiply by .37. For instance, a 130-pound woman would multiply 130 by .37 to get 48.1 grams of protein per day.

Seems simple, but scientists, nutritionists, and dieticians have recently noted that adults who exercise or who are dieting, pregnant, or elderly may need as much as 20 percent of their calories to be lean protein (multiply your weight by .45 to .54). And because infants and children are still growing, they need more protein relative to their body weight, about 20 to 28 grams per day for kids 4 to 10 years old and 12 to 15 grams per day for kids under the age of 4.★

There's no need to panic about all these numbers. Getting enough protein isn't really all that difficult for omnivores, vegetarians, or vegans as long as they eat a balanced diet with a variety of foods. If you are concerned about transitioning to a vegetarian or vegan diet, consult your doctor first.

The following table will give you an idea of how easy it is to get the recommended grams of protein just by eating a healthy, balanced diet.

## *Grams of Protein in Foods*★★

| FOOD | GRAMS PROTEIN |
|------|---------------|
| BROCCOLI, RAW FLORETS (3.5 OUNCES) | 2.98 |
| BROWN RICE (3.5 OUNCES) | 2.58 |
| CHICKEN (3.5 OUNCES) | 26 |
| EGG (LARGE, HARD-BOILED) | 6.29 |
| GARBANZO BEANS (3.5 OUNCES) | 8.86 |
| GROUND BEEF (3.5 OUNCES) | 26 |
| KIDNEY BEANS (3.5 OUNCES) | 8.6 |
| LENTILS (3.5 OUNCES) | 9 |
| 2% MILK (8 OUNCES) | 9.72 |
| MOZZARELLA CHEESE, PART SKIM (3.5 OUNCES) | 24.26 |
| MUESLI CEREAL (3.5 OUNCES) | 9.7 |
| PARMESAN CHEESE (3.5 OUNCES) | 38.46 |
| PLAIN YOGURT (8 OUNCES) | 12.86 |
| SOY MILK (8 OUNCES) | 7–8 |
| TEMPEH (3.5 OUNCES) | 18.1 |
| TOFU, FIRM (3.5 OUNCES) | 9 |
| TOFU, SOFT (3.5 OUNCES) | 6.55 |

★ National Academy of Sciences. "Dietary Reference Intakes (DRIs): Recommended Intakes for Individuals, Vitamins." 2004.

★★ Values derived from www.nal.usda.gov/fnic/foodcomp/search, the USDA National Agricultural Library's searchable food database.

# ALTERNATIVE PROTEIN PRIMER

Several products can help both vegetarians and vegans get the essential proteins they need and boost the texture and flavor of their meals. The array of soy and other plant-based meat alternatives may seem daunting at first, but after trying just a few, I'm sure you'll find them to be workable and valuable additions to your pantry.

EDAMAME (pronounced *ed-ah-MOM-eh*): These fresh, unshelled soybean pods have been a popular snack in Asia for thousands of years, and for good reason. They are a dietary goldmine, not only because they are high in protein (11 grams per half cup shelled) but also because they contain all the essential amino acids. Edamame are also a great source of plant hormones called isoflavones, phytoestrogens that have been linked to regulating insulin and lowering cholesterol. Edamame come frozen and fresh, in the pod or shelled. For a simple snack, try edamame steamed or boiled. Sprinkle them with sea salt mixed with a pinch of ground ginger powder and pop the sweet little beans out of their inedible shells right into your mouth. Shelled edamame can be used wherever a recipe calls for peas (see Vegetable and Chicken Korma with Cashews on page 171, or Primavera Potpies on page 137).

MISO: Miso is a fermented soybean and grain paste used in Asian cooking. Though high in sodium, miso adds lots of flavor and protein to soups, dressings, and stews. It is available in refrigerated plastic tubs at Asian and health food stores in a range of colors from white to rich brown, depending on the grains used and the fermentation time. The darker the color, the stronger the flavor. Try miso in Japanese Eggplant and Halibut with Miso Glaze (page 69). Miso will keep in the refrigerator indefinitely.

QUORN: Quorn is a brand of meat alternative made from a naturally occurring mycoprotein from the fungus family called *Fusarium venenatum*. Its texture is something like chicken and its flavor is neutral. It's most common in frozen convenience foods like MorningStar Farms' Chik'n Nuggets, cutlets, and ground-meat substitutes. Some people suffer intestinal distress from eating it; try a small amount before diving in.

SEITAN (pronounced *SAY-tan*): Also called "wheat meat," this high-protein product (20 to 26 grams for a 4-ounce serving) has a dense, chewy texture and a mild flavor. Seitan is made from high-protein wheat that has all the starch rinsed away until only the insoluble gluten remains. The resulting springy ball of dough is simmered in stock, deep fried, or steamed. Originally a Chinese invention, seitan commonly appears on Asian menus with whimsical names like "Mock Duck," "Mock Chicken," or "Mock Abalone." Packaged seitan, available at health food stores and some grocery stores, is often expensive and high in sodium, though it is handy in a pinch. Making seitan is quite easy, so I encourage you to try my Homemade Seitan recipe (page 229); it takes only minutes to mix and freezes well.

**SOY CRUMBLES:** Also labeled "recipe crumbles" or "smart ground" among other names, soy crumbles are made of textured vegetable protein TVP blended with other texture-giving ingredients like chicory-root fiber (inulin) to make a reliable ground-beef alternative. Try it in the Homemade Sloppy Joes and Josephines (page 86).

**TEMPEH:** A traditional Indonesian food, tempeh (pronounced *TEMP-ay*) is a dense cake of whole soybeans inoculated with an edible white mold (similar to the one used to make blue cheese) that makes the soy more digestible and lends the tempeh a savory, yeasty flavor. Tempeh is best when crisped up in a bit of oil by pan frying, deep frying, or oven roasting. It's an acquired taste, but some find it a welcome addition to stir-fries and casseroles like Red Chile Enchiladas with Chicken or Tempeh (page 118).

**TEXTURED VEGETABLE PROTEIN:** TVP, as it's often called, is a dried granular product made from defatted soy flour (the byproduct of making soybean oil). It must be reconstituted in water or stock, thereby making a rich, crumbly product that does well as a stand-in for ground beef. It is a primary ingredient of many meatless soy crumbles on the market. Try the Orecchiette and Meatballs recipe (page 101) to learn how adaptable TVP can be.

**TOFU, DEEP-FRIED:** Found at Asian markets, often labeled *age* (pronounced *AH-jay*), these deep-fried cubes are handy when you need tofu that will keep its shape. It is popular in Southeast Asia as a noodle-soup ingredient, and it absorbs marinades well, as in Thai Satays with Spicy Cucumber Salad (page 12). You may wish to soak fried tofu briefly in boiling water to remove excess oil and press dry with paper towels before using, especially when adding it to soups. Deep-fried tofu freezes well without damaging its spongy texture.

**TOFU, FRESH:** Fresh tofu is made from soy milk that is coagulated with lemon juice, magnesium, calcium chloride, or calcium sulfate so curds form, similar to the cheese-making process. The curds are drained and pressed to create cakes in varying degrees of firmness, from soft to extra firm. Firm and extra-firm fresh tofu is the best choice for stir-fries and other preparations when you want the tofu to hold its shape, like Bibimbap (page 175). Soft, fresh tofu is best puréed in soups and dips.

**TOFU, NIGARI** (pronounced *KNEE-gar-ee*): *Nigari* tofu, often labeled "Japanese-style tofu," is a fresh tofu coagulated with nigari (magnesium chloride). This tofu is generally firm and spongy, which makes it a favorite for searing, grilling, and stir-frying in recipes like Kung Pao Chicken or Tofu (page 179).

**TOFU, SILKEN:** Silken tofu is produced in a process similar to yogurt, thickened with glucono-delta-lactone (a naturally occurring food additive) instead of being coagulated, drained, and pressed. Its texture is softer than fresh tofu thanks to a higher water content; it also has a milder flavor. It is sold in aseptic boxes on grocery shelves and does not need to be refrigerated until the package is opened. It is generally fragile and works best blended into puddings, smoothies, or soups like Roasted Squash or Shrimp Bisque (page 53). It can also be added as a garnish to clear soups, such as the Miso Soup with Tofu or Clams (page 29).

**TOFURKY:** Tofurky is a brand of organic tofu-seitan products owned by Turtle Island Foods Company. Among the myriad meat substitute products on the market, I like Tofurky because soy isolates and other mega-processed ingredients are not used to create products like sausages and the popular Tofurky Roast, a roast turkey alternative popular with vegetarians and vegans. I use their sausages—bratwurst, kielbasa, and Italian—as a stand-in for meat sausage in recipes like Deep-Dish Chicago-Style Pizzas (page 91).

# ▼ IS FOR VEGAN

Vegans choose to go beyond the standard vegetarian diet to avoid all animal-derived products, including dairy products, eggs, gelatin, and honey. Many recipes in this book are already suitable for vegan diets, and they are labeled with a large ▼ beside the recipe title. In addition, recipes that can be converted from vegetarian to vegan easily have Vegan Variation instructions at the end of the recipe. For the most part, cooking for omnivores and vegans at the same time can be as easy as cooking for vegetarians and omnivores.

Some common foods, however, are of concern to those wishing to completely eliminate animal products from their diet. If you are cooking for a vegan, you must become a label reader. Hidden animal products like casein, whey, lactose, honey, and gelatin are added to packaged foods that would otherwise seem animal product–free. The following ingredients either have hidden animal sources or are not technically vegan. For more information on veganism and vegan ingredients, see Recommended Reading.

**CHEESE:** Cheese is made from dairy products and sometimes animal-derived rennet. Though there are vegetarian cheeses made without rennet, the use of dairy milk makes cheese a nonvegan food. Vegan cheeses are on the market, but most do not melt and are an acquired taste at best. Try a range of vegan cheeses, available at health food stores, to find one that suits you. In place of Parmigiano-Reggiano, try using nutritional yeast to taste in recipes (see Glossary) to give vegan foods a nutty, cheesy flavor.

**GELATIN:** Used in packaged foods to thicken and stabilize them, gelatin is made from collagen derived from animal bones, hides, and skin. Some vegan alternatives are agar-agar, kudzu, and xanthan gum.

**HONEY:** Bees produce honey, so honey is technically an animal product. Some vegans avoid honey. A good alternative is maple syrup or agave nectar (see Glossary).

**MAYONNAISE:** Mayo is made from eggs and oil. A good alternative is tofu-based Nayonaise, made by Nasoya, available where tofu products are sold.

**MILK (COW'S, SHEEP'S, GOAT'S):** Substitute with soy, rice, or nut milk. When cooking savory foods or baking, be sure to use unsweetened nondairy milks—many have sweeteners in them even when labeled "plain."

**PASTA:** Some commercial dried pastas contain eggs. Read the labels to be sure.

**SUGAR:** Some vegans eschew refined cane sugar because about half of all sugar is processed with charcoal that is sometimes made from bone char. Beet sugar, which looks exactly like cane sugar, is not refined in the same way and is therefore vegan. Unfortunately, labels seldom disclose the sugar's source. Ditto for powdered sugar and brown sugar. Unrefined sugar, available at natural food stores, and certain brands that have been confirmed vegan (see Resources) are acceptable for vegans.

## VEGANISM AND NUTRITION

According to the American Dietetic Association, vegan diets can be healthy and nutritionally adequate for people of any age, provided they are well planned and supplemented with multivitamins. Of particular concern is the intake of the vitamin B-12. This vitamin is naturally occurring in meat, but reliable sources cannot be found in plant foods with the exception of certain brands of nutritional yeast.* Since B-12 is essential for cell division and blood formation, a deficiency can result in serious health problems. Vegan vitamin supplements that contain B-12 and B-vitamin-fortified foods like nutritional yeast, soy milk, cereals, and meat alternatives are important additions to all vegan diets. The bottom line? If you are considering transitioning to a vegan diet, consult a doctor, naturopath, or dietician to learn how to make it work for you.

---

*Mangels, Reed, Ph.D., R.D. "Vitamin B12 in the Vegan Diet." www.vrg.org/nutrition/b12.htm.

# 1

## APPETIZERS AND SALADS

There's nothing better than a little nibble or light salad to start out a memorable meal. Since the first course sets the tone for any meal or get-together, it's important to make something that welcomes everyone, no matter what the diet.

The appetizers here range from satisfying salads to elegant finger food, and though they are great warm-ups to a main course, most can be made into light entrées by adding rice, a vegetable side dish, or a green salad.

Making appetizers for a mixed-diet crowd is a snap, but serving them can be a bit of challenge. No matter what sort of note or polite explanation you give that some of the food is **FOR VEGETARIAN GUESTS ONLY**, omnivores will inevitably be curious and gobble them up, despite your best efforts. One solution is to make equal numbers of vegetarian and meat appetizers so you're less likely to run out of the vegetarian nibbles. Another, more reliable tactic is to pass the vegan or vegetarian version only to your vegetarian or vegan guests.

# CRUNCHY SALAD ROLLS WITH COCONUT PEANUT SAUCE

*Makes 4 vegetarian and 6 omnivore rolls*

Salad rolls are a guaranteed hit, the delicate rice paper wraps filled with rice vermicelli, veggies, and peanut sauce are a favorite with kids and adults alike. Sadly, the rolls offered at most restaurants are filled with iceberg lettuce and little else. These rolls are full of tons of fresh herbs and other goodies like Chinese barbecued pork (found at Asian markets and grocery stores) or marinated baked tofu, so they are much tastier than your average salad roll.

Working with rice paper wraps can seem difficult at first, but you'll get the technique down after just a few tries, I promise. If the filling bursts out of the wrapper, just start over with a fresh wrapper and a little less filling.

**SAUCE:** 1 cup coconut milk, stirred

1½ teaspoons Thai red curry paste, such as Thai Kitchen (see **KEEPING IT VEGETARIAN**)

4 teaspoons Vegan Fish Sauce (page 228)

1 tablespoon sugar

½ cup all-natural sugar-free peanut butter (I use Adams 100% Natural)

**SALAD ROLLS:** 8 ounces rice vermicelli noodles

2 cups grated carrots

½ cup basil leaves, loosely packed

1 cup cilantro leaves, loosely packed

2 green onions, cut into thin 2-inch-long strips

4 ounces firm, baked tofu, such as Wildwood Royal Thai Flavor, cut into 2-inch-long by ½-inch-thick sticks

10 rice paper wrappers

5 ounces Chinese barbecued pork, cut into 18 thin slices

12 cooked shrimp, peeled and deveined

1. Combine the coconut milk, curry paste, vegan fish sauce, sugar, and peanut butter in a blender and blend until combined. Add more vegan fish sauce or curry to taste if you like. Set aside. (The sauce can be refrigerated in an airtight container for up to 4 days.)

2. Bring 8 cups of water to a boil. Add the noodles, stir, and turn off the heat. Let the noodles sit, stirring from time to time until they are pliable and tender when bitten into, 8 to 10 minutes. Drain and rinse well with cold water, drain again, and put them in a bowl.

3. Fill a teakettle or pot with about 8 cups of water and bring to a boil. Set out the carrots, basil leaves, cilantro leaves, green onions, and tofu on a dinner plate.

4. **VEGETARIAN: Fill a pie plate with some of the boiling water and slip 1 rice paper wrapper into the water. Let the paper soften for a few seconds. When it is pliable, carefully take it out with your fingers and place it flat on a cutting board. Put about ¼ cup of the noodles in the center of the bottom half of the rice paper. Top with some carrots, basil leaves, cilantro leaves, and green onions and 2 strips of the tofu. Bring the bottom edge of the rice paper up and over the filling and tuck it under the filling. Fold the left and right sides over the filling as if wrapping up a burrito, and roll up the wrapper to make a tight cylinder. Place it seam side down on a plate and cover with plastic wrap. Make 3 more vegetarian rolls, cover, and set aside.**

5. Replace the water in the pie plate with fresh hot water. To make the omnivore rolls, place ¼ cup of the noodles and some of the basil leaves, cilantro, and green onions on a wrapper, lift the bottom edge up and over, and tuck the wrapper under the filling. Place 3 slices of pork and 2 shrimp on the wrapper just where you've tucked the wrapper under the noodles. Fold in the sides and roll up tightly, place on another plate, and cover with plastic wrap. Make 5 more omnivore rolls and cover with plastic wrap.

6. Pour the peanut sauce into individual dipping bowls and serve the salad rolls immediately. (Leftover salad rolls can be wrapped individually in plastic

wrap and refrigerated for up to 1 day. Let rolls come to room temperature for 30 minutes before serving.)

**KEEPING IT VEGETARIAN:** Be sure to read the label—some prepared Thai curry pastes contain shrimp paste. Thai Kitchen red curry paste is vegan.

# HUM BAO: STEAMED BUNS WITH BARBECUED PORK OR BAKED TOFU

*Makes 15 vegan and 15 omnivore buns*

I love dumplings of all types, especially Chinese *hum bao*. The fluffy steamed dumplings filled with marinated *char siu* (barbecued pork loin) are great fun to make at home, but the process is quite time consuming if you make the dough and filling from scratch. I cheat and use frozen raw bread-dough rolls and stuff the buns with ready-to-eat Chinese barbecued pork or marinated baked tofu.

I steam the buns in a two-level bamboo steamer; the bamboo absorbs moisture so the *hum bao* cook to fluffy perfection without being doused in condensation. You can bake the rolls as well.

> 30 small balls of frozen bread dough (I like Rhodes Bake-N-Serve dinner rolls)
> ¼ cup hoisin sauce
> 4 teaspoons soy sauce
> 4 teaspoons Chinese rice wine or dry sherry
> 2 teaspoons cornstarch
> ¼ cup water
> 6 ounces savory baked tofu, cut into ¼-inch dice (1 cup)
> 4 ounces Chinese barbecued pork, cut into ¼-inch dice (1 cup)

1. Four hours before making the *hum bao*, let the dough thaw. Spray a baking sheet with nonstick cooking spray and place the rolls at least 2 inches apart on the sheet. Spray a piece of plastic wrap large enough to cover the baking sheet with nonstick cooking spray and then loosely cover the rolls. Let them thaw and rise at room temperature until doubled in size, about 4 hours.

(Alternatively, cover and let the rolls thaw on a baking sheet in the refrigerator for up to 24 hours.)

2. Combine the hoisin sauce, soy sauce, and rice wine in a small saucepan. Place the cornstarch in a small measuring cup and gradually whisk in the water; add the mixture to the saucepan. Bring to a simmer over medium heat and cook until thick and bubbly, about 2 minutes. Spray both racks of a bamboo steamer with nonstick cooking spray. Cut thirty 1- by 3-inch strips of parchment paper.

3. **VEGETARIAN: In a small bowl, combine half of the hoisin mixture with the tofu.**

4. In another small bowl, combine the remaining hoisin mixture with the pork. Hold 1 roll in your palm and flatten it slightly in the center. Spoon 1 tablespoon of the pork filling into the center; bring the edges up and over the filling and pinch together at the top to create a small purse. Place the bun, pinched side down, on a strip of the parchment paper. Repeat with the remaining pork filling and dough to make 15 buns. Place half the buns, resting on the parchment strips, in the lower rack of a bamboo steamer leaving at least 1 inch of space between each bun. You will need to steam the buns in 2 batches; keep the remaining pork buns covered with plastic wrap.

5. **VEGETARIAN: Repeat the process with the remaining dough balls and the tofu filling to make 15 tofu buns. Place half of the tofu buns in the upper rack of the steamer, and cover with the lid. Set aside the remaining buns, cover with plastic wrap, and mark a "V" on the plastic wrap with a marker.**

6. Place the stacked steamer over several inches of boiling water in a wok or large sauté pan, making sure the bottom of the steamer is not resting in the water. Reduce the heat to maintain a simmer and steam the buns for 20 to 25 minutes or until they are fluffy and a skewer inserted into the dough comes out clean. (Alternatively, line a baking sheet with parchment paper and bake the buns at 350 degrees F until golden brown and cooked through, 20 to 25 minutes.)

7. Carefully remove the steamer racks and transfer the buns to separate serving platters, noting which buns are vegetarian by placing some lettuce or parsley on that platter. Serve buns while steaming the second batch. (The *hum bao* can be steamed up to 24 hours in advance. Cool completely and wrap the buns individually in plastic wrap and refrigerate. To reheat, unwrap the buns, cover them with a moist paper towel, and microwave until heated through. Or, reheat in a bamboo steamer over simmering water for 10 minutes.)

# INDIAN SAMOSAS WITH HERB-TOFU DIP

*Makes 12 vegetarian and 12 omnivore appetizers*

Samosas—buttery pastry dough stuffed with spiced vegetables and sometimes lamb—are usually deep-fried. This recipe streamlines the procedure by using phyllo dough and baking the pastries instead: same crunch, less fat. The vegetable filling is delicious on its own, but I add ground lamb to some of it for meat eaters. The creamy, cooling dip is a great counterpoint to the slightly spicy filling. Since it's tofu based, it's a great source of lean protein; try it as a dip for raw vegetables.

**DIP:** 10 ounces silken tofu, drained
1 tablespoon soy milk
1 teaspoon lemon juice
¼ cup cilantro leaves
2 tablespoons mint leaves
1 pinch cayenne
Salt

**SAMOSAS:** 2 tablespoons vegetable oil
1 teaspoon brown mustard seeds
½ teaspoon cumin seeds
½ cup finely chopped onion
1 medium carrot, finely chopped
1 tablespoon peeled, minced ginger

1 large Yukon Gold potato (12 ounces), peeled and cut into
  ¼-inch dice

½ cup shelled edamame

½ teaspoon salt

½ teaspoon turmeric

½ cup water

2 teaspoons lemon juice

1½ teaspoons garam masala (see Glossary)

2 tablespoons minced cilantro

6 ounces ground lamb or beef, browned and drained

¼ pound phyllo dough (24 sheets), thawed

⅓ cup butter, melted

2 tablespoons olive oil

1. Combine the tofu, soy milk, lemon juice, cilantro, mint leaves, and cayenne in a blender until smooth. Season with the salt and set aside.

2. Heat the vegetable oil in a large sauté pan over medium heat. Add the mustard seeds and cumin seeds, cover, and cook until the mustard seeds have popped, about 1 minute. Add the onion, carrot, and ginger and sauté, stirring frequently until the onion is translucent, about 3 minutes. Add the potato, edamame, salt, turmeric, and water. Bring to a simmer, cover, and cook, stirring with a spatula once until the potatoes are tender when pierced with a fork, about 10 minutes. Remove from the heat and mash with a potato masher until the mixture is chunky but holds together easily when pressed together. Stir in the lemon juice, garam masala, and cilantro; season with additional salt if necessary.

3. **VEGETARIAN: Put 1½ cups of the potato mixture in a small bowl and set aside.**

4. Preheat the oven to 350 degrees F and line 2 baking sheets with parchment paper. Stack 2 sheets of phyllo dough on a cutting board with the long side facing you. Cover the remaining dough with a clean dish towel to keep it from drying out. Combine the butter and olive oil in a measuring cup. Pick up the right half of the top phyllo sheet, as if turning the page of a book. Lightly brush the bottom sheet with the butter mixture, lower the top

sheet onto the buttered sheet, and press together to seal the sheets. Repeat with the left side. Cut the dough into four 3½-inch-wide vertical strips.

5. **VEGETARIAN: Place 1 tablespoon of the vegetarian filling on the bottom left corner of 1 strip. Fold the bottom edge upward, lining the bottom edge up with the right edge of the strip to make a triangular pocket. Fold the pocket upward, then to the left, then to the right, and so on, as if folding a flag. Brush the pocket lightly with butter mixture and place it on the prepared baking sheet. Mark the corner of the parchment paper with a "V" in pencil to keep track of which samosas are vegetarian. Repeat with the remaining vegetarian filling; you will have about 12 pockets.**

6. Combine the remaining potato mixture with the lamb. Repeat the process with the lamb filling, placing the meaty samosas on the other prepared baking sheet. Bake both batches of samosas, rotating the baking sheets once, until the samosas are golden brown, about 40 minutes. Serve on separate plates with the dip on the side. (The pockets can be prepared ahead and frozen, unbaked, on baking sheets until solid. Transfer to 2 separate, labeled, airtight plastic containers, and freeze for up to 3 months. Bake frozen samosas at 350 degrees F for about 45 minutes, or until hot in the center.)

∨∨∨∨∨∨∨∨∨∨∨∨∨∨∨∨∨∨∨∨∨∨∨∨∨∨∨∨∨∨∨∨∨∨∨∨∨∨

**VEGAN VARIATION:** Brush the vegetarian phyllo pockets with melted nonhydrogenated vegan margarine such as Earth Balance, or use all olive oil instead of butter.

# ENDIVE STUFFED WITH SPANISH GOODIES

*Makes 15 vegetarian and 15 omnivore appetizers*

These elegant hors d'oeuvres feature the tanginess of Spanish blue cheese and the sweetness of ripe pears, with added crunch coming from either Marcona almonds (the small, tender Spanish almonds available at specialty food shops) or crisped Serrano ham for the omnivores' endive. Make these right before serving; the pears and endive will oxidize once cut.

> 3 heads endive
>
> 1 ripe pear, cored and finely chopped
>
> 1 teaspoon sherry vinegar
>
> 2 ounces Spanish blue cheese, crumbled (Valdeon, Picón, or Cabrales)
>
> ¼ cup chopped Marcona almonds or toasted, chopped almonds
>
> 1 tablespoon olive oil
>
> 2 thin slices Serrano ham or prosciutto

1. Cut the base away from the endive heads and separate the leaves. Rinse the leaves well and spin dry in a salad spinner or pat dry with paper towels. Gently mix the pear, vinegar, and cheese in a bowl. Spoon the mixture into endive leaves and arrange on 2 platters.

2. **VEGETARIAN: Sprinkle the almonds over the filled leaves on 1 platter.**

3. Heat the oil in a small sauté pan over medium-high heat. Add the ham and sauté until crisp and golden on both sides, about 1 minute total. Transfer to a cutting board, blot with paper towels, and finely chop. Sprinkle over the filled leaves on the other platter and serve immediately.

ᵛ ᵛ ᵛ ᵛ ᵛ ᵛ ᵛ ᵛ ᵛ ᵛ ᵛ ᵛ ᵛ ᵛ ᵛ ᵛ ᵛ ᵛ ᵛ ᵛ ᵛ ᵛ ᵛ ᵛ ᵛ ᵛ ᵛ ᵛ ᵛ ᵛ ᵛ ᵛ ᵛ ᵛ ᵛ ᵛ ᵛ ᵛ ᵛ ᵛ

**VEGAN VARIATION:** Omit the cheese in the vegetarian endive and add a pinch of salt to the pears before loading them onto the endive leaves.

# THAI SATAYS WITH SPICY CUCUMBER SALAD

*Makes 3 tofu and 9 chicken skewers*

This is a lovely starter for warm weather when you're in a grilling mood. You can make the satays a meal for four by simply flipping on the rice cooker and serving them with steamed jasmine rice, or try them alongside the Crunchy Salad Rolls with Coconut Peanut Sauce (page 3) for a Southeast Asian feast.

**MARINADE AND SKEWERS:**
1 teaspoon cumin seeds
1 teaspoon coriander seeds
1 teaspoon turmeric
½ teaspoon mace
1 tablespoon minced garlic
½ cup canned coconut milk, stirred
1 tablespoon Vegan Fish Sauce (page 228)
2 tablespoons brown sugar
8 ounces fried tofu (see page xviii) or extra-firm nigari tofu
8 ounces boneless, skinless chicken breast, frozen until semi-firm
1 tablespoon fish sauce, also called *nam pla*
12 bamboo skewers soaked in cold water

**SALAD:**
1 small garlic clove
½ small red Thai chile pepper (also called "bird chile")
1 tablespoon Vegan Fish Sauce (page 228)
4 teaspoons sugar
2 tablespoons lime juice
1 medium cucumber, halved lengthwise and cut into ¼-inch slices
¼ cup cilantro
½ teaspoon kosher salt

1. In a small saucepan, toast the cumin and coriander seeds over medium heat until fragrant, about 2 minutes. Grind in a mortar and pestle or clean spice grinder. Put the mixture into a medium bowl, add the turmeric, mace, garlic, coconut milk, vegan fish sauce, and brown sugar; stir to dissolve the sugar.

2. VEGETARIAN: **Slice the tofu into 6 triangles about ½ inch thick. Place the tofu in a shallow bowl, add half the coconut milk mixture, and carefully rub it into the tofu pieces; set aside.**

3. Slice the chicken breast into 2-inch-long strips about ½ inch thick (you should have 18 to 20 pieces). Combine the chicken with the fish sauce and remaining coconut milk mixture; toss to coat. Cover and let both the tofu and chicken marinate in the refrigerator at least 1 hour. (The marinated proteins can be covered and refrigerated for up to 2 days.)

4. For the salad, mash the garlic and Thai chile pepper in a mortar and pestle to a paste. (Alternatively, chop and smash them with the side of a chef's knife.) Combine the paste with the vegan fish sauce, sugar, and lime juice in a medium bowl; stir to dissolve the sugar. Add the cucumber, cilantro, and salt; toss to combine.

5. Preheat the grill over medium-high heat.

6. VEGETARIAN: **Thread the tofu carefully onto 3 skewers so the pieces grill evenly.**

7. Thread the chicken on the remaining skewers, spacing the meat so that it cooks evenly; 2 pieces of meat will fit on a 6-inch skewer. Place the meat skewers on one side of the grill and cook until the chicken is no longer pink in the center, about 3 minutes per side.

8. VEGETARIAN: **Meanwhile, place the tofu on the other side of the grill and grill until the pieces are singed on the edges, about 2 minutes per side. Be sure to use separate tongs to turn the vegetarian skewers.**

9. Serve the skewers from separate serving platters with the cucumber salad on the side.

   TIP: Wait at least 2 minutes before moving the chicken skewers after placing them on the grill to allow the meat to sear; properly seared meat won't stick to the grill.

# CRUSTLESS QUICHE-ETTES

*Makes 24 small appetizer bites or 8 standard muffin-size quiches*

These rich, savory custards offer all the fun and flavor of quiche without fiddling with a crust. I bake them in a standard muffin tin if I will be serving them as a plated first course or as a light main course for four with a salad. You can also use mini-muffin pans; the little bites make great finger food to serve with cocktails. The "quiche-ettes" are vegetarian until the ham is added in the last step before baking.

2 teaspoons olive oil
3 cups baby spinach leaves, roughly chopped (about 1 ounce)
½ cup roughly chopped Roasted Red Peppers (page 232) or jarred
6 large eggs
½ cup half-and-half
¼ teaspoon salt
⅛ teaspoon freshly ground black pepper
1 pinch ground nutmeg
2 ounces Black Forest ham, julienned
3 tablespoons Boursin or other spreadable cheese with herbs
1 sprig parsley

1. Preheat the oven to 350 degrees F. Spray 8 muffin cups or 24 mini-muffin cups (you will need 2 pans) liberally with nonstick cooking spray. Heat the oil in a small skillet over medium-high heat; add the spinach and sauté, turning with tongs until the leaves are wilted, about 1 minute. Remove from the heat. Divide the spinach and red peppers among the muffin cups.

2. Whisk together the eggs, half-and-half, salt, pepper, and nutmeg in a medium bowl. Fill each cup with the egg mixture and put dabs of the cheese on top of each well. Add the ham to 4 large wells or 12 mini-wells.

3. Place the muffin pans on top of baking sheets and place in the oven. Bake until the custard is just set and a knife comes out clean when inserted in

the center, 20 to 25 minutes for large quiches, 15 to 20 minutes for mini-quiches. (The quiches can be made ahead, wrapped, and refrigerated for up to 2 days. Reheat in a moderate oven.)

4. Let the quiches stand for 5 minutes, then run a knife around the sides of each quiche to release it from the pan. Place the ham quiches on a serving plate.

5. **VEGETARIAN: Place the ham-free quiches on a separate serving plate and garnish with parsley.**

# PICADILLO EMPANADAS

*Makes 15 vegetarian and 15 beef empanadas*

Picadillo is a Latin American combo of ground beef, onions, tomatoes, and spices served with rice and beans or used as a stuffing. Here, the filling is made with meat or soy crumbles and is stuffed into flaky pastry pockets (made from store-bought pie dough), and voilà, sophisticated appetizers for everyone.

The smoky flavor in the filling comes from smoked paprika. It's my go-to spice when I want to add smokiness to a dish. Be careful when adding it to recipes—a little goes a long way! Smoked paprika can be found at some grocery stores or by mail order (see Resources).

1 tablespoon golden raisins

1 tablespoon boiling water

1 tablespoon plus 1½ teaspoons olive oil

¼ cup finely chopped onion

½ cup finely chopped red bell pepper

1½ teaspoons minced garlic

1 Roma tomato, finely chopped, or ¼ cup canned tomatoes, drained and finely chopped

½ teaspoon ground cumin

½ teaspoon New Mexican chile powder

⅛ teaspoon smoked paprika (see Glossary)

1 tablespoon sliced pimento-stuffed green olives (about 6 small)

½ teaspoon hot sauce (I use Cholula)

2 ounces soy crumbles or reconstituted textured vegetable protein (TVP) (see page xviii)

2 ounces lean ground beef

One 15-ounce box premade pie dough (2 rounds)

½ cup grated cheddar cheese

1 egg

1 tablespoon water

1. Preheat the oven to 375 degrees F and line 2 baking sheets with parchment paper. Put the raisins in a small bowl, cover with the water, and set aside.

2. Heat 1½ teaspoons of the oil in a large sauté pan over medium heat. Add the onion and red pepper and sauté, stirring frequently, until the onions are tender, about 5 minutes. Add the garlic and sauté until fragrant, about 30 seconds. Add the tomatoes, cumin, chile powder, paprika, and olives and simmer, stirring occasionally, until the tomatoes break down, about 5 minutes. Chop the raisins and add them, their soaking liquid, and the hot sauce to the pan; stir to combine. Divide the mixture between 2 small bowls.

3. **VEGETARIAN: In the same pan, heat 1½ teaspoons of the oil and add the soy crumbles. Cook, stirring constantly until just heated through, about 1 minute. Combine with 1 of the bowls of onion-pepper mixture.**

4. Heat the remaining 1½ teaspoons of oil over medium heat and add the ground beef. Cook, stirring frequently, until the meat is browned and cooked through, about 3 minutes. Combine the meat in the other bowl with the onion-pepper mixture.

5. Roll 1 pie dough disk on a lightly floured surface into a roughly rectangular shape, about 10 by 15 inches. Cut the dough into 3- by 3-inch squares.

6. **VEGETARIAN: Place 1 scant tablespoon of the soy crumble filling on half of 1 square of dough. Top with a pinch of the cheese; fold the dough over to form a triangle-shaped turnover. Crimp the edges with fork tines to seal and place on 1 prepared baking sheet. Repeat with the remaining squares and veggie filling. Whisk together the egg and the water; brush each empanada with some of the egg wash. Using a sharp paring knife, cut a small "V" in the dough of each veggie empanada.**

7. Roll out the second disk of pie dough and cut into 3-inch squares. Fill the squares with meat filling and cheese, as with the vegetarian empanadas. Place the empanadas on the second baking sheet and brush with the remaining egg wash.

8. Bake until the empanadas are golden brown, about 20 minutes; rotate the baking sheets once. Serve with your favorite salsa for dipping. (The empanadas can be par-baked for 15 minutes and kept in the refrigerator,

loosely wrapped with plastic, for up to 2 days. Reheat in a 350-degree F oven until heated through, about 15 minutes.)

**KEEPING IT VEGETARIAN:** Be sure to read the label on the pie dough package. Some commercial brands contain lard!

v v v v v v v v v v v v v v v v v v v v v v v v v v v v v v v v v v v v

**VEGAN VARIATION:** Check the label on the pie dough package to make sure it contains no dairy or other animal products. Omit the cheese and egg wash.

# SALMON AND VEGGIE SUSHI ROLLS

*Makes 24 vegetarian and 32 salmon pieces*

Sliced sushi rolls are the ideal finger food for entertaining—they can be made several hours in advance and can feed both fish lovers and vegetarians from basically the same ingredients. If you make the sushi roll in advance, be sure to let the chilled rolls sit at room temperature for at least thirty minutes before slicing and serving, or the cold rice will be gummy.

| | |
|---|---|
| **RICE:** | 4 cups medium-grain sushi rice such as Calrose |
| | 4½ cups cold water, plus additional |
| | ¾ cup *unseasoned* rice vinegar |
| | 3 tablespoons sugar |
| | ¾ teaspoon salt |
| **VEGETABLE ROLL:** | 1 small cucumber (about 6 ounces), seeded and cut into thin strips |
| | 1 medium carrot, julienned |
| | 8 snow peas, trimmed, strings removed, cut into thin strips |
| | 2 green onions, chopped |
| | 6 tablespoons garlic-and-chive cream cheese |
| **SALMON ROLL:** | 8 ounces wild salmon fillet, skinless, pin bones removed |
| | 2 teaspoons lemon zest |
| | 1½ teaspoons freshly squeezed lemon juice |
| | 2 tablespoons fresh dill, roughly chopped |
| | 4 tablespoons garlic-and-chive cream cheese |

**ASSEMBLY:** Sushi-rolling mat

8 nori (toasted seaweed) sheets

4 tablespoons prepared wasabi

Soy sauce, for dipping

1. Put the rice in a large bowl, add water, swish, and drain. Repeat 3 more times. Cover with cold water and let the rice soak for 30 minutes. Drain in a fine mesh sieve and transfer to a rice cooker. Add the 4½ cups of cold water and turn on the cooker. (Alternatively, simmer the rice in a large saucepan with a tight-fitting lid until tender, about 20 minutes.) Spread the cooked rice onto a rimmed baking sheet, making a single layer. Set the rice near an open window or with a desk fan trained on it to cool it quickly.

2. In a measuring cup, combine the vinegar, sugar, and salt and microwave for 1 minute. Stir to dissolve the sugar. Pour all but 2 tablespoons over the cooled rice and stir until the rice has absorbed the liquid; set aside the remaining vinegar mixture. (The rice can be made up to 2 days in advance. Let it come to room temperature before rolling the sushi.)

3. With a sharp slicing knife, thinly slice the salmon at a 45-degree angle. Lay slices on a plate in a single layer, sprinkle with the lemon zest, lemon juice, and dill. Let the salmon marinate for 10 minutes.

4. Wrap a sushi-rolling mat with two layers of plastic wrap. Lay the mat with slats running horizontally on a clean cutting board. Place a piece of seaweed, shiny side down, on the mat with the long end facing you. Dip your fingers in the reserved vinegar-sugar mixture and distribute ¾ cup of rice evenly over the seaweed, leaving a ½-inch border at the far end. Press rice down with fingertips to make it adhere to the seaweed. Spread 1 tablespoon of the cream cheese in a horizontal line across the rice on the end nearest you. Spread a quarter of the salmon over the rice in an even layer. Lift the part of the mat nearest you up and over the end nearest you, then gently squeeze the top of the mat to make a firm cylinder. Open the mat and roll the cylinder away from you into a tight log, using the mat to make the roll uniformly sized. Transfer the roll, seam side down, to a clean plate. Repeat the process, using ¾ cup of rice for each roll, plus the remaining salmon and cream cheese to make 3 more rolls. Set aside.

5. **VEGETARIAN: Distribute ¾ cup of rice on a nori sheet as with the salmon rolls; spread with 2 tablespoons of cream cheese and a small strip of vegetables on the end nearest you. Roll up as you did with the salmon rolls. Repeat the process with the remaining rice, cream cheese, and vegetables to make 2 more rolls.**

6. Slice the vegetarian rolls crosswise with a sharp knife into about 8 pieces per roll and arrange on a serving platter. Repeat with the salmon rolls, placing them on a separate platter. Serve with the wasabi and soy sauce on the side. (The rolls can be made up to 4 hours in advance; cover tightly with plastic wrap and refrigerate. Let sit at room temperature for 30 minutes before slicing and serving.)

v v v v v v v v v v v v v v v v v v v v v v v v v v v v v v v v v v v v v v

**VEGAN VARIATION:** Omit the cream cheese.

# GRILLED CAESAR SALADS WITH OR WITHOUT ANCHOVIES

*Serves 1 vegetarian and 3 omnivores*

Romaine hearts—the light green inner leaves sold in bags in the produce section of grocery stores—become smoky and almost meaty when they are grilled. In this substantial salad, I pair them with grilled marinated onions, focaccia croutons, and creamy homemade Caesar dressing.

The recipe is essentially vegetarian, but if you love anchovies, you won't be disappointed. Anchovies are draped over the omnivores' salads, and a little of the oil the fishies are packed in is used to brush the lettuce before it hits the grill, too. If you're not a fan of anchovies, omit them from the recipe and use olive oil instead, as with the vegetarian portion.

**DRESSING:** 1 egg yolk

½ teaspoon minced garlic

½ teaspoon vegetarian Worcestershire sauce (see **KEEPING IT VEGETARIAN**)

½ teaspoon Dijon mustard

2 tablespoons fresh lemon juice

¼ cup extra-virgin olive oil

Salt and freshly ground black pepper

**SALAD:** 1 small red onion, cut into ¼-inch-thick rings

1 tablespoon plus 2 teaspoons extra-virgin olive oil

2 tablespoons balsamic vinegar

6 ounces focaccia, sliced

2 heads hearts of romaine, halved lengthwise (12 ounces)

12 anchovies packed in oil, oil reserved

1 ounce Parmigiano-Reggiano cheese, shaved into strips with a vegetable peeler

1. If using a gas grill, preheat over medium-high heat. If using a charcoal grill, start the charcoal and grill the ingredients when it has ashed over.

2. While the grill is preheating, combine the egg yolk, garlic, Worcestershire sauce, mustard, and lemon juice in a blender. With the machine running,

gradually add the oil in a slow, steady stream. Transfer the dressing to a small bowl, season with the salt and pepper, and set aside.

3. Brush the onion slices with 1 tablespoon of the oil. Grill the onions until just tender, about 3 minutes per side. Place them in a small bowl, sprinkle with the vinegar, and set aside. Grill the focaccia until lightly charred and crisp, about 3 minutes per side. Cut into 1-inch cubes and set aside.

4. **VEGETARIAN: Brush 1 romaine half with the remaining 2 teaspoons of oil.**

5. Brush the remaining romaine halves with the reserved anchovy oil. Grill all the romaine halves, keeping the vegetarian portion separate, until they are slightly wilted and charred, about 3 minutes per side.

6. **VEGETARIAN: Place the vegetarian romaine half on a dinner plate and set to the side.**

7. Divide remaining grilled heads among 3 dinner plates. Sprinkle all the salads with the onions, focaccia croutons, and cheese. Drizzle each with a few tablespoons of the dressing. Top the omnivores' salads with anchovies. Serve immediately with a fork and steak knife.

> **KEEPING IT VEGETARIAN:** Most brands of Worcestershire sauce contain anchovies. Look for vegetarian or vegan Worcestershire sauce, like Wizard's, at natural food stores.

∨∨∨∨∨∨∨∨∨∨∨∨∨∨∨∨∨∨∨∨∨∨∨∨∨∨∨∨∨∨∨∨∨∨∨∨∨∨∨

**VEGAN VARIATION:** Roast 1 head of garlic as in the instructions for Cassoulet for the Whole Crowd (page 132). Squeeze the garlic out of its papery skin and mash with a fork. Whisk the garlic with 1 tablespoon lemon juice, 1 teaspoon Dijon mustard, and 3 tablespoons extra-virgin olive oil. Season with salt and pepper, and use in place of the egg-based dressing. Omit the cheese topping.

# FRIED GREEN TOMATOES (AND SOMETIMES BACON) WITH SMOKEY BLUE CHEESE

*Serves 1 vegetarian and 3 omnivores*

Ever wonder what to do with those green tomatoes still on the vine in autumn? This recipe from Chef Derek Hanson at the now-defunct vegetarian restaurant Nutshell in Portland, Oregon, is your answer. This combination of crispy on the outside, juicy on the inside fried green tomatoes and smoky blue cheese dressing is so "meaty" and satisfying that you'll never notice the tomatoes aren't ripe.

The salad itself is vegetarian; I add a bit of bacon to the omnivores' salads because bacon makes everything taste better. I recommend Nueske's bacon (see Resources): the small company based in the tiny town of Wittenberg, Wisconsin, smokes lean pork cuts over applewood, so their bacon is chewy, sweet-salty, and pure heaven for bacon lovers.

8 small shallots

¼ cup sugar

¼ cup plus 1 tablespoon champagne vinegar or white wine vinegar

½ cup smoked blue cheese, crumbled (I recommend Rogue Creamery's Smokey Blue cheese; see Resources)

¼ cup half-and-half

1 pinch cayenne

Salt and freshly ground black pepper

2 pounds green tomatoes

½ cup fine-ground (instant) polenta

Vegetable oil, for frying

4 cups mesclun salad mix

6 strips pepper bacon, cooked until crisp

1. Peel and thinly sliced the shallots; place in a small bowl and set aside.

2. Combine the sugar and vinegar in a small saucepan over high heat. Bring to a boil and stir to dissolve the sugar. (Alternatively, combine in a measuring cup and microwave until hot, about 1½ minutes.) Pour over the shallots

and marinate for 20 minutes. (Shallots can be made ahead and refrigerated in an airtight container for up to 3 weeks.)

3. Preheat the oven to 200 degrees F and line a baking sheet with paper towels. Blend ¼ cup of the cheese with the half-and-half, vinegar, and cayenne in a processor or blender until smooth. Stir in the remaining ¼ cup of cheese and season to taste with the salt and pepper. (The dressing can be made ahead and refrigerated in an airtight container for up to 3 days.)

4. With a sharp, serrated knife cut the tomatoes crosswise into ¼-inch slices. Cut out the hard core in the center of the topmost slices and discard. Spread the polenta on a large plate. Dredge each tomato slice in the polenta, pressing to adhere. Cover the bottom of a heavy skillet with ½ inch of the oil and heat over high heat until hot but not smoking. Reduce the heat to medium and carefully add 3 or 4 tomato slices. Cook until they are golden brown, about 3 minutes per side. Transfer to the prepared baking sheet, sprinkle with the salt, and keep warm in the oven while frying the remaining tomatoes.

5. Arrange the tomatoes on 4 salad plates in concentric circles. Top with the shallots and the salad mix. Spoon the dressing around the outside edges of the tomatoes.

6. **VEGETARIAN: Set aside 1 salad without bacon.**

7. Place 2 strips of bacon on top of the remaining 3 salads and serve.

# 2

## SOUPS AND STEWS

Soups in a mixed-diet family can be a tricky proposition. It seems most soup recipes are based on chicken stock, the ubiquitous golden liquid that delivers savory flavor without stealing the stage from other ingredients. Since vegetarians do not eat chicken or other meat stocks, I've devised ways for all of us to have our soup and eat it, too.

The first solution is to make soups with vegetable stock instead of chicken stock. This works for most recipes in this book. I recommend making your own vegetable stock and varying the vegetables and seasonings to fit the type of soup you are making. In the Basics chapter there are recipes for all-purpose No-Chicken Stock, a richer Roasted Vegetable Stock for heartier soups, a clear brown Asian-Style Stock, and a simple Roasted Mushroom Stock that will cover all the bases. Though making homemade vegetable stock is almost as easy as boiling water, I know not everyone has the time. And that's fine; several recipes specify homemade or packaged vegetable stock where store-bought will do just fine. Try several of the vegetable stocks on the market to decide which work best for you, and don't be shy about diluting them slightly if they are too strongly flavored or salty.

In other recipes, like the French Onion Soup (page 31) or the Tom Kha Gai or Tofu (page 37), I add a high-quality bouillon cube or demi-glace base to the omnivores' portion to add the meaty flavor that defines certain soups for meat eaters. I've listed some of my favorite bouillon and soup-base brands in the Resources section.

When stewed meat or seafood provides additional flavor for the soup or stew, as with the Curry Laksa (page 33), Beet and Beef or Lentil Borscht (page 41), and Cuban Black Bean Soup with DIY Toppings (page 49), I stew the meat separately and add it to the pot after setting aside some soup for vegetarians.

Whichever method you adopt, this chapter will provide many ways for your mixed-diet family to be wrapped in the warmth of homemade soup. So, when the wicked winds blow and the sniffles set in, bring out the soup pot and get simmering!

# MISO SOUP WITH TOFU OR CLAMS

*Serves 1 vegetarian and 3 omnivores*

Miso soup starts with an easy-to-prepare stock called *dashi*, made from kelp (kombu) and smoked bonito tuna flakes. In this version, the tuna is added to the omnivore's stock only; the other portion remains vegan. You can get creative when it comes to garnishes with this simple Japanese staple—fresh vegetables, seafood, and even a beaten egg (à la egg-drop soup) can be added to make it your own.

6 dried shiitake mushrooms

2 cups boiling water

Two 9- by 4-inch kombu pieces (1 ounce) (see Glossary)

4 tablespoons white miso paste

3 green onions, thinly sliced on the bias

¼ cup diced firm silken tofu

1 cup bonito flakes (see Glossary)

1 pound manila clams, scrubbed and rinsed in cold water

Soy sauce

1. Place the mushrooms in a small bowl and pour the boiling water over them. Cover with a small saucer to submerge them completely and set aside for 30 minutes. Stem the mushrooms and thinly slice the caps, reserving soaking liquid.

2. Put the kombu and 7 cups of water in a large soup pot. Pour the mushroom soaking liquid into the pot, stopping before you get to any sediment in the bottom of the bowl. Heat over medium-high heat; as soon as the water comes to a simmer, remove the kombu and discard it. Reduce the heat to low. (The stock can be made up to 3 days in advance and refrigerated in an airtight container.)

3. **VEGETARIAN: Ladle 2 cups of the stock into a small saucepan. Whisk 1 tablespoon of the miso into the stock. Stir in one quarter of the mushrooms and the green onions. Carefully add the tofu cubes; keep warm over medium-low heat.**

4. Add the bonito flakes to the remaining stock. As soon as they sink to the bottom, strain the stock through a fine-mesh sieve, discard the bonito flakes, and return the stock to the pot. Add the remaining mushrooms and all the clams, bring to a simmer, and cook until the clams open, about 3 minutes. Discard any clams that do not open. Whisk the remaining 3 tablespoons of miso and green onions into the soup.

5. Season both soups to taste with the soy sauce; serve immediately.

# FRENCH ONION SOUP

*Serves 1 vegetarian and 3 omnivores*

French onion soup, full of caramelized onions, rich brown stock, and a gooey crust of cheese, is the ultimate cold weather comfort food, but vegetarians usually have to sit out on the joys of this French classic because it is made with veal or beef stock. This recipe relies on the richness of well-caramelized onions, mushroom stock, and a Parmigiano-Reggiano rind for a similar, satisfying flavor—a little beef bouillon in the omnivore's soup helps, too. *Quelle* solution!

1½ pounds yellow onions (about 2 large)

2 tablespoons plus 2 teaspoons olive oil

3 sprigs fresh thyme

1 cup dry vermouth or dry white wine

8 cups Roasted Mushroom Stock (page 226) or packaged mushroom stock (see Resources)

1 bay leaf

One 2-inch piece Parmigiano-Reggiano rind (see **TIP**)

¼ teaspoon dried savory leaves

Twelve ½-inch-thick slices crusty baguette

½ teaspoon minced garlic

Salt and freshly ground black pepper

2 cups grated Gruyère cheese (about 8 ounces)

1 beef bouillon cube (I use Knorr brand), or 1 tablespoon veal demi-glace base (see Resources)

4 oven-safe soup bowls

1. Preheat the oven to 350 degrees F. Cut off the onion root ends and tops and discard. Halve the onions lengthwise, peel, and slice thinly through the root end. Heat 2 tablespoons of the oil in a large sauté pan or skillet over medium heat. Add the onions and thyme sprigs and cook, stirring frequently, until the onions begin to brown, about 15 minutes. Reduce the heat if the onions begin to burn—blackened onions will make the soup bitter.

2. Add ½ cup of the vermouth and scrape up browned bits on the bottom of the pan with a wooden spoon. Cook until the vermouth has evaporated,

about 4 minutes. Add the remaining ½ cup of vermouth; simmer and scrape until it has evaporated, about 4 minutes. Transfer the onions to a 3-quart stockpot and add the mushroom stock, bay leaf, Parmigiano-Reggiano rind, and savory leaves. Bring to a simmer, cover, and cook for 30 minutes. (The soup can be made up to this point and refrigerated in an airtight container for up to 2 days.)

3. Place the baguette slices on a baking sheet. Smash the garlic to a paste with the side of a chef's knife and combine with the remaining 2 teaspoons of oil in a small bowl. Brush the baguette slices with the mixture, sprinkle with the salt and pepper, and bake until golden brown, about 20 minutes. Remove from the oven. Place 1 slice of baguette at the bottom of each oven-proof soup bowl. Adjust the oven rack so the soup bowls will be a few inches from the broiler element; preheat the broiler.

4. **VEGETARIAN: Remove the thyme sprigs, bay leaf, and Parmigiano-Reggiano rind from the soup and discard. Transfer 2½ cups of the soup to a small saucepan, season with the salt and pepper, and keep warm over low heat.**

5. Add the bouillon cube to the remaining soup in the large pot, bring to a simmer, and cook for 5 minutes to meld flavors. Season the soup with the salt and pepper.

6. **VEGETARIAN: Ladle the vegetarian soup into 1 of the bowls, top with 2 baguette slices, and sprinkle with one quarter of the cheese. Set the bowl to one side of a rimmed baking sheet.**

7. Fill the remaining bowls with the bouillon-flavored soup; top with the remaining baguette slices and cheese, as with the vegetarian soup. Place on the other side of the baking sheet. Broil the soups, watching closely, until the cheese is bubbly and brown, about 2 minutes. Serve immediately.

TIP: The hard rind of Parmigiano-Reggiano cheese can be used to impart soups and sauces with a savory flavor, much as a bay leaf is used. Always remove the rind before serving.

v v v v v v v v v v v v v v v v v v v v v v v v v v v v v v v v v v v v

**VEGAN VARIATION:** Omit the cheese rind in the soup, omit the cheese topping; serve with garlicky baguette toasts only.

# CURRY LAKSA (MALAYSIAN CURRY RICE NOODLE SOUP)

*Serves 1 vegetarian and 3 omnivores*

This addictive Malaysian noodle soup has a loyal following in Southeast Asia and Australia, and it's no wonder why. The mixture of fragrant curry broth, slippery rice noodles, and herbs is a slurpy feast for all the senses. Canned curry paste can be used if you're in a hurry, but read labels—some contain shrimp paste. Though Maesri makes a good canned Penang vegetarian curry paste, I urge you to try your hand at making homemade curry paste at least once. It's great fun to bash and pound away at the ingredients (and your frustrations) in a mortar and pestle, and homemade curry paste is much more fragrant than the canned variety.

10 cups water

4 ounces dry flat rice noodles (commonly used for pad thai)

1 tablespoon vegetable oil

5 tablespoons Malaysian Curry Paste (recipe follows) or canned Penang curry paste

3 cups Asian-Style Stock (page 224) or packaged vegetable stock

One 14-ounce can coconut milk

3 tablespoons Vegan Fish Sauce (page 228), plus additional for seasoning

8 kaffir lime leaves

1 teaspoon sugar

2 cups broccoli florets cut into bite-size pieces

4 ounces fried tofu (see page xviii), cut into bite-size cubes

1 cup snow peas, strings removed

8 ounces shrimp, peeled and deveined

1 heaping cup bean sprouts

¼ cup cilantro, roughly chopped

¼ cup fresh mint leaves, roughly chopped

4 tablespoons fried shallots (see **TIP**)

1 lime, quartered

1. Bring the water to a boil in a pot. Put the rice noodles in the water, remove the pot from the stove, and soak until the noodles are pliable, about 10 minutes. Drain and rinse with cool water, and pat dry with paper towels; set aside.

2. Heat the oil in a large soup pot over medium heat. Add the curry paste and stir and fry until it is fragrant, about 1 minute. Add the vegetable stock, coconut milk, 3 tablespoons of the vegan fish sauce, lime leaves, and sugar. Bring to a simmer and cook for 10 minutes.

3. Add the broccoli and tofu; cook until the broccoli is crisp-tender, about 5 minutes. Reduce the heat to medium low, add the snow peas and rice noodles, and season to taste with the vegan fish sauce.

4. Transfer 1 cup of the liquid part of the soup into a small saucepan. Add the shrimp and bring to a simmer over medium heat. Cook until the shrimp curl and turn opaque, about 3 minutes.

5. **VEGETARIAN: Ladle a little over a quarter of the soup and the majority of the tofu in 1 bowl, and set aside this portion for the vegetarian.**

6. Divide the remaining soup among 3 bowls for the omnivores. Ladle the shrimp and its cooking liquid into the bowls.

7. Top all servings with the bean sprouts, cilantro, mint leaves, and fried shallots. Serve with lime quarters on the side.

TIP: Fried shallots are available in Asian markets. To make your own, thinly slice ¼ cup of shallots, toss them with 1½ teaspoons of cornstarch, and deep-fry them until crisp and golden. Use immediately.

## Malaysian Curry Paste

*Makes ¾ cup*

In Malaysian cuisine candlenuts are used in *laksa* curry pastes to boost their richness. Candlenuts are fairly difficult to find and must be cooked before they are eaten—they are toxic when raw. I substitute macadamia nuts or walnuts, which are easier to find.

6 dried New Mexican chiles
3 cups boiling water
1 teaspoon coriander seeds
1½ teaspoon cumin seeds
6 black peppercorns
¾ teaspoon turmeric
½ teaspoon salt
2 tablespoons minced, peeled galangal root (see Glossary)
2 tablespoons chopped garlic
2 tablespoons chopped shallot
1 stalk lemongrass, white and light green parts only, minced
1 teaspoon lime zest
½ cup macadamia nuts or walnuts, finely chopped
1 tablespoon finely chopped cilantro

1. Stem and seed the chiles. Put the chiles in a medium bowl. Pour the boiling water over the chiles, weight them down with a small saucer, and soak them for 20 minutes or until softened. Drain and finely chop them with a knife.

2. In a small pan over medium heat, toast the coriander seeds and cumin seeds until fragrant and lightly browned, about 5 minutes. Transfer to an electric spice grinder. Add the peppercorns, turmeric, and salt and grind to a fine powder. (Alternatively, pound the spices in a mortar and pestle.)

3. Combine the chiles, toasted spice powder, galangal root, garlic, shallot, lemongrass, lime zest, nuts, and cilantro in a food processor or mortar and pestle and process or pound until smooth, stopping to scrape the sides of the work bowl occasionally. Add up to ¼ cup of warm water to the processor if necessary to help the ingredients blend. (The curry paste can be frozen in an airtight container for up to 3 months before the flavors begin to fade.)

# TOM KHA GAI OR TOFU (CREAMY COCONUT-GALANGAL SOUP WITH CHICKEN OR TOFU)

*Serves 2 vegetarians and 3 omnivores*

*Tom kha gai*, literally "soup galangal chicken" in Thai, is a rich, aromatic coconut broth infused with lemongrass, kefir lime leaves, and galangal—a tough rhizome that looks a bit like plump, thin-skinned ginger. Galangal's subtle eucalyptus-like flavor is crucial to this dish; find it at Asian markets and freeze what you don't use in a plastic freezer bag. Freezing the chicken breast until it is semi-firm makes it possible to slice the meat very thinly, which adds to the elegance of this creamy soup.

3½ cups No-Chicken Stock (page 225) or mild packaged vegetable stock

2¾ cups coconut milk, stirred

1½ teaspoons brown sugar

3 stalks lemongrass

1½ small red Thai chiles (often labeled "bird chiles")

One 4-inch piece fresh galangal (3 ounces), cut into ½-inch-thick slices

15 fresh kaffir lime leaves

3 ounces oyster mushrooms, tough base discarded, torn into pieces (2 cups)

¾ cup sliced shallots

4 ounces firm tofu, cut into bite-size cubes

1 boneless, skinless chicken breast (6 to 8 ounces), frozen until semi-firm

1 chicken bouillon cube, crumbled

3 tablespoons fish sauce

2 tablespoons plus 1 teaspoon lime juice

4 teaspoons Vegan Fish Sauce (page 228)

½ cup cilantro, chopped

1. Put the stock, coconut milk, and brown sugar in a medium pot. Cut the hard root end and dry, grassy ends off the lemongrass stalks and discard. Cut stalks into 1-inch lengths and bash them a few times with a meat

tenderizer or bottom of a bottle to help release their fragrant oils. Add to the pot. Gently bruise the chiles the same way and add to the pot with the galangal and lime leaves. Bring to a simmer over medium-high heat, cover, and simmer gently for 30 minutes. Use a slotted spoon to remove the chiles, lemongrass, galangal, and lime leaves; discard.

2. **VEGETARIAN: Transfer 2 cups of the soup to a small saucepan. Add a third of the mushrooms and shallots and all the tofu; bring to a gentle simmer over medium-low heat.**

3. Add the remaining mushrooms and shallots to the large pot and bring to a simmer over medium heat. Cut the semi-frozen chicken breast crosswise (against the grain) into ¼-inch-thick slices and add to the large pot with the bouillon cube. Simmer until the chicken is just cooked through, about 5 minutes. Add the fish sauce and 2 tablespoons of the lime juice to the large pot.

4. **VEGETARIAN: Add the vegan fish sauce and the remaining teaspoon of lime juice to the small pot, stirring very gently so you don't break up the tofu.**

5. Serve both soups garnished with cilantro.

# PROVENÇAL TOMATO-FENNEL SOUP WITH OR WITHOUT SEAFOOD

*Serves 1 vegetarian and 3 omnivores*

This soup is inspired by bouillabaisse, the dazzling two-course fish soup from the south of France served with toasts spread with rouille (a peppery garlic sauce). The original soup is an endeavor—it requires several kinds of fish, fish stock, and lots of simmering, straining, and time. This recipe mimics the flavors of the classic soup but serves vegetarians and omnivores—and it's lots easier.

**SOUP:**
- 2 tablespoons olive oil
- 1 large onion, halved and sliced through root end (2 cups)
- One 8-ounce fennel bulb, cored and chopped
- 1 tablespoon minced garlic
- ½ cup dry white wine
- 1 bay leaf
- 2 cups tomato sauce
- 3 cups Roasted Vegetable Stock (page 227) or packaged vegetable stock
- 2 pinches saffron threads
- ½ cup canned garbanzo beans, rinsed and drained
- 3 teaspoons chopped fresh tarragon
- 8 ounces firm white fish such as halibut, cut into 1½-inch pieces
- 8 ounces shrimp, peeled and deveined
- 6 ounces squid tubes, thinly sliced
- Salt and freshly ground black pepper

**TOASTS AND ROUILLE:**
- Six ¼-inch-thick slices crusty baguette
- 1 tablespoon olive oil
- 1 egg
- ¼ teaspoon minced garlic
- 1 tablespoon lemon juice
- ½ teaspoon smoked paprika (see Glossary)
- 2 pinches cayenne
- ½ teaspoon salt
- ⅔ cup extra-virgin olive oil

1. Preheat the oven to 350 degrees F. Heat the 2 tablespoons of oil in a large soup pot over medium heat. Add the onion and fennel and sauté, stirring frequently, until the onions are translucent but not browned, about 10 minutes. Add the garlic and cook until fragrant, about 30 seconds. Add the wine and simmer until nearly evaporated, about 3 minutes. Stir in the bay leaf, tomato sauce, vegetable stock, and saffron; bring to a gentle simmer. Cover and cook, stirring occasionally, until the vegetables are tender and the flavors have melded, about 40 minutes.

2. While the soup is cooking, prepare the toasts and rouille. Lay the baguette slices on a baking sheet and brush with 1 tablespoon of the olive oil. Transfer to the oven and bake until golden brown and crisp, about 15 minutes.

3. Combine the egg, garlic, lemon juice, paprika, cayenne, and salt in a blender. With the blender running, gradually add the ⅔ cup of extra-virgin olive oil in a slow, steady stream, stopping to scrape down the sides of the blender once or twice. Add a few tablespoons of water to make it a spreadable consistency, pour into a small serving bowl, and set aside.

4. **VEGETARIAN: Transfer 2 cups of the soup to a small saucepan. Add the garbanzo beans and 1 teaspoon of the tarragon, cover, and keep warm over low heat.**

5. Add the halibut, shrimp, and the remaining 2 teaspoons of tarragon to the large pot and simmer gently until the halibut is cooked through and the shrimp have curled and turned opaque, about 4 minutes. Add the squid and cook until they have just turned opaque, about 1 minute.

6. Season both soups with the salt and pepper. Serve the soups, passing baguette slices spread with a generous amount of the rouille to float on the top of the soup.

v v v v v v v v v v v v v v v v v v v v v v v v v v v v v v v v v v v v v

**VEGAN VARIATION:** Serve the vegetarian soup without the rouille.

# BEET AND BEEF OR LENTIL BORSCHT

*Serves 2 vegetarians and 3 to 4 omnivores*

Put a pot of this hearty Russian goodness on the stove, grab a copy of *Anna Karenina*, and curl up in your favorite reading chair while the soup simmers and fills your home with its comforting aroma. Serve it with dark rye bread and a generous dollop of sour cream (or vegan sour cream) and you'll feel just a little Tolstoy-esque.

¼ ounce dried porcini mushrooms (about ½ cup)

2 cups boiling water

1 tablespoon plus 2 teaspoons olive oil

1 pound beef chuck steak, trimmed of fat, cut into
   ½-inch pieces

1¾ cups packaged low-sodium beef stock

1½ cups finely chopped onion

1 large carrot, finely chopped

1 celery stalk, finely chopped

1 tablespoon minced garlic

1 medium Yukon Gold potato (6 ounces), peeled and chopped

1 cup roughly chopped green cabbage

½ teaspoon dried savory

1½ teaspoons dried dill

12 ounces red beets, peeled and grated (see **TIP**)

2 tablespoons tomato paste

2 bay leaves

1 tablespoon plus 2 teaspoons red wine vinegar

Salt and freshly ground black pepper

½ cup brown lentils

1 cup sour cream or vegan sour cream

1. Place the mushrooms in a small bowl. Pour the boiling water over the mushrooms; set aside. In a 3-quart saucepan, heat 2 teaspoons of the oil over medium-high heat; brown the beef in 2 batches. Return all the beef to the pan, add the beef stock, and bring to a simmer. Reduce the heat to medium low to maintain a gentle simmer.

2. In a 3-quart pot, heat the remaining 1 tablespoon of oil over medium-high heat. Add the onions, carrot, and celery and cook until the onions are softened, about 5 minutes. Add the garlic and cook for 30 seconds. Turn off the heat and add the potatoes, cabbage, savory, dill, beets, and tomato paste; stir well to combine.

3. Transfer 3 cups of the vegetable mixture to the saucepan with the beef. Add 1 bay leaf and bring to a simmer over medium heat. Cover and simmer until the beef is tender, about 1 hour and 15 minutes. Immediately before serving, add 1 tablespoon of vinegar and season with salt and pepper to taste.

4. **VEGETARIAN: Meanwhile, coarsely chop the mushrooms and reserve the soaking liquid. Add the mushrooms to the pot with the remaining vegetables. Carefully pour the reserved soaking liquid into the pot, stopping when you reach the sediment at the bottom of the bowl. Add the lentils and remaining bay leaf, bring to a simmer, cover, and cook for 1 hour. Add the remaining 2 teaspoons vinegar and season to taste with the salt and pepper.**

5. Serve both soups with the sour cream passed separately.

TIP: To avoid dyeing your fingers with beet juice, peel them under cold running water and use a food processor fitted with the grating disc attachment to grate them.

# SAVORY SPRINGTIME WONTON SOUP

*Serves 2 vegetarians and 3 omnivores as a first course*

When asparagus and young peas are just coming into season, I love to make this light Asian-style soup to highlight their spring flavors. In the fall, try the soup with wild mushrooms, like piney-flavored matsutake mushrooms, and diced root vegetables instead. The soup itself is vegetarian; the omnivores' version includes pork wontons and thinly sliced Chinese barbecued pork (available at Asian markets and grocery stores).

**WONTONS:**
- 2 teaspoons vegetable oil
- 1 teaspoon minced garlic
- 1 teaspoon peeled, minced ginger
- 1 cup finely chopped green cabbage
- 2 tablespoons finely grated carrot
- 2 green onions, finely chopped
- ½ teaspoon sugar
- ½ teaspoon dark sesame oil
- 1 teaspoon soy sauce
- ½ teaspoon cornstarch
- 1 pinch white pepper
- 4 dried shiitake mushrooms, reconstituted in boiling water for 30 minutes
- 30 wonton wrappers
- 3 ounces lean ground pork (about ⅓ cup)

**SOUP:**
- 8 cups Asian-Style Stock (page 224), Roasted Mushroom Stock (page 226), or packaged mushroom stock (see Resources)
- 1 ounce Chinese barbecued pork, thinly sliced (about ½ cup)
- 6 thin asparagus spears cut into 1-inch pieces
- 12 snow peas cut into ½-inch pieces
- 2 green onions, finely chopped

1. Heat the vegetable oil in a small sauté pan over medium heat. Add the garlic and ginger and sauté until fragrant, about 30 seconds. Add the cabbage and carrot and sauté until they are tender, about 3 minutes. Transfer

the mixture to a bowl and let it cool for 10 minutes. Add the green onions, sugar, sesame oil, soy sauce, cornstarch, and pepper; stir well to combine.

2. **VEGETARIAN: Transfer 2 heaping tablespoons of the vegetable mixture to a small bowl. Stem the reconstituted mushrooms and finely chop the caps. Add the caps to the bowl and stir well to combine.**

3. **VEGETARIAN: Line a dinner plate with parchment paper and set out a small cup of water. Hold 1 wonton wrapper with 1 corner facing you. Dip your finger in the water and moisten the top 2 edges of the wrapper. Place a scant tablespoon of the mushroom filling in the center of the wonton wrapper, fold the wrapper in half to create a triangle, and press the edges together to seal. Bring the left and right corners downward and pinch together to seal them to create a tortellini shape. Repeat with the remaining filling and wrappers to make 8 to 10 vegetarian wontons; set aside on the parchment-lined plate.**

4. Add the pork to the remaining vegetables and stir well until slightly fluffy, about 2 minutes. Line another plate with parchment paper and fill and fold 15 to 20 wontons with the pork mixture.

5. Place 6 cups of the stock in a medium saucepan, over medium-high heat. Add the pork wontons, sliced pork, and two thirds of the asparagus and snow peas. Bring to a gentle simmer (do not boil or wontons will break apart) and cook for 5 minutes. Remove a pork wonton and cut into it to check that the pork is cooked through. Cook for another minute if it is not done.

6. **VEGETARIAN: Meanwhile, heat the remaining 2 cups of stock in a small saucepan over medium-high heat. Add the vegetarian wontons and remaining asparagus and snow peas; bring to a gentle simmer and cook for 5 minutes.**

7. Divide the soup among bowls, sprinkle with the green onions, and serve.

# CREAMY CORN SOUP WITH DUNGENESS CRAB AND TOASTED CORN

*1 vegetarian and 3 omnivore servings*

This soup is all about the simple flavor of sweet summer corn, so it is best to make it with super-fresh corn at its absolute peak. Though the soup is rich and creamy, it is vegan. The creamy texture comes from the starchy corncobs and fiber-rich oatmeal, which melts into the soup undetected. The pièce de résistance is a sprinkle of buttery broiled corn kernels or crabmeat as a garnish.

8 ears fresh yellow corn

2 tablespoons olive oil

1½ cups finely chopped onion

1 cup finely chopped carrot

½ cup finely chopped celery

1 tablespoon minced garlic

8 cups No-Chicken Stock (page 225) or packaged vegetable stock

½ cup rolled oats

1 bay leaf

Salt and freshly ground black pepper

1 pinch cayenne

1 tablespoon extra-virgin olive oil

2 tablespoons finely chopped basil

1½ cups Dungeness crabmeat (from a 1½ pound crab)

1. Shuck the corn and brush away any silk with a clean toothbrush. To shave off the kernels, place the ear stem side down on a cutting board. Hold the top of the cob and saw off the kernels with a sharp chef's knife, being careful not to cut into the cob. Repeat with the remaining corn; you will need about 4 cups of corn kernels. Set aside the cobs and kernels.

2. Heat the oil in a soup pot over medium heat. Add the onions, carrots, and celery and sauté until tender but not browned, about 10 minutes. Add the garlic and sauté until fragrant, about 30 seconds. Add the cobs, 3 cups of the corn kernels, stock, oats, and bay leaf; bring to a boil. Reduce the heat

to maintain a simmer, cover, and cook for 30 minutes. Remove the cobs and bay leaf and discard.

3. Blend the soup with an immersion blender or in batches in a blender with the lid slightly ajar, and return to the pot. Season with the salt, pepper, and cayenne; keep warm over low heat.

4. Preheat the broiler and adjust the oven rack so it is 4 inches below the broiling element. Line a rimmed baking sheet with foil and spray with nonstick cooking spray. Combine the remaining corn kernels with the extra-virgin olive oil and spread on the prepared sheet. Broil, stirring once until the corn is browned in places, about 4 minutes. (Be careful when stirring: the kernels pop and spit a bit!) Transfer to a small bowl and stir in 1 tablespoon of the basil.

5. **VEGETARIAN: Fill 1 soup bowl with soup and top with a few table-spoons of the corn–basil mixture.**

6. Combine the crabmeat with the remaining 1 tablespoon of basil. Divide remaining soup among the soup bowls and top with both the corn mixture and crab mixture.

# CUBAN BLACK BEAN SOUP WITH DIY TOPPINGS

*Serves 2 vegetarians and 6 omnivores*

This satisfying Caribbean-inspired soup is flavored with smoked pork hock for omnivores, but vegetarians won't miss a thing in their portion of this protein-rich soup.

I love to serve this soup for casual dinner parties—I just set out all the toppings, plop the pots of soup on the table, and invite guests to personalize their bowls with the toppings. I use soft, crumbly Mexican *queso fresco* cheese here (available at some grocery stores and Latin markets), but you can substitute grated cheddar or Monterey Jack if *queso fresco* is unavailable.

1 pound dried black beans (about 2½ cups)

1 bay leaf

1 smoked pork hock or ham bone

2 tablespoons extra-virgin olive oil

1½ cups finely chopped onion

2 medium poblano peppers, seeded and ribs removed, chopped (¾ cup)

1 tablespoon sliced garlic

1½ teaspoons ground cumin

1 tablespoon Mexican oregano (see Glossary)

1 tablespoon salt

1½ tablespoons finely chopped canned chipotle pepper in adobo

2 teaspoons brown sugar

2 tablespoons dry sherry

Zest of 1 lime

Freshly ground black pepper

8 strips bacon, cooked and crumbled

Sour cream

1 red onion, minced

1 cup *queso fresco* (see Glossary), crumbled

4 tablespoons chopped cilantro

1 lime, cut into 8 wedges

1. Put the beans in a large bowl, add cold water to cover by 2 inches, and soak for 8 hours or overnight. Drain and rinse well. Transfer the beans to a large soup pot and add cold water just to cover (about 8 cups). Add the bay leaf and bring to a boil. Reduce the heat and simmer until the beans are tender but not mushy, about 1 hour and 20 minutes, skimming off the white foam that surfaces.

2. Meanwhile, in a medium pot, combine 8 cups of water and the pork hock; bring to a boil. Reduce the heat to medium and simmer, skimming off the foam that surfaces and adding water if needed to keep the pork covered in water. When the pork is tender (about 1 hour and 20 minutes), remove it and reserve 1½ cups of the cooking liquid. Discard any rind and fat, cut the pork into small pieces, and set aside.

3. Heat the oil over medium-high heat in a large sauté pan; add the onions and poblano pepper and cook for 5 minutes, stirring frequently. Add the garlic, cumin, and oregano and cook for 1 minute, stirring constantly. Add 1 cup of water to the pan and bring to a boil, scraping up any browned bits on the bottom of the pan. Transfer the mixture to the bean pot. Stir in the salt, chipotle pepper, brown sugar, sherry, and lime zest and simmer for 30 minutes. Blend with an immersion blender or mash with a potato masher until about half the beans are mashed and the soup is slightly thickened.

4. **VEGETARIAN: Transfer 3 cups of the soup to a small saucepan and keep warm over low heat.**

5. Add the pork and cooking liquid to the remaining soup and bring to a simmer over medium-high heat; simmer for 10 minutes. Discard bay leaf.

6. Season both soups with salt and pepper. Set out the bacon, sour cream, onion, cheese, cilantro, and lime wedges in small bowls on the dining table. Serve the soup and let the guests decorate their bowls of soup with toppings of their choice.

v v v v v v v v v v v v v v v v v v v v v v v v v v v v v v v v v v v v v v

**VEGAN VARIATION:** Offer vegan sour cream and shredded soy cheese instead of dairy toppings.

# POSOLE STEW WITH PORK OR NOT

*Serves 2 vegetarians and 4 omnivores*

I fell in love with posole on a visit to New Mexico, where it is served at just about every meal as a soup, side dish, or a main-event stew like this recipe. Traditionally, the puffy dried corn kernels called hominy are simmered for hours in a chile-spiked pork broth. In this recipe I use canned hominy, and the pork and its broth are cooked separately and added to the omnivores' portion toward the end of cooking. You may want to prepare the pork broth a few hours or the day before serving.

**PORK AND BROTH:**
- 2 pounds pork leg roast or pork butt, trimmed of fat and cut into bite-size pieces
- 1 cup roughly chopped onion
- 1 large garlic clove, smashed
- 1 bay leaf

**STEW:**
- 1 small dried New Mexican red chile
- 1½ cups boiling water
- 1 Anaheim chile (if you like spicy food, use 2)
- 2 tablespoons olive oil
- 1½ cups finely chopped onion
- ¾ cup thinly sliced carrot
- ¾ cup finely chopped celery
- 4 teaspoons finely chopped garlic
- 1½ teaspoons Mexican oregano (see Glossary)
- 1 teaspoon ground cumin
- One 29-ounce can hominy, rinsed and drained
- 10 ounces red new potatoes cut into ½-inch dice
- 4 cups No-Chicken Stock (page 225) or mild packaged vegetable stock
- 2 tablespoons lime juice
- Salt and freshly ground black pepper
- ¼ cup finely chopped cilantro

1. Cut the pork into 1-inch cubes and put them in a medium saucepan. Add the onion, garlic, bay leaf, and enough of the water to cover the pork by 1 inch (3 to 4 cups). Bring to a boil and reduce the heat to a simmer. Cook, skimming off any foam until the meat is fork tender, about 1½ hours. (Alternatively, cook in a slow cooker on low heat until tender, about 4 hours.)

2. Place the dried chile in a small bowl. Pour the 1½ cups boiling water over it and soak for 30 minutes. Discard the water, seeds, and stem, finely chop the chile, and set aside.

3. Roast the Anaheim chile over a gas flame or on a baking sheet set 4 inches below the broiler until charred all over, turning with tongs occasionally, about 10 minutes. When it is cool enough to handle, peel and seed the chile and finely chop the flesh. Combine with the reserved red chile and set aside.

4. Heat the oil in a large soup pot over medium heat. Add the onion, carrots, and celery; sauté until the onion is translucent, about 10 minutes. Add the garlic, oregano, and cumin and sauté until fragrant, about 30 seconds. Remove from the heat and stir in the hominy and potatoes.

5. **VEGETARIAN: Transfer 2 cups of the vegetable mixture to a small saucepan. Add the vegetable stock and 1 tablespoon of the chile mixture. Bring to a gentle simmer over medium-low heat and partially cover.**

6. Skim the fat off the top of the pork broth and discard. Add the pork, pork broth, and remaining chiles to the large pot with the remaining vegetable mixture and simmer until the flavors have melded and the potatoes are tender, about 30 minutes.

7. **VEGETARIAN: Add 2 teaspoons of the lime juice to the vegetarian posole and season with the salt and pepper to taste.**

8. Stir the remaining lime juice into the omnivore posole. Season with the salt and pepper to taste.

9. Serve both soups sprinkled with the cilantro.

# ROASTED SQUASH OR SHRIMP BISQUE

*Serves 2 vegetarians and 4 omnivores*

Bisques are an elegant French invention that often feature shrimp or lobster and always tip the scale of creamy luxuriousness and calories. This soup has a similar silky texture, but it is thick and creamy thanks to protein-rich silken tofu, not cream. A touch of curry powder gives the vegetarian bisque its earthy flavor; the omnivores' version is shellfish-errific thanks to chopped shrimp and a simple stock made from shrimp shells.

1½ pounds butternut or other winter squash, such as Hubbard
2 tablespoons olive oil
Salt and freshly ground black pepper
8 ounces shrimp, peeled and deveined, shells reserved
1 chicken bouillon cube, crumbled
1½ cups water
1½ cups chopped onion
1 small leek, white and green parts only, chopped
1 large carrot, finely chopped
1 medium celery stalk, finely chopped
1 tablespoon minced garlic
2 tablespoons tomato paste
1 cup dry white wine
3 to 4 cups Roasted Vegetable Stock (page 227) or packaged vegetable stock
1 bay leaf
8 ounces silken tofu, drained
4 teaspoons dry sherry
Cayenne
2 pinches curry powder
Chopped chives for garnish

1. Preheat the oven to 400 degrees F. Line a rimmed baking sheet with foil and spray with nonstick cooking spray. Peel the squash, halve it lengthwise, and scrape out the seeds and stringy bits. Cut the flesh into 1-inch cubes and toss with 1 tablespoon of the oil. Place on the prepared baking sheet,

sprinkle with the salt and pepper, and roast until the cubes are tender, about 40 minutes. Turn on the broiler and broil the cubes until they are browned and caramelized around the edges, about 3 minutes. Remove and set aside.

2. While the squash is roasting, put the shrimp shells, bouillon cube, and the water in a small saucepan. Bring to boil, reduce the heat, and simmer gently for 20 minutes. Strain and set aside.

3. Heat the remaining tablespoon of oil in a soup pot over medium heat. Add the onions, leeks, carrots, and celery and cook, stirring occasionally, until the vegetables have softened, 8 to 10 minutes. Add the garlic and tomato paste and sauté until fragrant, about 1 minute. Add the wine and bring to a simmer, scraping browned bits from the bottom of the pan, and cook until reduced by half, about 2 minutes. Stir in the squash, 3 cups of the vegetable stock, and bay leaf. Reduce heat to a maintain a gentle simmer. Cover and cook for 20 minutes. Remove the bay leaf. Add the tofu and blend with an immersion blender, or blend in batches in a blender with the lid slightly ajar to allow steam to escape. Return to the pot, stir in the sherry, and season with salt, pepper, and cayenne.

4. **VEGETARIAN: Transfer 2 cups of the bisque to a small pan. Add the curry powder and enough vegetable stock to reach the desired consistency. Keep warm over medium-low heat.**

5. Add the strained shrimp-shell stock and shrimp to the remaining bisque in the pot and bring to a gentle simmer over medium heat. Cook until the shrimp are cooked through, about 3 minutes.

6. Divide the soups among the bowls, sprinkle with the chives, and serve.

# FIDEOS WITH CHICKEN OR A POACHED EGG

*Serves 1 vegetarian and 3 omnivores*

*Fideos* is a popular first course in Spain and Mexico that features thin nests of vermicelli cooked in a rich red chile and chicken stock. I use vegetarian stock instead and poach an egg in one portion to make the vegetarian soup protein-rich, while shredded rotisserie chicken (yes, the grab-and-go kind available at supermarkets) completes the omnivores' portions. The result is a simple, satisfying soup that chases the sniffles away with one bite.

4 tablespoons vegetable oil

6 ounces vermicelli nests or broken angel hair pasta (about 2 heaping cups)

1 cup finely chopped onion

½ cup finely chopped red bell pepper

1 tablespoon minced garlic

4 cups Roasted Vegetable Stock (page 227) or packaged vegetable stock

One 14-ounce can diced tomatoes with juice

¾ teaspoon Mexican oregano (see Glossary)

1½ teaspoons ground cumin

1 scant tablespoon finely chopped canned chipotle chiles in adobo

Salt and freshly ground black pepper

Hot sauce (optional)

1 egg

2 cups shredded rotisserie chicken, plus any accumulated juices in bottom of container

½ cup crumbled *queso fresco* (see Glossary), or feta cheese

3 tablespoons finely chopped cilantro

1 lime, cut into wedges

1. Heat 2 tablespoons of the oil in a large sauté pan over medium-high heat. Add the pasta nests and sauté, stirring constantly until the noodles are golden brown, about 1 minute. With tongs, turn over the nests and cook

for 30 seconds. (If using angel hair pasta, cook, stirring constantly with a spatula until pasta is golden brown, about 2 minutes, reducing the heat if it begins to burn.) Transfer to a bowl and set aside.

2. Heat the remaining oil in the pan; add the onions and bell pepper and sauté until the onions are translucent, about 5 minutes. Add the garlic and cook for 30 seconds.

3. Return the pasta nests to the pan. Add the stock, tomatoes, oregano, cumin, and chiles; bring to a simmer. Reduce the heat to medium low, cover, and gently simmer until the pasta is almost tender, about 5 minutes. Season with the salt, pepper, and hot sauce.

4. **VEGETARIAN: Transfer 1½ cups of the soup and pasta mixture to a small sauté pan and bring to a gentle simmer over medium-low heat. Use a spoon to push the noodles and vegetables away from the center of the pan to make a little well. Break the egg and gently slip it into the well. Spoon a bit of the stock over the top of the egg, cover, and cook until the whites are just set and the yolk is still runny, about 5 minutes.**

5. Meanwhile, stir the shredded chicken and any juices from the bottom of the rotisserie container (the juices will be like jelly if the chicken is cold, but that's fine) into the sauté pan with remaining stock and noodles. Cover and bring to a gentle simmer over medium-low to low heat.

6. Serve the soups sprinkled with the cheese and cilantro, with lime wedges on the side.

ˇ ˇ ˇ ˇ ˇ ˇ ˇ ˇ ˇ ˇ ˇ ˇ ˇ ˇ ˇ ˇ ˇ ˇ ˇ ˇ ˇ ˇ ˇ ˇ ˇ ˇ ˇ ˇ ˇ ˇ ˇ ˇ ˇ ˇ ˇ ˇ ˇ ˇ ˇ ˇ ˇ ˇ

**VEGAN VARIATION:** Omit the eggs and cheese from the vegetarian portion; add ½ cup rinsed and drained canned pinto beans.

# CHILI WITH CORNBREAD BISCUIT TOPPING

*Serves 1 to 2 vegetarians and 3 omnivores*

The combination of corn, squash, and beans makes this spicy chili much more interesting than the rather uninspired (and sodium-laced) canned chilis we are all familiar with. I add ground buffalo meat to the omnivore portion; buffalo has more flavor and less fat than traditional ground beef. Both versions are capped with a fluffy cornbread biscuit topping to make this much jazzier than your everyday bowl o' soup.

**CHILI:**
- 2 tablespoons vegetable oil
- 2 cups chopped onion
- 1 Anaheim chile, seeded and chopped
- 1 tablespoon minced garlic
- 2 tablespoons New Mexican chile powder
- 5 teaspoons ground cumin
- 1 teaspoon paprika
- 2 pinches ground cloves
- One 28-ounce can diced tomatoes with juice
- 1½ cups Roasted Vegetable Stock (page 227) or packaged vegetable stock
- 1 teaspoon brown sugar
- 1 teaspoon salt
- 1 cup corn kernels, fresh or frozen
- One 15-ounce can pinto beans, rinsed and drained
- 1 cup peeled and finely diced winter squash (see **TIP**)
- 1 pound ground buffalo meat or lean ground beef, browned and drained

**TOPPING:**
- 1½ cups all-purpose flour
- 2 teaspoons baking powder
- ½ cup yellow cornmeal
- ½ teaspoon salt
- ⅓ cup cold butter, finely diced
- ⅔ cup plus 1 tablespoon buttermilk
- 1 cup grated cheddar cheese

1. Heat the oil in a 3-quart oven-safe sauté pan or skillet over medium heat. Add the onions and chile and sauté until the onions are translucent and begin to brown, about 10 minutes. Add the garlic, chile powder, cumin, paprika, and cloves; continue to sauté for 1 minute. Add the tomatoes, stock, brown sugar, and salt and bring to a simmer. Cover, reduce the heat to maintain a gentle simmer, and cook for 30 minutes. Stir in the corn and beans and continue to cook over low heat.

2. Preheat the oven to 350 degrees F. Whisk together the flour, baking powder, cornmeal, and salt in a medium mixing bowl. Add the butter and rub it into the flour mixture with your fingertips until the butter is in tiny pieces. Add the buttermilk and toss with a fork until the dough begins to come together. Gather the dough with your hands and knead it gently on a lightly floured surface 2 or 3 times to create a cohesive dough. Divide the dough into 7 pieces and flatten them into 2- to 2½-inch-round biscuits about ½ inch thick.

3. **VEGETARIAN: Ladle 2 cups of the chili into a 1-quart baking dish and stir in the squash. Top with 2 biscuits and ¼ cup of the cheese.**

4. Stir the browned meat into the remaining chili. Place the remaining 5 biscuits on top of the chili in the sauté pan, spacing the biscuits 1 inch apart (they will expand while baking). Sprinkle with the remaining cheese.

5. Transfer both the pan and baking dish to the oven. Bake until the biscuits are golden brown and a knife inserted in the center of the largest biscuit comes out clean, about 30 minutes. Serve immediately.

TIP: If peeling and dicing winter squash is on your list of least favorite chores, take heart! Uncooked diced squash is available in the freezer section of grocery stores and can be used instead.

# 3

## QUICK FIXES

The following recipes are not of the "open a can of mushroom soup . . ." or "pick up the phone and order a pizza" variety, but they are fairly simple to throw together, and they cater to both meat eaters and vegetarians or vegans. With a bit of careful shopping and some creative shortcuts, you need to spend only a short bit of time in the kitchen, perhaps with a glass of wine while you're stirring, to come up with a good meal that doesn't come from a box or the freezer. Not a bad a way to unwind after work, if you think about it.

# HALOUMI AND CHICKEN SOUVLAKI SKEWERS

*Makes 6 vegetarian and 6 omnivore skewers*

*Haloumi* is a slightly salty Greek cheese that is firm enough to grill. Paired with garlic- and herb-marinated vegetables, grilled *haloumi* makes a nice alternative to the usual veggie burger or tofu hot dog vegetarians normally get at barbecues. Find *haloumi* at grocery stores with good cheese departments and at Middle Eastern shops; Indian *paneer* cheese makes a fine substitute. For omnivores, the same vegetables are skewered along with chicken breast pieces marinated in a Greek-inspired yogurt mixture so that the meat stays moist and juicy.

> 12 bamboo skewers, soaked in cool water for 1 hour
>
> ¼ cup extra-virgin olive oil
>
> 2 tablespoons finely chopped garlic
>
> 1 tablespoon chopped fresh oregano, or 1½ teaspoons dried oregano
>
> Zest of 1 lemon
>
> 1 tablespoon lemon juice
>
> ½ teaspoon salt
>
> ½ teaspoon freshly ground black pepper
>
> 6 ounces baby pattypan squash, or mature pattypan squash cut into ½-inch wedges
>
> 8 ounces zucchini (1 large), cut into ½-inch-thick rounds
>
> 12 large cremini mushrooms
>
> ½ medium red onion, cut into ½-inch-thick wedges through root end
>
> ½ cup plain full-fat yogurt
>
> 1 pound boneless, skinless chicken breasts cut into 1-inch pieces
>
> 8 ounces *haloumi* or *paneer* cheese, cut into 1-inch cubes
>
> ½ lemon, thinly sliced and quartered

1. Preheat the grill over medium-high heat. In a medium nonreactive bowl, whisk ¼ cup of the oil with the garlic, oregano, lemon zest, lemon juice, salt, and pepper. Transfer 2 tablespoons of the marinade to a small mixing

bowl, add the squash, zucchini, mushrooms, and onions; toss to coat. Let marinate for 20 minutes.

2. Stir the yogurt into the remaining marinade and add the chicken, tossing to coat. Marinate for 20 minutes. (The vegetables and chicken can be marinated separately up to 1 day in advance; cover and refrigerate until ready to use.)

3. **VEGETARIAN: Thread two thirds of the vegetables and all the *haloumi* onto 5 or 6 skewers, alternating the cheese with the vegetables and lemon pieces.**

4. Thread the chicken, remaining vegetables, and lemon pieces in alternating layers on the remaining skewers. Do not overcrowd the meat or the chicken won't cook evenly. Grill on one side of the grill until the chicken is opaque white on one side, about 4 minutes. Turn with tongs and grill on until the chicken is no longer pink in the center, about 5 minutes.

5. **VEGETARIAN: Grill the *haloumi* skewers on the other side of the grill at the same time, using a separate pair of tongs to turn the skewers. Grill until the vegetables are crisp-tender and the *haloumi* is browned in places, about 3 minutes per side.**

6. Transfer the chicken skewers to 1 platter and the vegetarian skewers to another platter; serve.

v v v v v v v v v v v v v v v v v v v v v v v v v v v v v v v v v v v v v v v

**VEGAN VARIATION:** Use cubes of firm tofu instead of cheese.

# SPAGHETTI CARBONARA

*Serves 1 vegetarian and 3 omnivores*

This recipe remains essentially the same for both bacon-lovers and vegetarians: hot pasta is tossed with eggs, herbs, and Parmigiano-Reggiano cheese to create a rich, simple sauce; bacon is added at the end to the omnivore's pasta.

I like to add sautéed seasonal vegetables to make the dish healthier and more interesting. In fall and winter, meaty wild mushrooms are wonderful; in spring, fresh peas or asparagus are great; and in summer, zucchini, golden pattypan squash, and red bell peppers are lovely. The recipe is easily adapted to whatever tender vegetables you have on hand.

4 free-range, organic eggs

4 tablespoons cream

2 tablespoons finely chopped Italian parsley

1 tablespoon chopped fresh thyme leaves

¾ cup grated Parmigiano-Reggiano cheese, plus additional for serving

¾ teaspoon freshly ground black pepper

3 tablespoons olive oil

8 ounces thick-cut bacon, roughly chopped

6 teaspoons minced garlic

3 cups chopped seasonal vegetables (see headnote)

Salt and freshly ground black pepper

1 pound spaghetti

1. Bring a large pot of water to a boil. Whisk together the eggs, cream, parsley, thyme, cheese, and pepper in a large serving bowl.

2. Heat 1 tablespoon of the oil in a medium sauté pan over medium-high heat. Add the bacon and sauté until crisp, about 3 minutes. Add 4 teaspoons of the garlic and cook until fragrant, about 30 seconds. Set aside in a warm place.

3. Heat the remaining 2 tablespoons of oil in a clean medium sauté pan over medium-high heat. Add the vegetables and sauté, stirring occasionally, until

they are tender, about 5 minutes. Add the remaining 2 teaspoons of garlic, season with the salt and pepper, and sauté for 30 seconds; set aside.

4. Boil the pasta until it is al dente, about 8 minutes. Drain and quickly add it to the egg mixture. Add the vegetables and toss with salad spoons; the heat of the pasta will cook the eggs and create a creamy sauce.

5. VEGETARIAN: **Transfer one quarter of the pasta mixture to a bowl, topping it with lots of the vegetables.**

6. Add the bacon to the remaining pasta mixture and toss to combine; divide among 3 bowls. Serve immediately; pass additional cheese at the table.

# ANTIPASTO CALZONES

*Makes 1 vegetarian and 3 omnivore calzones*

The idea of making calzones may not sound like a quick recipe option, but this recipe relies on prepared raw pizza dough and store-bought antipasto ingredients; so "home-made" calzones are certainly a possibility on a weeknight. Look for raw pizza dough in cartons or bags in the refrigerated section of natural food markets and gourmet grocery stores. An easy pizza dough recipe follows in case you can't find the premade stuff or you're feeling more ambitious.

> 1 pound store-bought raw pizza dough, or 1 batch Calzone Dough (recipe follows)
>
> 1 tablespoon olive oil
>
> 1 small zucchini, diced (¾ cup)
>
> ¾ cup sliced Roasted Red Peppers (page 232), or jarred
>
> One 14-ounce can artichoke hearts in water, drained and roughly chopped
>
> ¼ cup pitted olives, sliced
>
> ½ cup fresh basil leaves
>
> 2 cups (8 ounces) part-skim mozzarella cheese, grated
>
> Salt and freshly ground black pepper
>
> 8 ounces bulk Italian sausage, browned and drained
>
> 1 ounce vegetarian pepperoni (optional) (I like Yves brand)
>
> 2 tablespoons coarse cornmeal
>
> 1 tablespoon truffle oil (optional) (see Resources)
>
> 2 cups jarred marinara sauce, warmed

1. Place a pizza stone on the center rack of the oven and preheat the oven to 450 degrees F. (Alternatively, line a baking sheet with foil and brush it with olive oil, but *do not* place it in the preheating oven.) Set out the pizza dough to sit at room temperature for 30 minutes, loosely covered with plastic wrap.

2. Heat the oil in a small sauté pan until hot; add the zucchini and sauté, stirring once, until tender and beginning to brown, about 4 minutes. Gently combine the zucchini, red peppers, artichoke hearts, olives, basil, and cheese in a large bowl. Season with the salt and pepper and set aside.

3. Divide the dough into 4 balls. On a lightly floured surface, roll and stretch each ball into an 8-inch round. (If the dough springs back as you roll it out, allow it to rest for 15 minutes before giving it another try.) Divide the vegetable mixture among the dough rounds. Distribute the Italian sausage on 3 of the calzones, and fold the dough over the filling, pinching the edges to seal.

4. **VEGETARIAN: Place the vegetarian pepperoni on the remaining calzone and pinch the edges to seal. Using a sharp paring knife, cut a "V" into the dough.**

5. Sprinkle a pizza peel or the back of a clean cookie sheet with a little of the coarse cornmeal and slide the calzones onto the preheated pizza stone or baking sheet. Be sure to space them so any escaping sausage juices won't touch the vegetarian calzone. Bake until the crusts are golden brown and juices are bubbly around the edges, about 40 minutes.

6. Brush the calzones with truffle oil and serve immediately with individual dipping bowls of marinara sauce.

## Calzone Dough

*Makes 1 pound*

> ¾ cup lukewarm water
> 1 teaspoon honey
> 1 package (¼ ounce) quick-rising active dry yeast
> 1½ cups all-purpose unbleached white flour, plus additional for kneading
> 1 cup whole-wheat flour
> 1 tablespoon plus 1 teaspoon olive oil
> 1 pinch salt

1. Stir the water and honey together in a mixing bowl. Add the yeast and stir until it is dissolved. Add the white flour, whole-wheat flour, 1 tablespoon of the oil, and salt and knead in a stand mixer with the dough hook for 4 minutes. (Alternatively, knead by hand on a lightly floured surface for 10 minutes.) The dough will be a little sticky; the moister the dough the crisper the crust.

2. Rub a clean bowl with the remaining 1 teaspoon of oil, transfer the dough to the bowl, cover loosely with plastic wrap, and let rise in a warm spot for 1 hour. (The dough can be made up to 2 days ahead; cover with plastic wrap and refrigerate. Let the dough come to room temperature before using.)

# JAPANESE EGGPLANT AND HALIBUT WITH MISO GLAZE

*Serves 1 vegetarian and 3 omnivores*

A fishmonger friend of mine introduced me to the simple Japanese method of marinating fish in a mixture of white miso, sweet rice cooking wine, and sake. When broiled, the fish crisps and caramelizes around the edges to a delicious golden brown. The mixture is equally good on Japanese eggplant. Large European eggplant won't work, however; the texture will not cook to the custardy deliciousness of long, slim Japanese eggplant. You can find Japanese eggplant at farmers markets in late summer to early fall and all year at Asian markets and some grocery stores.

> ¼ cup dry sake
> 1 tablespoon sugar
> ½ cup white miso paste, also labeled *shiromiso*
> ¼ cup mirin (sweet rice cooking wine)
> 1 tablespoon soy sauce
> Zest of ½ lemon
> 1 pound firm white fish fillet such as halibut, black cod, or turbot
> 1 pound (4 large) Japanese eggplant, halved lengthwise
> 1 lemon, quartered
> 4 green onions, chopped
> 6 cups steamed white rice

1. Combine the sake and sugar in a small saucepan. Bring to a boil and cook, stirring constantly until the sugar dissolves, about 30 seconds. Whisk in the miso, mirin, soy sauce, and lemon zest.

2. Place the fish in a baking dish just large enough to hold it and pour ½ cup of the miso mixture over the fish. Rub the marinade into the fish and marinate for at least 10 minutes and up to 30 minutes. Set aside the remaining miso mixture for the eggplant.

3. Preheat the broiler. Line 2 small rimmed baking sheets with foil and spray with nonstick cooking spray. Transfer the fish fillets to 1 of the prepared baking sheets, discarding any excess marinade in the baking dish. Broil, rotating pan once, until the fish is caramelized around the edges and cooked through, 8 to 12 minutes (see **TIP**). Cover loosely with foil and set aside.

4. **VEGETARIAN: Score the cut sides of the eggplant with a paring knife. Lay the eggplant cut side down on the other prepared baking sheet. Broil for 3 minutes. With tongs, turn over the eggplant and brush with the remaining miso mixture. Continue to broil until the eggplant are browned and tender when pierced with a fork, about 3 minutes.**

5. Transfer the fish and eggplant to separate serving dishes, squeeze a little lemon over the fish, sprinkle both dishes with the green onions, and serve with the hot rice.

**TIP:** To test fish for doneness, insert a paring knife in the thickest part of the fillet and hold it there for 3 seconds. Carefully touch the knife against your lower lip, *sharp end angled away from you.* The knife's metal will pick up the temperature of the fish: if the knife is cold, the fish is still rare; if the knife is warm, the fish is medium; if the knife is hot, the fish is well done.

# RIZO QUESADILLAS WITH CREAMY AVOCADO DIP AND LAZY SPANISH RICE

*Serves 1 vegetarian and 3 omnivores*

Quesadillas are a great "get out of jail free" card when it comes to dinner. Just take a tortilla, top with grated cheese, heat in a skillet until toasty, fold in half, and dinner is ready! In this version, sautéed onions, peppers, and chorizo add a flavorful punch. I use Soyrizo, a soy-based stand-in for pork chorizo in the vegetarian quesadilla. It tastes so much like the real thing, I often use it for everyone's quesadillas. If you're feeling ambitious (but not overly so), I have included a recipe for quick Spanish rice to accompany the quesadillas.

DIP: 1 ripe avocado

¼ cup chopped cucumber

⅓ cup sour cream or plain yogurt

¼ cup cilantro, loosely packed

2 tablespoons chopped fresh mint leaves

1 tablespoon lime juice

1 tablespoon water

¼ teaspoon ancho or New Mexican chile powder

Salt and freshly ground black pepper

QUESADILLAS: 1 tablespoon olive oil

1 small onion, thinly sliced

1 small red bell pepper, thinly sliced

¼ cup (2 ounces) Soyrizo, plastic casing removed

¾ cup (6 ounces) chorizo, casing removed

2½ cups grated cheddar cheese

1 teaspoon vegetable oil

Four 8-inch whole-wheat flour tortillas

Lazy Spanish Rice (recipe follows) (optional)

1. Preheat the oven to 200 degrees F. Halve the avocado, remove the pit, and scrape the flesh into a blender. Add the cucumber, sour cream, cilantro, mint, lime juice, water, and chile powder. Blend until smooth. Season with the salt and pepper, cover with plastic wrap, and set aside.

2. Heat the olive oil in a large sauté pan over medium-high heat. Add the onion and bell pepper and sauté, stirring frequently, until they are tender and beginning to brown, about 4 minutes. Pour into a bowl and set aside.

3. **VEGETARIAN: Return the pan to medium-high heat and sauté the Soyrizo until heated through, about 1 minute. Transfer to a small bowl.**

4. Sauté the chorizo in the same pan, breaking up the meat with a wooden spoon, until cooked through, about 4 minutes. Drain well in a small fine-mesh sieve and transfer to another small bowl.

5. **VEGETARIAN: Lightly brush a large skillet with the vegetable oil and set over medium heat. Put a tortilla in the pan and sprinkle ⅔ cup of the cheese over the tortilla. Sprinkle a quarter of the sautéed vegetables and all the Soyrizo on half the tortilla. Cook until the cheese is melted and the tortilla is golden brown underneath, about 3 minutes. Fold the tortilla in half and transfer it to a baking sheet; keep warm in the oven.**

6. Repeat with the remaining tortillas, cheese, vegetables, and meat chorizo to make 3 quesadillas. Transfer finished quesadillas to the baking sheet in oven to keep them warm. While cooking the remaining quesadillas, be sure to keep the omnivore quesadillas separate from the vegetarian one.

7. Cut the vegetarian quesadilla into wedges and place on a plate. Cut the omnivore quesadillas and divide among 3 more plates. Serve with the dip and rice.

# Lazy Spanish Rice

*Serves 4 as a side dish*

This easy side dish is cooked with pantry staples in a rice cooker, so it is as easy as flipping a switch. The secret is a good-quality salsa and a slightly spicy chipotle bouillon cube, available at some grocery stores and Latin markets. You can use canned chipotle chiles instead if you can't find the chipotle cubes.

1½ cups long-grain white or brown rice

5 tablespoons mild or medium salsa

1 Knorr chipotle bouillon cube, crumbled, or 2 teaspoons chopped canned chipotle chiles

2¾ cups water

1 tablespoon butter

2 tablespoons sliced black olives

2 green onions, chopped

1. Combine the rice, salsa, bouillon cube, water, and butter in a rice cooker. Cook until the rice is tender. Fluff with a fork and fold in the olives and green onions.

∨ ∨ ∨ ∨ ∨ ∨ ∨ ∨ ∨ ∨ ∨ ∨ ∨ ∨ ∨ ∨ ∨ ∨ ∨ ∨ ∨ ∨ ∨ ∨ ∨ ∨ ∨ ∨ ∨ ∨ ∨ ∨ ∨ ∨ ∨ ∨ ∨ ∨ ∨ ∨ ∨

**VEGAN VARIATION:** Use olive oil instead of butter.

# QUICK TOMATO BASIL SOUP WITH TORTELLINI

*Serves 1 vegetarian and 3 omnivores as a main course*

This recipe is a little guilty pleasure I have been making since I was in college. Back then I used canned tomato soup and cheap dried tortellini. I've upgraded the recipe since then—now I use canned imported Italian tomatoes and fresh tortellini, but the idea is the same and the taste is as comforting as ever. I use prosciutto- or sausage-stuffed tortellini for the omnivore portion because I love the authentic Italian flavor; but you can streamline the recipe a little by using cheese tortellini for both the vegetarians and omnivores, if you like.

3 tablespoons butter

¾ cup thinly sliced shallots

1 tablespoon minced garlic

One 28-ounce can San Marzano tomatoes (see Resources)

4 cups Roasted Vegetable Stock (page 227) or mild packaged
   vegetable stock

1 teaspoon dried basil

1 bay leaf

¼ teaspoon ground cloves

Salt and freshly ground black pepper

Sugar

3 ounces fresh cheese tortellini

8 ounces prosciutto or sausage tortellini

1 teaspoon minced Italian parsley

1 baguette, warmed

1. Melt the butter over medium heat in a soup pot. Add the shallots and sauté until they are translucent, about 10 minutes. Add the garlic and cook until it is fragrant, about 30 seconds. Add the tomatoes and their juice, stock, basil, bay leaf, and cloves. Bring to a simmer and cook partially covered for 25 to 30 minutes. Remove the bay leaf and blend the soup with an immersion blender or in batches in a blender with the lid slightly ajar until smooth. Return the soup to the pot, season with the salt, pepper, and sugar to taste, and keep warm over low heat.

**2. VEGETARIAN: Bring a large pot of water to a boil. Add the cheese tortellini and simmer until tender, about 5 minutes. Use a slotted spoon to transfer the tortellini to 1 bowl, cover with foil, and set aside.**

3. Return the water to a boil and add the meat-filled tortellini. Simmer until tender, about 5 minutes; divide among 3 bowls.

4. Ladle the soup over the tortellini, and sprinkle the vegetarian bowl of soup with parsely. Serve with the baguette.

# CHINESE BROCCOLI WITH NO-OYSTER SAUCE AND CASHEWS OR CHICKEN

*Serves 1 vegetarian and 3 omnivores as part of a rice meal*

Oyster sauce is made with oyster extract, a food naturally high in glutamates that gives the thick sauce loads of umami flavor (see Mmm, Umami on page xii). Since it is made with seafood, it is off-limits for vegetarians. Fortunately there are some good vegetarian equivalents made with shiitake mushrooms. Look for vegetarian oyster sauce at Asian markets and specialty stores, and double-check the ingredients list to make sure it is oyster-free. If you can't find vegetarian oyster sauce, try the recipe for homemade No-Oyster Sauce that follows.

The sweet-salty flavor of vegetarian oyster sauce balances the slight bitterness of Chinese broccoli in this vegetarian stir-fry. I serve it alongside chicken stir-fried with real oyster sauce for omnivores to complete the meal.

> 2 cups water
> 1 pound Chinese broccoli, cut into ¾-inch pieces (see Glossary)
> 3 tablespoons vegetable oil
> ½ cup thinly sliced shallots
> 1 tablespoon sliced garlic
> 2 tablespoons peeled, minced ginger
> ¼ cup No-Oyster Sauce (recipe follows) or vegetarian oyster sauce

1 cup unsalted cashews, toasted

12 ounces boneless, skinless chicken breast, thinly sliced

2 tablespoons regular (or vegetarian) oyster sauce

6 cups hot steamed rice

1. Bring the water to a boil in a large wok. Place the broccoli in a steamer basket and set it over the boiling water. Cover and steam until the stalks are tender, about 3 minutes. Remove the broccoli, discard the water, and return the wok to high heat. When the wok is dry, heat 2 tablespoons of the oil. Add the shallots and stir-fry until they begin to brown, about 1 minute. Add the garlic and ginger and stir-fry for 20 seconds. Add the broccoli and ¼ cup of the vegetarian oyster sauce and stir-fry for 1 minute.

2. **Place half of the broccoli mixture on a serving platter, sprinkle with cashews, cover loosely with foil, and set aside.**

3. Put the remaining broccoli on another serving platter, cover with foil and set aside. Return the wok to high heat and add the remaining 1 tablespoon of oil. Add the chicken and stir-fry until it is cooked through, about 3 minutes. Add the regular oyster sauce and stir-fry for 1 minute. Place the chicken on the top of the cashew-free broccoli.

4. Serve the stir-fries with rice.

# No-Oyster Sauce

*Makes 2¼ cups sauce*

> 1 ounce (about 8 medium) dried shiitake mushrooms
> ½ cup soy sauce or mushroom soy sauce
> ¾ cup water
> 1 tablespoon cornstarch
> 1 tablespoon cold water
> 3 tablespoons brown sugar

1. Stem the mushrooms and discard stems. Grind the caps in a clean spice or coffee grinder in batches until they are a fine powder. Combine with the soy sauce and water in a small saucepan; bring to a simmer. Reduce the heat to medium low, cover, and simmer gently for 5 minutes. Remove the pan from the heat and let steep for 30 minutes.

2. Strain the mixture through a fine-mesh sieve, pressing on the solids to extract as much liquid as possible. Rinse the saucepan and return the strained liquid to the pan.

3. Combine the cornstarch and cold water in a small cup. Add the mixture and the brown sugar to the pan and simmer until thickened and bubbly, about 2 minutes. (The sauce can be prepared in advance and refrigerated in an airtight container for several weeks. Reheat gently over medium heat in a small pan, adding water if necessary to make a thick sauce.)

# STUFFED CHICKEN BREASTS AND PORTOBELLO MUSHROOMS

*Serves 1 to 2 vegetarians and 3 omnivores*

This all-in-one recipe is a great option for weeknight dinners when you're in the mood for something a little special but don't have the time to make multiple dishes. The zucchini keeps the stuffing extraordinarily moist and works equally well stuffed under the chicken breast skin as mounded in portobello mushrooms. The cooking time for both is about the same. Serve this with some buttered broccoli and you're done!

2 tablespoons butter

½ cup finely chopped onion

¼ cup finely chopped red bell pepper

1¼ cups grated zucchini (1 medium)

2 tablespoons finely chopped fresh basil

2 tablespoons finely chopped Italian parsley

3 cups fresh whole-wheat bread crumbs (from 4 slices of bread) (see **TIP**)

¼ cup grated Parmigiano-Reggiano cheese

Salt and freshly ground black pepper

1 egg, beaten

2 medium portobello mushrooms, stemmed

2 tablespoons olive oil

3 bone-in skin-on chicken breasts

½ cup dry white wine

1. Preheat the oven to 375 degrees F. Line a small rimmed baking sheet or baking dish with parchment paper.

2. Melt the butter in a large ovenproof sauté pan over medium-high heat. Add the onions and bell pepper and sauté, stirring constantly, until the vegetables are tender and beginning to brown, about 5 minutes. In a medium bowl, combine the onion mixture with the zucchini, basil, parsley, bread crumbs, and cheese. (Set the pan aside for later use.) Season the stuffing with the salt and pepper to taste. Stir in the egg and set aside.

3. **VEGETARIAN: Rub the mushrooms with 1 tablespoon of the olive oil, season both sides with the salt and pepper, and place them gill side up on the prepared baking sheet. Mound each mushroom with ½ cup of the stuffing; set aside.**

4. Carefully slide your fingers under the chicken breasts' skin to loosen it. Stuff ½ cup of the stuffing under the skin of each breast. Season both sides of the chicken with the salt and pepper and place in the ovenproof sauté pan. (The recipe can be prepared to this point up to 24 hours in advance, covered with plastic wrap, and refrigerated.)

5. Drizzle the chicken with the remaining 1 tablespoon of oil and transfer to the oven in the pan. Bake for 10 minutes.

6. **VEGETARIAN: Transfer the stuffed mushrooms to the oven.**

7. Bake both entrées until an instant-read thermometer registers 165 degrees F when inserted in the thickest part of the chicken and the mushrooms are tender when cut into with a paring knife, about 35 minutes more.

8. **VEGETARIAN: Put the mushrooms on 1 or 2 dinner plates and cover loosely with foil until ready to serve.**

9. Place the chicken breasts on 3 dinner plates. Place the sauté pan on the stove over high heat. Add the wine and bring to a simmer, scraping the browned bits off the bottom of the pan with a wooden spoon. Simmer until the wine has reduced by half, about 4 minutes. Spoon the sauce over the chicken breasts and serve.

   TIP: Do not use canned, sandy-textured bread crumbs in this recipe! To make soft fresh bread crumbs, tear whole-wheat sandwich bread into small pieces and pulse in a food processor until fine (or finely chop with a chef's knife). Fresh bread crumbs freeze well in a resealable freezer bag for up to 3 months.

∨∨∨∨∨∨∨∨∨∨∨∨∨∨∨∨∨∨∨∨∨∨∨∨∨∨∨∨∨∨∨∨∨∨

**VEGAN VARIATION:** Substitute olive oil for the butter in the stuffing and omit the egg and cheese from the vegetarian portion of the stuffing. Season the vegan stuffing with nutritional yeast instead of Parmigiano-Reggiano cheese.

# JAMBALAYA FOR EVERYONE

*Serves 1 to 2 vegetarians and 3 omnivores*

Jambalaya is a humble one-skillet dish of Cajun origin that uses rice and bits of this and that to feed many mouths. And so, though plenty of Cajuns will accuse me of heresy for even suggesting it, I use both spicy andouille and vegetarian sausages here. I do so in the spirit of feeding everyone, which is what jambalaya is all about, after all.

3 tablespoons olive oil

2 cups finely chopped onion

2 ribs celery, chopped

1 medium green bell pepper, finely chopped

1 tablespoon finely chopped garlic

4 teaspoons Cajun seasoning (see **TIP**)

1 cup long grain rice

One 14.5-ounce can diced tomatoes with juice

1¾ cups Roasted Vegetable Stock (page 227) or packaged
 vegetable stock

1 bay leaf

2 andouille sausage links or other spicy sausage (8 ounces)

2 vegetarian sausages (7 ounces) cut into ½-inch-thick slices

8 ounces shrimp, peeled and deveined

Hot sauce (optional)

1. Preheat the oven to 400 degrees F. In a large sauté pan with a lid, heat 2 tablespoons of the oil over medium-high heat until hot. Add the onion, celery, and green pepper and sauté, stirring occasionally until the onion is translucent, about 5 minutes. Add the garlic, Cajun seasoning, and rice; cook for 30 seconds. Add the tomatoes, stock, and bay leaf and bring to a simmer. Cover, reduce the heat to medium low, and cook for 20 minutes. Do not stir or the rice will become mushy.

2. Meanwhile, place the andouille sausages in a small baking dish and bake until just cooked through, about 20 minutes. Cut into bite-size pieces and cover with foil.

3. **VEGETARIAN: Heat the remaining 1 tablespoon of oil in a medium sauté pan over medium-high heat. Add the vegetarian sausage and sauté until brown and crisp, about 3 minutes per side. Fluff the rice mixture with a fork and toss a quarter of it with the vegetarian sausage in a small bowl. Cover with foil and set aside.**

4. Add the shrimp to the sauté pan used to cook the vegetarian sausage. Cook over medium-high heat until they are curled and just cooked through, about 2 minutes. Toss the shrimp and andouille sausage with the remaining rice mixture and place in a serving bowl. Serve both jambalayas with the hot sauce.

> **TIP:** Cajun seasonings vary widely between brands, but they usually contain cayenne, paprika, thyme, ground celery seed, and copious amounts of salt. I recommend using a salt-free Cajun seasoning (see Resources) in this recipe so you can control the amount of sodium in the dish.

# PHILLY CHEESE STEAKS

*Serves 1 vegetarian and 3 omnivores*

This recipe is written in homage to Philadelphia's famous gooey cheese-sauce-topped steak sandwiches. Slicing the steak when it is partially frozen makes it possible to get super-thin slices of meat, just like the sandwich stands in Philly. The vegetarian version uses seitan, which is a great protein-rich stand-in for steak. If you are in a real hurry, substitute thin slices of provolone cheese for the cheese sauce, and stick the sandwiches under the broiler for a moment to melt the cheese.

4 ounces Homemade Seitan (page 229) or packaged, cut into
½–inch strips

¼ teaspoon black pepper

¼ teaspoon garlic powder

1½ teaspoons soy sauce or Bragg Liquid Aminos All Purpose
Seasoning (see Glossary)

1¼ cups milk

1 bay leaf

4 peppercorns

2 tablespoons unsalted butter

3 tablespoons all-purpose flour

2 teaspoons Dijon mustard

1 pinch cayenne

2 cups grated sharp cheddar cheese

Salt

2 tablespoons vegetable oil

1 medium onion, halved, peeled, and sliced through the root end

1 large green bell pepper, thinly sliced

4 whole–wheat hoagie rolls, split lengthwise and toasted

12 ounces rib eye steak, trimmed of fat, frozen until semi-firm,
and thinly sliced

1. **VEGETARIAN: Toss the seitan strips with the pepper, garlic powder, and soy sauce; set aside.**

2. In a microwave-safe measuring cup, combine the milk, bay leaf, and peppercorns. Microwave for 2 minutes. (Alternatively, cook in a small saucepan over medium heat until bubbles form around the edges, about 8 minutes.) Set aside and let the milk steep for 5 minutes. Discard the bay leaf and peppercorns.

3. Melt the butter in a saucepan over medium heat, whisk in the flour, and cook for 1 minute. Gradually whisk in the hot milk and cook until the mixture is thick and bubbly, about 3 minutes. Turn the heat to low and whisk in the mustard, cayenne, and cheese. Season with salt and pepper, cover, and keep warm over the lowest possible heat.

4. In a large cast iron skillet or sauté pan, heat 1 tablespoon of the oil over high heat until hot but not smoking. Add the onion and bell pepper and sauté, stirring occasionally until they are limp and beginning to brown around the edges, about 5 minutes. Pour into a bowl, cover, and set aide.

5. **VEGETARIAN: Return the skillet to the heat add the remaining 1 tablespoon of oil and when it is hot, add the seitan. Sauté until the slices are crisp around the edges and heated through, about 2 minutes. Mound the strips on the bottom part of 1 roll.**

6. Place the skillet over medium-high heat. Season steak strips with salt and pepper and place them to the pan. Sear for 1 minute, flip with tongs, and cook until they are browned on the other side, about 1 minute. Divide among the bottom parts of the remaining 3 rolls.

7. Top the sandwiches with the sautéed vegetables and cheese sauce and serve.

v v v v v v v v v v v v v v v v v v v v v v v v v v v v v v v v v v v

**VEGAN VARIATION:** Serve the vegetarian sandwich without the cheese sauce.

# HOMEMADE SLOPPY JOES AND JOSEPHINES

*Serves 1 vegetarian and 3 omnivores*

Nostalgia for childhood foods is a funny thing; the dishes we wistfully remember (and crave) seldom measure up to our fond memories of them. So it goes with my hankering for sloppy joes, the messy "sandwich that eats like a meal" that was ubiquitous in the '70s. A quick glance at the ingredients list of the canned sloppy joe sauce I was familiar with had me gasping—high-fructose corn syrup and a long list of preservatives play starring roles. So much for my wholesome childhood memory!

This homemade recipe is a healthier alternative, there's lots less sugar, and soy crumbles stand in quite well for the ground beef in the vegetarian portion. To add a grown-up touch, garnish the sandwiches with thinly sliced red onion, avocado, or even a little baby arugula.

> 2 tablespoons olive oil
> ½ cup finely chopped onion
> ½ cup finely chopped green bell pepper
> 1 tablespoon minced garlic
> One 10.75-ounce can tomato purée
> 3 tablespoons ketchup
> ¼ cup water
> 2 tablespoons Dijon mustard
> 2 tablespoons loosely packed brown sugar
> ¼ teaspoon cayenne
> 1 teaspoon salt
> ½ teaspoon freshly ground black pepper
> 4 ounces soy crumbles (I like MorningStar Farms' Grillers
>     Recipe Crumbles)
> 1 pound lean ground beef or ground turkey
> 4 whole-wheat hamburger buns

1. Heat 1 tablespoon of the olive oil in a 12-inch skillet over medium heat. Add the onion and bell pepper and sauté, stirring occasionally, until the onion is translucent, about 10 minutes. Add the garlic and sauté until fragrant, about 30 seconds. Stir in the tomato purée, ketchup, water, mustard,

brown sugar, cayenne, salt, and pepper; cover and simmer gently for 20 minutes over low heat.

**2. VEGETARIAN: In a small bowl, gently combine the soy crumbles and 1 cup of the tomato mixture. Set aside and keep warm.**

3. Heat 1 tablespoon of the oil in a medium sauté pan. Add the ground beef and cook, breaking up the meat with a spatula, until it is thoroughly browned; drain. Stir the meat into the remaining sauce and bring to a simmer over medium heat.

4. Place the vegetarian mixture on 1 bun and the ground beef mixture on the remaining 3 buns and serve.

# QUICKIE CANNELLONI

*Serves 2 vegetarians and 3 omnivores*

Cannelloni are quite a bit of work when done the old-fashioned way—making home-made pasta sheets or boiling and filling dried pasta tubes usually forces this comfy favorite into the special-occasion category. Enter no-boil lasagna noodles, which can be transformed into pliable pasta sheets after a quick soak in hot water. Add good-quality jarred marinara and this special-occasion dish can be made any night.

6 ounces medium or firm tofu, drained

2 tablespoons minced fresh basil or jarred pesto sauce

1 tablespoon minced Italian parsley

2 pinches ground nutmeg

2 cups grated part-skim mozzarella cheese

6 tablespoons grated Parmigiano-Reggiano cheese

Salt and freshly ground black pepper

1 package no-boil lasagna noodles (I like Barilla's Oven Ready Lasagne Noodles)

One 25-ounce jar high-quality pasta sauce (I like Amy's brand Family Marinara)

12 ounces bulk turkey or pork Italian sausage, browned and drained

1 egg

1. Preheat the oven to 375 degrees F and bring a teakettle or 3-quart pot of water to a boil. Remove the kettle from the heat.

2. **VEGETARIAN: Mash the tofu, basil, parsley, 1 pinch nutmeg, ½ cup of the mozzarella cheese, and 3 tablespoons of the Parmigiano-Reggiano cheese together in a medium bowl. Season with salt and pepper and set aside.**

3. **VEGETARIAN: Fill a large baking dish with half of the hot water. Add 6 lasagna noodles, spreading them so they are all in contact with the water but are not uniformly stacked. (This will prevent the sheets from sticking together.) Soak the sheets until they are pliable, about 3 minutes. Put ½ cup of the pasta sauce in a small**

baking dish. Remove 1 sheet of pasta from the water and place it on a cutting board. Put 2 heaping tablespoons of the tofu-cheese mixture across the short side of the pasta sheet and roll it into a cylinder shape. Place it seam side down in the baking dish. Repeat, making 6 tofu cannelloni. Top with ½ cup of tomato sauce and ¼ cup of the mozzarella cheese; set aside.

4. Combine the sausage, ½ cup of the mozzarella cheese, the remaining 3 tablespoons of the Parmigiano-Reggiano cheese, and egg in a medium bowl; stir to combine.

5. Replace the pasta-soaking water with the remaining hot water from the kettle and add 10 pasta sheets. Soak until the sheets are pliable, about 3 minutes. Spoon ½ cup of the tomato sauce on the bottom of a medium baking dish. Fill the pasta as with the tofu batch, using 2 heaping table-spoons of sausage-cheese filling per roll. Place them seam side down in the medium baking dish. Spoon the remaining tomato sauce over the sausage cannelloni and sprinkle with the remaining ¾ cup of mozzarella cheese. (Both batches of cannelloni can be made up to 2 days ahead. Wrap with plastic wrap and refrigerate. If baking chilled cannelloni, bake for an additional 15 minutes.)

6. Spray 2 pieces of foil with nonstick cooking spray and cover the baking dishes tightly. Bake for 40 minutes. Uncover, and bake until the sauce is bubbly and the cheese is golden brown, about 10 minutes.

ᐯ ᐯ ᐯ ᐯ ᐯ ᐯ ᐯ ᐯ ᐯ ᐯ ᐯ ᐯ ᐯ ᐯ ᐯ ᐯ ᐯ ᐯ ᐯ ᐯ ᐯ ᐯ ᐯ ᐯ ᐯ ᐯ ᐯ ᐯ ᐯ ᐯ ᐯ ᐯ ᐯ ᐯ ᐯ ᐯ ᐯ ᐯ ᐯ ᐯ

VEGAN VARIATION: Make sure the pasta is egg-free; omit the cheeses in the tofu filling and top with grated vegan mozzarella.

# DEEP-DISH CHICAGO-STYLE PIZZAS

*Serves 1 to 2 vegetarians and 1 to 2 omnivores*

This recipe for gooey deep-dish pizza is really embarrassingly easy—store-bought pizza dough is baked in oven-safe skillets instead of fussing with pizza peels and baking stones, and the toppings are just as simple. If you don't have oven-safe skillets, bake the pizzas in 8-inch cake pans brushed with olive oil instead.

> 2 tablespoons olive oil, plus additional for the pans
> 1 meatless Italian sausage (about 4 ounces), roughly chopped
> ½ teaspoon fennel seeds
> 2 pounds prepared pizza dough, at room temperature
> 2½ cups shredded mozzarella cheese
> One 15-ounce can diced tomatoes with Italian herbs, drained
> 1 Italian pork sausage (about 4 ounces), casing removed

1. Preheat the oven to 425 degrees F.

2. **VEGETARIAN: Heat 1 tablespoon of the oil in an 8- to 10-inch oven-safe skillet over medium-high heat. Add the meatless sausage and ¼ teaspoon of the fennel seeds; sauté until the sausage is golden brown, about 4 minutes. Transfer to a small plate. Brush the bottom and sides of the skillet with some of the oil. Roll one portion of dough on a lightly floured surface into a 10-inch round and place it in the prepared skillet, letting the dough come up the sides. Sprinkle with half the cheese, half the tomatoes, and all the meatless sausage; set aside.**

3. Stir the remaining ¼ teaspoon of fennel seeds into the pork sausage. Heat the remaining 1 tablespoon of oil in another 8- to 10-inch oven-safe skillet over medium heat. Form the sausage into small clumps and sauté until browned and just cooked through, about 8 minutes. Transfer to a small plate, scraping out any browned bits with a spatula. Brush the bottom and sides of the skillet with some of the oil. Roll the remaining dough into an 10-inch round on a lightly floured surface and place it in the prepared

skillet, letting the dough come up the sides. Sprinkle with the remaining cheese, tomatoes, and all the pork sausage.

4. Bake both pizzas until the edges are deep golden brown and the cheese is bubbly, about 35 minutes. Serve from the skillets immediately.

# CEDAR PLANK SALMON AND PORTOBELLO MUSHROOMS WITH GRILLED TOMATO-FENNEL SALAD

*Serves 1 to 2 vegetarians and 3 omnivores*

Grilling on cedar planks imparts a subtle smoky flavor to fish and vegetables without requiring a smoker or other expensive gear. Find the planks at gourmet stores in bundles of four or more, or seek out less expensive untreated cedar planks at home improvement stores; just make sure they have not been treated with chemicals. You must soak the planks in cool water for 3 hours before grilling so that they will smoke but not catch fire when on the grill.

Two 13- by 8-inch cedar planks
1 medium fennel bulb
1 pound small heirloom tomatoes
½ small red onion
⅓ cup plus 1 tablespoon olive oil
½ cup kalamata olives, pitted
1 tablespoon capers, roughly chopped
1 tablespoon balsamic vinegar
½ cup basil leaves
Salt and freshly ground black pepper
2 tablespoons garlic, smashed to a paste
2 tablespoons chopped fresh thyme leaves
2 large portobello mushrooms, stemmed
Three 6-ounce wild salmon fillets, pin bones removed, skin on

1. Submerge the planks in cold water and allow them to soak for at least 3 hours. Preheat the grill to medium high, or prepare charcoal and wait until it has just ashed over.

2. To make the salad, remove any feathery leaves from the fennel and reserve for another use. Halve the bulb lengthwise, cut out the hard core in the bottom, and discard. Brush the fennel, tomatoes, and onion lightly with 1 tablespoon of the oil. Grill the fennel and onions for 5 minutes; add the

tomatoes and grill, turning once until they are charred in places, about 5 minutes. Remove the fennel, onions, and tomatoes from the grill. Finely chop and combine in a serving bowl with the olives, capers, vinegar, and basil. Season with salt and pepper and set the salad aside.

3. Combine the remaining ⅓ cup of the oil, garlic, and thyme in a small bowl; set aside. Put the cedar planks on the grill, cover, and grill until the planks just begin to smoke, about 10 minutes. While the planks heat up, prepare the mushrooms and salmon.

4. **VEGETARIAN: With a soup spoon, scrape off the dark gills on the underside of the mushrooms and discard. Brush the mushrooms liberally with the garlic-oil mixture and season with salt and pepper. Place the mushrooms gill side down on 1 plank.**

5. Brush the salmon with some of the garlic-oil mixture. Season with the salt and pepper and place the fish fillets skin side down on the other plank.

6. Cover the grill, open the ventilation holes about halfway, and grill until the mushrooms are tender when pierced with a fork and the salmon is medium rare, 10 to 15 minutes (see **TIP** on page 70). With a spatula, remove the salmon from the grill and place on 3 dinner plates.

7. **VEGETARIAN: Turn the mushrooms gill side up, spoon any of the remaining garlic-oil mixture into the caps, and top with the cheese. Cover and continue to grill for another 2 minutes, until the cheese has melted. Put the mushrooms on 1 or 2 plates and fill with some of the tomato-fennel salad.**

8. Spoon the remaining salad over the salmon and serve.

ⅴ ⅴ ⅴ ⅴ ⅴ ⅴ ⅴ ⅴ ⅴ ⅴ ⅴ ⅴ ⅴ ⅴ ⅴ ⅴ ⅴ ⅴ ⅴ ⅴ ⅴ ⅴ ⅴ ⅴ ⅴ ⅴ ⅴ ⅴ ⅴ ⅴ ⅴ ⅴ ⅴ ⅴ ⅴ ⅴ ⅴ ⅴ ⅴ ⅴ
**VEGAN VARIATION:** Omit the cheese from the mushrooms.

# MOROCCAN VEGETABLES, FISH, AND COUSCOUS EN PAPILLOTE

*Serves 1 vegetarian and 3 omnivores*

The cooking method *en papillote* (cooking ingredients in parchment parcels) may have a fancy-sounding French name, but the flavors of this simple recipe are purely Moroccan. Fish and/or julienne vegetables are anointed with lemon-spice butter and roasted in easy-to-assemble parchment parcels, which lets the ingredients steam-bathe in their own juices, resulting in al dente vegetables and perfectly cooked fish in no time.

You'll have to be a bit bossy come mealtime: the parcels take only 12 minutes to bake, and it's important everyone is at the table the moment dinner comes out of the oven so they can open the packets and breathe in all the delicious steam.

**COUSCOUS:** 1 cup Roasted Vegetable Stock (page 227) or packaged vegetable stock

¾ cup whole wheat couscous

2 tablespoons finely chopped Italian parsley

2 tablespoons lemon juice

¼ cup shelled pistachios, coarsely chopped

Salt and freshly ground black pepper

**LEMON BUTTER:** 4 tablespoons unsalted butter, at room temperature

1 teaspoon ground cumin

1 tablespoon finely chopped Italian parsley

Zest of ½ lemon

1 large garlic clove, chopped and smashed to a paste (about 1 teaspoon)

⅛ teaspoon cayenne

½ teaspoon kosher salt

**FISH AND VEGETABLES:** 1 small red pepper, thinly sliced into 3-inch lengths

6 ounces thin asparagus, tough ends discarded, cut into 3-inch lengths

1 large carrot, julienned and cut into 3-inch lengths

3 firm white fish fillets (snapper, tilapia, halibut), about 6 ounces each

Salt and freshly ground black pepper

1. Preheat the oven to 450 degrees F. Cut 4 pieces of parchment paper into 15-inch lengths. Fold each length in half crosswise; starting at the fold, cut each piece of folded paper into a large half-heart shape, as if you were making a valentine.

2. Bring the stock to a boil in a small saucepan. Add the couscous, parsley, and lemon juice; stir, cover, and set aside for 10 minutes. Fluff with a fork, stir in the pistachios, and season with the salt and pepper.

3. In a small bowl, combine the butter, cumin, parsley, lemon zest, garlic, cayenne, and salt; set aside.

4. **VEGETARIAN: Open 1 piece of parchment. In the center of the half closest to you, mound about ⅔ cup of the couscous. Top with one third of the red pepper, asparagus, and carrot and dot with a generous tablespoon of the lemon-butter mixture. Fold the top part of the paper over the ingredients so the edges meet. Make small overlapping folds in the paper to seal the edges together. Crimp the folds with your thumbnail to tightly seal the folds and prevent steam from escaping. Mark the packet with a "V" in pencil and place it on a baking sheet.**

5. Divide the couscous and vegetables among the remaining 3 parchment parcels. Season the fish liberally with the salt and pepper and put 1 fillet on top of each couscous-vegetable mound. Dot the tops of the fish with the remaining lemon-butter mixture and fold and crimp the parcels closed. Carefully transfer them to the baking sheet.

6. Bake all of the packets for 12 minutes, or until the fish is cooked through (see **TIP** on page 70). Using a wide spatula, transfer each packet to a dinner plate, making sure the vegetarian receives the "V" packet.

v v v v v v v v v v v v v v v v v v v v v v v v v v v v v v v v v v v v v v

**VEGAN VARIATION:** Omit the butter in the vegetarian packet. Drizzle the vegetables with lemon-infused olive oil (available at gourmet stores) and sprinkle with minced garlic, ground cumin, salt, and freshly ground black pepper.

# 4

## CLASSIC RECIPES FOR EVERYONE

**W**ho doesn't love steaming potpies, ribbons of pasta tossed with rich, chunky Bolognese sauce, or saucy red chile enchiladas? The recipes in this chapter cover the dishes we all grew up with and have had love affairs with longer than we could even say "comfort food."

Just because most of these favorites normally contain a heaping helping of meat doesn't mean vegetarians and vegans must resort to cold salads or frozen veggie burgers for dinner. Just an extra step or two and everyone at your table can be included in these timeless family favorites.

# ORECCHIETTE AND MEATBALLS

*Serves 1 to 2 vegetarians and 3 omnivores*

Pasta and meatballs is one of those wonderfully comforting dishes we can all relate to. Fortunately, vegetarians don't have to give up the dish; these vegetarian meatballs have a little chew and loads of flavor, just like "real" meatballs.

Though the recipe may seem long, don't be put off! The ingredients are nearly the same for both the meatball and the "meat"ball recipes, so the dish comes together quickly. I use ear-shaped orecchiette pasta because I love the way it acts like little catchers' mitts for the meatballs and sauce. You can use spaghetti or any other shape of pasta you like.

8 ounces lean ground beef or ground dark-meat turkey

2 teaspoons minced garlic, smashed to a paste

2 tablespoons very finely minced onion

1½ teaspoons Italian seasoning

½ cup fresh bread crumbs (from about 1 slice of stale sandwich bread)

1 egg, separated

3 tablespoons buttermilk, milk, or plain yogurt

7 tablespoons grated Parmigiano-Reggiano cheese

¾ teaspoon salt

¼ teaspoon freshly ground black pepper, plus additional

4 tablespoons olive oil

One 24-ounce jar marinara sauce (I like Amy's brand Family Marinara)

¼ cup textured vegetable protein (TVP) (see page xviii)

¼ cup boiling vegetable stock or water

1½ teaspoons tomato paste

3 tablespoons vital wheat gluten flour (see Glossary)

1 pound orecchiette or other pasta

3 tablespoons minced fresh basil

1. In a medium bowl combine the ground beef, 1½ teaspoons of the garlic, 2 teaspoons of the onion, 1 teaspoon of the Italian seasoning, bread crumbs,

egg yolk, buttermilk, 5 tablespoons of the cheese, and ½ teaspoon of the salt. Season with ¼ teaspoon of the pepper and mix well. Using 1 heaping tablespoon per meatball, roll the mixture into about 24 meatballs.

2. Heat 3 tablespoons of the oil in a 12-inch or larger skillet over medium-high heat. Add half the meatballs, reduce the heat to medium, and cook until browned and cooked through, about 10 minutes total. Drain off the fat, add 2¼ cups (about two thirds) of the marinara sauce, and return the pan to medium-low heat. Bring a large pot of water to a boil for the pasta.

3. **VEGETARIAN: In a medium bowl, combine the TVP and the boiling stock or water; set aside for 5 minutes. Add the tomato paste, the remaining ½ teaspoon of garlic, 4 teaspoons of onion, ½ teaspoon of Italian seasoning, egg white, 2 tablespoons of cheese, ¼ teaspoon of salt, vital wheat gluten flour, and a few grinds of pepper. Combine with a wooden spoon. Using a scant tablespoon per ball, roll the mixture into 10 to 12 balls. Heat the remaining 1 tablespoon of oil in a nonstick sauté pan over medium heat. Add the "meat"balls and cook until they are golden brown, about 10 minutes total (watch carefully and reduce the heat if they begin to brown too quickly). Add the remaining marinara sauce and reduce the heat to medium low. Do not stir too much or the "meat"balls may break apart.**

4. Add the pasta to the boiling water, stir, and boil until al dente according to package instructions. Drain the pasta and place one third of the pasta in a small serving bowl; top with the vegetarian meatballs and sauce. Place the remaining pasta in a medium serving bowl. Top with the meatballs and sauce. Sprinkle both bowls with the basil and serve.

TIP: Both the meatballs and "meat"balls can be cooked, cooled, and frozen in resealable freezer bags for up to 2 months. Just reheat them in marinara sauce for 30 minutes and serve.

# HANGER STEAK AND CRISP POLENTA TRIANGLES WITH SHIITAKE–RED WINE SAUCE

*Serves 1 vegetarian and 3 omnivores*

This rich mushroom gravy is so earthy and satisfying that it's good on just about anything, including steak or polenta. Hanger steak, sometimes labeled "hanging tenderloin," is a relatively inexpensive cut with a slightly chewy texture and loads of beefy flavor. Though the cut was found only in French restaurants just a few years ago, it has gained popularity among home cooks who love it for its flavor and price (it's often cheaper than flank or New York strip). If you can't find hanger steak, use your favorite cut instead.

If you are in a hurry, you can pan-fry packaged ready-to-eat polenta (available in 12-ounce tubes at grocery stores) instead of making homemade polenta.

**POLENTA:** 1 teaspoon softened butter

4 cups water

1 teaspoon salt

1 cup polenta

1 teaspoon nutritional yeast (see Glossary)

¼ cup grated Parmigiano-Reggiano cheese

3 tablespoons olive oil, for frying

**SAUCE:** 2 tablespoons butter

3 tablespoons minced shallots

8 ounces (4 cups) shiitake mushrooms, stemmed, caps sliced

½ teaspoon salt

½ teaspoon chopped fresh thyme

½ cup Pinot Noir wine

1 tablespoon tomato paste

1½ cups Roasted Mushroom Stock (see page 226) or
    packaged mushroom stock (see Resources)

1½ teaspoons cornstarch

1 tablespoon water

| STEAK AND | 1 pound asparagus (finger-thick stalks work best), tough ends |
| ASPARAGUS: | snapped off and discarded |

1 tablespoon extra-virgin olive oil

1 tablespoon lemon zest

Kosher salt and freshly ground black pepper

1 tablespoon vegetable oil

Two 8-ounce hanger steaks

1. Rub one 9-inch pie plate with the softened butter. Bring 4 cups of water and the salt to a boil over high heat. Reduce the heat to medium and gradually whisk in the polenta. Gently simmer, stirring frequently with a wooden spoon, until the polenta has thickened, about 20 minutes. Stir in the nutritional yeast and cheese and pour the polenta into the prepared pie plate. Refrigerate until the polenta is firm to the touch, 1 hour. Cut the polenta into 6 triangles and set aside. (The polenta can be made up to 2 days in advance. Cool completely, cover with plastic wrap, and refrigerate until ready to use.)

2. Preheat the oven to 450 degrees F. For the sauce, melt the 2 tablespoons of butter in a medium saucepan over medium-high heat. Add the shallots and sauté until they are softened, about 1 minute. Add the mushrooms, sprinkle with the ½ teaspoon of salt and thyme, and sauté, stirring once, until the mushrooms are browned and have given off their liquid, about 4 minutes. Reduce the heat to medium, add the wine, and simmer, scraping any browned bits on the bottom of the pan until the wine has almost evaporated, about 1 minute. Add the tomato paste and stock and bring to a simmer. Combine the cornstarch and the water in a small bowl, stir into the gravy, and simmer until bubbly, about 1 minute. Reduce the heat and keep warm over low heat.

3. Pan-fry the polenta. Heat the olive oil in a large sauté pan over medium-high heat until hot. Carefully add the polenta triangles, reduce the heat to medium, and cook without moving them until they are golden around the edges, about 5 minutes. Reduce the heat to medium low and carefully flip the triangles with a spatula. Continue to cook while preparing the steaks; reduce the heat if the polenta becomes too brown.

4. On a small baking sheet, toss together the asparagus, olive oil, lemon zest, and season with salt and pepper to taste; set aside.

5. Heat the vegetable oil in a large oven-safe sauté pan or cast iron skillet until hot. Season the steaks with the kosher salt and pepper and sear on 1 side until browned, about 3 minutes. With tongs turn the steaks over and transfer the pan to the oven. Place the baking sheet with asparagus in the oven on the rack above the steaks. Roast the asparagus until tender and the steaks until an instant-read thermometer registers 120 degrees F when inserted in the thickest part of the steak, about 5 minutes (the steaks will be medium rare to medium; cooking hanger steaks beyond this point is not advisable). Place the steaks on a cutting board, cover them loosely with foil, and let them rest for 10 minutes.

6. Slice the steaks thinly against the grain. Place 1 piece of polenta and a small bundle of the asparagus on 3 plates. Arrange the steak slices in a fan-shape on the polenta, top with sauce, and serve.

7. **VEGETARIAN: Place 2 to 3 triangles of the polenta on the vegetarian's plate, top with mushroom sauce and serve with the remaining asparagus.**

v v v v v v v v v v v v v v v v v v v v v v v v v v v v v v v v v v v v v v

**VEGAN VARIATION:** Make the polenta without cheese. Brush the polenta dish with olive oil, and make the sauce with olive oil instead of butter.

# CRISPY BAJA FISH OR BLACK BEAN AND CHAYOTE SQUASH TACOS

*Serves 2 vegetarians and 4 omnivores*

Baja-style fish tacos are everywhere on the West Coast, from mobile carts to upscale eateries. The standard recipe includes crisp, batter-fried white fish tucked into griddle-warmed corn tortillas topped with crisp cabbage slaw and sour cream sauce.

In this recipe, a bean, corn, and chayote squash succotash provide vegetarians with a protein-rich alternative to the fish. It goes so well with the crunchy coleslaw topping that omnivores will probably want to try a vegetarian taco as well; there is enough succotash in this recipe for everyone.

| | |
|---|---|
| **SUCCOTASH:** | 1 tablespoon olive oil |
| | ¾ cup finely chopped red onion |
| | 1 tablespoon minced jalapeño pepper (about ½ medium) |
| | 10 ounces chayote squash (see Glossary), peeled, pitted, and cut into ½-inch dice (about 1 cup) |
| | 1 teaspoon ground cumin |
| | One 10-ounce can black beans, rinsed and drained |
| | 2 ears fresh corn shaved off the cob or frozen sweet corn (about 1 cup) |
| | ½ cup tomato sauce |
| | ¼ cup water |
| | Salt |
| **COLESLAW AND SAUCE:** | 3 tablespoons white wine vinegar |
| | ½ teaspoon salt |
| | 1 teaspoon sugar |
| | 1 small fennel bulb (4 ounces) |
| | 3 cups shredded green cabbage |
| | ½ cup thinly sliced red onion |
| | 3 tablespoons minced cilantro |
| | ½ cup sour cream or plain yogurt |
| | 1 teaspoon yellow mustard |

| | |
|---|---|
| **FISH AND**<br>**ASSEMBLY:** | 24 small corn tortillas<br>½ cup all-purpose flour<br>½ teaspoon salt<br>1 tablespoon mustard powder<br>1 teaspoon New Mexican chile powder<br>½ teaspoon Mexican oregano<br>2 eggs, beaten<br>1 cup panko (see **TIP**)<br>Vegetable oil, for frying<br>12 ounces snapper, tilapia, halibut, or other white fish,<br>    cut into finger-size strips |

1. **VEGETARIAN: Heat the oil in a medium sauté pan over medium-high heat. Add the onion, jalapeño, and chayote and sauté, stirring occasionally, until the onions begin to brown, about 5 minutes. Add the cumin, beans, corn, tomato sauce, and water; bring to a simmer. Cover, reduce the heat to medium low, and simmer gently until the chayote is tender and translucent, about 20 minutes. Season with the salt and keep warm over low heat. (The succotash can be made up to 2 days ahead; cool and refrigerate in an airtight container. To reheat, microwave or heat gently in a small saucepan.)**

2. For the coleslaw, combine the vinegar, salt, and sugar in a small saucepan. Cook over medium heat until the sugar has dissolved, about 1 minute. (Alternatively, put in a microwave-safe bowl and microwave until hot.) Halve the fennel lengthwise, cut out the hard core in the center, and discard. Thinly shave the fennel on a mandoline or slice as thinly as possible with a sharp knife. Combine fennel, cabbage, onions, and cilantro with the hot vinegar mixture; set aside. In a small bowl, whisk together the sour cream and mustard and set aside.

3. Preheat the oven to 200 degrees F. Wrap the tortillas in a clean, moist towel and place them in the oven to warm while frying the fish.

4. Line a rimmed baking sheet with paper towels. Combine the flour, salt, mustard powder, chile powder, and oregano in a shallow bowl. Whisk the eggs in another shallow bowl and place the panko in a third bowl. Add

enough vegetable oil to a small saucepan so that it is at least 2 inches deep. Heat the oil over high heat until hot, about 350 degrees F on a deep-fry thermometer or until a cube of bread turns golden brown in 3 seconds when dropped into the oil.

5. While the oil heats, gently dredge 4 or 5 fish strips in the flour mixture, then the eggs, and finally the panko, pressing to help the panko adhere. Fry the fish in batches until crisp and golden brown, about 3 minutes. Reduce the temperature if the fish browns too quickly. Transfer the fish to the prepared baking sheet and keep warm in the oven while you bread and fry the remaining fish in small batches.

6. To serve, put the succotash, fish, coleslaw, and sour cream sauce in serving bowls. Let diners build their own tacos: place a few pieces of fish or spoonfuls of the succotash into a tortilla, top with coleslaw and drizzle with sauce.

TIP: Panko is a crisp breading available at grocery stores where Asian ingredients are sold. Coarse bread crumbs or cracker crumbs can be substituted in a pinch.

∨ ∨ ∨ ∨ ∨ ∨ ∨ ∨ ∨ ∨ ∨ ∨ ∨ ∨ ∨ ∨ ∨ ∨ ∨ ∨ ∨ ∨ ∨ ∨ ∨ ∨ ∨ ∨ ∨ ∨ ∨ ∨ ∨ ∨ ∨ ∨ ∨ ∨

VEGAN VARIATION: Omit the sour cream sauce from the vegetarian tacos or substitute vegan sour cream in the sauce.

# CREAMY CHICKEN OR PORTOBELLO LASAGNAS WITH SPINACH NOODLES

*Serves 2 vegetarians and 3 omnivores*

Making your own pasta sheets takes a bit of time, but the new pasta rolling attachments that fit into stand mixers make fresh pasta sheets a snap; this spinach pasta is so delicious it's definitely worth the effort. If you are short on time or don't have a pasta maker, use cooked boxed spinach lasagna noodles or plain no-boil noodles. The lasagnas in this recipe are layered in individual gratin dishes, so you can customize each lasagna—a real plus if you are cooking for a picky eater.

5 ounces (½ package) frozen leaf spinach, thawed

2 cups all-purpose flour, plus additional

1 egg

1 tablespoon salt, plus additional

5 cups low-fat milk

1 medium garlic clove crushed with side of a knife

1 bay leaf

2 sprigs fresh thyme

4 tablespoons butter

⅓ cup minced shallots

2 pinches white pepper

⅛ teaspoon freshly ground nutmeg

2 large portobello mushrooms, stemmed

2 tablespoons olive oil

1 teaspoon minced garlic

½ cup dry Marsala wine or dry sherry

3 cups bite-size broccoli florets

¼ cup water

1½ cups grated Parmigiano-Reggiano cheese

½ rotisserie chicken, skin and bones discarded, torn into
   bite-size pieces

1. Place the spinach in a colander and squeeze out all the moisture. Finely chop the spinach and put it in the bowl of a stand mixer. Add 1½ cups of the flour, egg, and a pinch of the salt; with the paddle attachment, mix until the ingredients come together. Switch to the dough hook and mix until the dough is smooth and elastic, about 3 minutes. (Alternatively, mix the dough and knead by hand for 10 minutes.) Wrap the dough in plastic wrap and let it rest while making the filling and sauce. (The dough can be made up to 2 days in advance; wrap tightly in plastic wrap and refrigerate until ready to use. Bring to room temperature before using.)

2. Preheat the oven to 350 degrees F. For the sauce, combine the milk, garlic, bay leaf, and thyme in a 2-quart saucepan. Cook over medium heat until bubbles form just around the edges of the pan, about 8 minutes. (Alternatively, microwave in a microwave-safe bowl until hot, about 3 minutes.) Remove from the heat and let the mixture steep for 10 minutes. Pour it through a fine-mesh strainer into a large bowl with a spout. Discard the garlic, bay leaf, and thyme. Wash out the pan and return it to medium heat. Add the butter and shallots and sauté for 2 minutes. Whisk in the remaining ½ cup of flour and cook for 1 minute, stirring constantly. Slowly whisk in the milk and cook, stirring frequently until the sauce is thickened and bubbly, about 10 minutes. (Decrease the heat as needed to keep the sauce from scorching on the bottom.) Season with the salt, pepper, and nutmeg; keep warm over low heat.

3. **VEGETARIAN: Scrape away the dark gills from the underside of the mushrooms and discard; thinly slice the caps. Heat the oil in a small sauté pan over medium-high heat; add the mushrooms and sauté, stirring occasionally, until they have given off their liquid, about 2 minutes. Add the garlic and continue to sauté until the mushrooms are tender, about 1 minute. Add the wine and simmer until it has nearly evaporated, about 1 minute. Pour the mixture into a small bowl and set aside.**

4. Return the pan to medium-high heat, add the broccoli and water, cover, and cook until the broccoli is crisp-tender, about 2 minutes. Drain and set aside.

**5.** Bring a large pot of water with the remaining 1 tablespoon of salt to a boil. Divide the dough into 4 pieces and dust them with the flour. Slightly flatten 1 piece and feed it through the pasta maker on the thickest setting. Fold the dough in half and feed it through again on the same setting. Dust with the flour and continue to feed through the rollers, turning to the next-thinnest setting each time through, until you reach the third-thinnest setting (number 5 on most pasta machines). Cut the sheets into lengths slightly shorter than the gratin dishes. Repeat with the remaining dough. You will need about 16 pieces of pasta. (Freeze any remaining pasta dough in a resealable freezer bag for up to 2 months.)

**6.** Preheat the oven to 350 degrees F. Spray 5 gratin dishes with nonstick cooking spray. Cook the pasta in the boiling water until tender, about 2 minutes. Drain in a colander and rinse with cold water. Toss the pasta sheets with nonstick cooking spray and lay them out on a clean work surface.

**7. VEGETARIAN: Ladle a few tablespoons of sauce on the bottom of 2 gratin dishes. Place a strip of pasta on top of the sauce in each gratin dish. Spoon half the mushrooms and a bit of the broccoli on top of the pasta; sprinkle with a few tablespoons of cheese and sauce. Add another layer of pasta, the remaining mushrooms, a bit more broccoli, 3 tablespoons of sauce, and a sprinkle of cheese.**

**8.** Layer the remaining pasta in gratin dishes with the chicken, remaining broccoli, cheese, and sauce. Place on baking sheet. (The lasagnas can be made up to 2 days in advance; cover with plastic wrap and refrigerate until ready to bake.)

**9.** Place the gratin dishes on a baking sheet. Bake until the sauce is bubbly and the cheese is golden brown, about 45 minutes. Let them cool for 5 minutes before serving.

# COUNTRY BENEDICT

*Serves 1 vegetarian and 3 omnivores*

Nothing says laid-back Sunday morning (or evening) like hot biscuits swathed with creamy, sausage-studded pan gravy. It's one of my favorite comfort foods. My vegetarian husband likes the dish, too, provided I make his portion with vegetarian breakfast links. I serve my biscuits and gravy with scrambled eggs cooked in a double boiler (it yields perfect, creamy eggs every time), so the recipe becomes a sort of countrified version of eggs Benedict. If you're as slow to wake up as I am, you can make the biscuits and gravy up to a day in advance and reheat them in the morning right before serving. Or better yet, make this dish for dinner when you're awake enough to appreciate it.

8 Home-Style Biscuits (recipe follows)

2¾ cups milk

1 garlic clove, halved lengthwise

1 bay leaf

6 peppercorns

1 teaspoon vegetable oil

2 ounces vegetarian breakfast sausage (I like Boca meatless breakfast links), roughly chopped

3 tablespoons butter

3 tablespoons flour

1 teaspoon poultry seasoning

1 teaspoon hot sauce

Salt and freshly ground black pepper

8 ounces bulk pork or turkey breakfast sausage, browned and drained

8 large eggs, lightly beaten

3 tablespoons finely chopped parsley or chives

1. Combine the milk, garlic, bay leaf, and peppercorns in a small saucepan. Cook over medium heat until bubbles form just around the edges of the pan, about 8 minutes. (Alternatively, microwave for 3 minutes in a microwave-safe measuring cup.) Remove from the heat and let the mixture steep for 10 minutes. Remove the garlic, bay leaf, and peppercorns and discard.

2. **VEGETARIAN: Heat the oil over medium-high heat in a large skillet or sauté pan. Add the vegetarian sausage and sauté until it is browned and crisp, about 3 minutes. Transfer to a small bowl, cover, and set aside.**

3. Return the skillet to medium heat and melt the butter. Whisk in the flour and poultry seasoning and cook for 1 minute. Gradually whisk in the hot milk and cook, whisking constantly until the gravy is thick and bubbly, about 2 minutes. Stir in the hot sauce and season with the salt and pepper to taste.

4. **VEGETARIAN: Transfer ⅔ cup of the sauce to the bowl with the vegetarian sausage. Cover and keep warm.**

5. Stir the browned pork sausage into the remaining sauce and keep warm over low heat. (Both gravies can be made up to 2 days ahead and refrigerated in airtight containers. Reheat gently and thin with additional milk, if necessary.)

6. In a medium pot bring 3 inches of water to a simmer. Spray a metal mixing bowl with nonstick cooking spray. Add the eggs and set the bowl over the simmering water. Cook, occasionally scraping the bottom and sides of the bowl with a rubber spatula, until the eggs are just set, about 5 minutes.

7. Halve the warm biscuits horizontally and divide them among 4 plates. Top with the scrambled eggs, sausage or vegetarian sausage gravy, and parsley. Serve immediately.

ᴠ ᴠ ᴠ ᴠ ᴠ ᴠ ᴠ ᴠ ᴠ ᴠ ᴠ ᴠ ᴠ ᴠ ᴠ ᴠ ᴠ ᴠ ᴠ ᴠ ᴠ ᴠ ᴠ ᴠ ᴠ ᴠ ᴠ ᴠ ᴠ ᴠ ᴠ ᴠ ᴠ ᴠ ᴠ ᴠ ᴠ ᴠ ᴠ ᴠ

**VEGAN VARIATION:** Make the gravy with unsweetened soy milk instead of dairy milk, and serve without eggs. If your omnivores are diehard dairy fans, whisk a few tablespoons of half-and-half into the gravy after setting aside the vegan portion.

# Home-Style Biscuits

*Makes eight 2½-inch biscuits*

> 2 cups all-purpose flour
> ½ teaspoon salt
> ½ teaspoon onion powder
> 1 tablespoon baking powder
> ½ cup (1 stick) cold unsalted butter, cut into small pieces
> ¾ cup cream or milk

1. Preheat the oven to 425 degrees F. Line a baking sheet with parchment paper. Combine the flour, salt, onion powder, and baking powder in a large mixing bowl. Add the butter and rub it into the flour mixture with your fingertips until the butter is in lentil-size pieces. Add the cream and stir until the dough just comes together.

2. Turn the dough onto a lightly floured work surface and roll into a ¾-inch-thick disk. Using a water glass or biscuit cutter, cut the dough into 2½-inch rounds, placing them on the prepared baking sheet as you work. Form the scraps into additional biscuits. Bake until the biscuits are golden brown, 12 to 15 minutes. (Biscuits can be made up to a day before serving. Cool completely and store in an airtight container.)

˅ ˅ ˅ ˅ ˅ ˅ ˅ ˅ ˅ ˅ ˅ ˅ ˅ ˅ ˅ ˅ ˅ ˅ ˅ ˅ ˅ ˅ ˅ ˅ ˅ ˅ ˅ ˅ ˅ ˅ ˅ ˅ ˅ ˅ ˅ ˅ ˅ ˅ ˅ ˅ ˅

**VEGAN VARIATION:** Substitute cold, vegan nonhydrogenated margarine like Earth Balance Vegan buttery sticks for the butter and unsweetened soy milk for the cream.

# PAELLA FOR EVERYONE

*Serves 2 vegetarians and 3 omnivores*

In Spain there are as many types of paella as there are cooks—seafood-packed feasts that serve whole villages to small pans of saffron-scented paellas with bits of rabbit. It shouldn't come as too much of a surprise, then, that there are authentic paella recipes that have no meat in them at all. This recipe makes both a vegetable and a seafood version using the same basic ingredients. You can omit the chicken, or the mussels, or the shrimp if you don't have them, but if at all possible do include the dried salami-style Spanish chorizo; it adds a smoky, distinctive flavor that makes the dish really special. Find it at gourmet grocery stores, or order it online from gourmet retailers (see Resources).

1 cup dry white wine or vermouth

1 pinch saffron threads

3 tablespoons olive oil

1 red bell pepper, cut into ½-inch-wide strips

3 bone-in skin-on chicken thighs

Salt and freshly ground black pepper

1½ cups finely chopped onion

4 teaspoons minced garlic

1½ cups uncooked Arborio rice

¾ cup hot vegetable stock

2 large tomatoes, grated (1½ cups), skins discarded, or one
    14.5-ounce can diced tomatoes with juice, finely chopped

⅓ cup canned garbanzo beans, rinsed and drained

¼ teaspoon smoked paprika (see Glossary)

¼ cup snap peas, trimmed

Three 2-inch sprigs fresh rosemary

1½ cups chicken stock

4 ounces Spanish chorizo, cut into ¼-inch-thick slices

12 large shrimp (6 to 8 ounces), deveined but not shelled (see **TIP**)

12 mussels, rinsed well and debearded

1 cup water

½ lemon, cut into 6 wedges

1. Preheat the oven to 400 degrees F. Microwave the wine in a glass measuring cup until hot, about 1 minute, or heat it in a small saucepan over gentle heat. Stir in the saffron and set aside.

2. Heat 1 tablespoon of the oil in a large sauté pan over medium-high heat. Add the bell pepper and sauté until the strips begin to brown, about 3 minutes. Remove from the pan and set aside. Return the pan to medium heat, season the chicken with the salt and pepper, and place skin side down in the pan. Cook until the skin is golden brown, about 7 minutes. Turn the chicken and cook until an instant-read thermometer inserted in the center of 1 thigh near the bone registers 150 degrees, about 3 minutes. Place the chicken on a plate and set aside.

3. Heat the remaining 2 tablespoons of oil in a clean 2-quart oven-safe sauté pan over medium-high heat. Add the onion and sauté until tender, about 5 minutes. Add the garlic, stir, and cook for 1 minute. Stir in the rice and cook for 1 minute, stirring constantly. Remove the pan from the heat.

4. **VEGETARIAN: Transfer ½ cup of the rice-onion mixture to a 3-cup baking dish. Add ¼ cup of the wine-saffron mixture, all the vegetable stock, ½ cup of the tomatoes, all of the garbanzo beans, and the paprika. Lay ⅓ cup of the red pepper strips, all the snap peas, and 1 sprig of the rosemary on top of the rice in a decorative pattern. Cover tightly with foil and place in the oven.**

5. Return the oven-safe sauté pan with the rice to medium-high heat, and add the remaining wine-saffron mixture, tomatoes, and chicken stock; bring to a boil. Nestle the chicken and chorizo into the rice, top with the remaining red pepper strips and 2 rosemary sprigs, cover, and place in the oven.

6. Bake both paellas until the rice is tender and the liquid is absorbed, about 30 minutes. Remove from the oven and keep warm.

7. Combine the shrimp, mussels, and the water in a small pan. Bring to a boil, cover, and cook until the mussels have opened and the shrimp are cooked through, about 5 minutes. Discard any mussels that do not open. Uncover the paellas and nestle the seafood into the chicken-chorizo paella.

8. Serve with lemon wedges.

**TIP:** I cook the shrimp with their shells intact in this recipe to help them retain their shape. To devein the shrimp with shells intact, snip down the back of the shrimp with small, sharp scissors, going just deep enough to reveal the dark intestinal tract that runs down the back. Rinse away with cold water leaving the legs, shell, and tail still attached.

# RED CHILE ENCHILADAS WITH CHICKEN OR TEMPEH

*Serves 2 vegetarians and 3 omnivores*

Vegetarians often get the short end of the stick when it comes to Mexican food. Time and again when dining out, I've seen my husband anticipate a good Mexican meal, only to find that gloppy beans and rice in various forms are the only items he can eat. Although beans and rice have their place, vegetarians deserve other options. These enchiladas feature tempeh or chicken and an easy homemade enchilada sauce that is head and shoulders above the bland packaged sauces you may be familiar with.

**CHILE SAUCE:**  2 tablespoons vegetable or olive oil

¾ cup minced red onion

2 tablespoons minced garlic

½ teaspoon dried Mexican oregano

2 teaspoons ground cumin

½ teaspoon ground cinnamon

2 tablespoons New Mexican chile powder

2 tablespoons all-purpose flour

One 15-ounce can tomato sauce

2 cups vegetable stock

1 bay leaf

1 tablespoon sugar

1 ounce bittersweet chocolate, chopped

**ENCHILADAS:**   1 tablespoon minced garlic

1 tablespoon ground coriander

2 teaspoons ground cumin

½ teaspoon smoked paprika (see Glossary)

¾ teaspoon kosher salt

4 tablespoons vegetable oil

8 ounces tempeh (see page xviii), cut into
½-inch squares

12 ounces boneless, skinless chicken breasts

4 ounces cream cheese

2 green onions, chopped

Ten 8-inch flour tortillas

1½ cups cheddar cheese

1. Preheat the oven to 375 degrees F. Heat the oil in a large saucepan over medium heat. Add the onion and sauté, stirring occasionally until translucent, about 10 minutes. Add the garlic, oregano, cumin, cinnamon, chile powder, and flour; cook for 1 minute, stirring constantly. Whisk in the tomato sauce, stock, and bay leaf and bring to a simmer. Cook, whisking occasionally until the sauce has thickened slightly, about 5 minutes. Whisk in the sugar and chocolate. Cover and keep warm over low heat.

2. Meanwhile, prepare the tempeh and chicken. In a small bowl, make a paste of the garlic, coriander, cumin, paprika, salt, and oil.

3. **VEGETARIAN: Line a small baking sheet with parchment paper. Place the tempeh on the prepared baking sheet and toss with half the spice paste. Bake for 25 minutes, tossing once with a spatula.**

4. Meanwhile, place the chicken breasts in a small baking dish and rub with the remaining spice paste. Bake until the chicken is no longer pink when cut into at the thickest part, or an instant-read thermometer registers 165 degrees F, about 25 minutes. When cool enough to handle, roughly chop the chicken. Stir the cream cheese and green onions into the chicken; set aside.

5. Place a damp paper towel in the bag with the tortillas and microwave for 1 minute to make them more pliable. (Alternatively, wrap the tortillas in a moist kitchen towel and place them in a 375 degree F oven for 5 minutes.)

6. Place 6 tortillas on a work surface. On the end closest to you, spoon a heaping ⅓ cup of the chicken mixture onto each tortilla. Roll up tightly to encase the filling and place seam side down in a large baking dish. Cover with two thirds of the sauce and ¾ cup of the cheddar cheese.

7. **VEGETARIAN: Crumble the tempeh and combine with ½ cup of the cheddar cheese. Roll filling up in the 4 remaining tortillas and place them seam side down in the small baking dish. Cover with the remaining enchilada sauce and remaining ¼ cup cheddar cheese.**

8. Bake the enchiladas until the cheese has melted and the sauce is bubbly around the edges, about 30 minutes.

   **KEEPING IT VEGETARIAN:** When purchasing tortillas, be sure to read the label. Some tortillas contain lard.

ᵛ ᵛ ᵛ ᵛ ᵛ ᵛ ᵛ ᵛ ᵛ ᵛ ᵛ ᵛ ᵛ ᵛ ᵛ ᵛ ᵛ ᵛ ᵛ ᵛ ᵛ ᵛ ᵛ ᵛ ᵛ ᵛ ᵛ ᵛ ᵛ ᵛ ᵛ ᵛ ᵛ ᵛ ᵛ ᵛ ᵛ ᵛ ᵛ ᵛ ᵛ ᵛ

**VEGAN VARIATION:** Omit the cheese from the tempeh enchiladas or substitute soy cheese for the cheddar.

# PULLED PORK OR BARBECUED TOFU SANDWICHES WITH SWEET AND SOUR SLAW

*Serves 3 vegetarians and 3 to 4 omnivores*

This recipe shares the same homemade spice rub and easy smoky-sweet barbecue sauce for both the oven-roasted pulled pork and the crispy tofu. There is ample barbecued tofu here for three sandwiches, or you can freeze the leftover tofu in a resealable freezer bag and reheat it when you need a vegetarian meal in a hurry.

**RUB:** 1½ teaspoons New Mexican chile powder

¾ teaspoon sweet paprika

¼ teaspoon smoked paprika (see Glossary)

¼ teaspoon ground cumin

¼ teaspoon granulated garlic

¼ teaspoon ground fennel seeds

1½ teaspoons packed brown sugar

½ teaspoon salt

⅛ teaspoon freshly ground black pepper

**SAUCE:** 3 large shallots, sliced (½ cup)

2 tablespoons chopped garlic

1½ cups ketchup

1 cup water

3 tablespoons dark sesame oil

3 tablespoons walnut or hazelnut oil

½ cup honey

3 tablespoons coarse-grain mustard

1 tablespoon hot sauce

**PROTEINS AND ASSEMBLY:** 3 pounds boneless pork ribs (often labeled "country ribs")

1 tablespoon olive oil

1 cup water

One 20-ounce package extra-firm nigari tofu (see **TIP**), cut into ½-inch cubes

6 to 7 hamburger buns

3 cups Sweet and Sour Slaw (recipe follows)

1. In a small bowl, combine the chile powder, sweet and smoked paprikas, cumin, garlic, fennel seeds, sugar, salt, and pepper; set aside.

2. To make the barbecue sauce, in a blender or food processor combine the shallots, garlic, ketchup, 1 cup water, sesame oil, walnut oil, honey, mustard, and hot sauce. Blend until smooth; set aside.

3. Preheat the oven to 325 degrees F. Pat the pork dry with paper towels, sprinkle with ¼ cup of the spice rub, and rub into the meat. Heat the oil in a Dutch oven over medium-high heat. Brown the meat in batches until browned on both sides. (Reduce the heat if the spice rub begins to burn.) Return all the meat to the Dutch oven, add the water, cover tightly with foil *and* a tight-fitting lid, and transfer to the oven. Bake until a fork inserted in the thickest piece of meat will easily twist it apart, 2½ hours. Halfway through the cooking, turn the meat over in the liquid.

4. VEGETARIAN: **When the pork has been in the oven for 2 hours, line 2 rimmed baking sheets with parchment paper and spray with nonstick cooking spray. Toss the tofu with 1 cup of the barbecue sauce, spread evenly on 1 baking sheet, and sprinkle with remaining heaping tablespoon of spice rub. Place the baking sheet on the oven rack above the pork and bake for 30 minutes.**

5. Remove the pork from the oven. Use tongs to transfer the pork to the other baking sheet; discard the cooking liquid. Slather the meat with 1 cup of the barbecue sauce. Keep the remaining barbecue sauce warm in a small saucepan over low heat. Return the baking sheet to the oven, increase the oven temperature to 400 degrees F, and bake both the pork and tofu until they are browned and crisp on the edges, about 30 minutes more.

6. VEGETARIAN: **In a medium bowl, combine the tofu, any crusty bits on the baking sheet, and 1 cup of the warm barbecue sauce.**

7. Use forks to pull the pork into shreds; discard any fat. Stir the pork into the remaining warm barbecue sauce.

8. Divide the pork and tofu among the hamburger buns and top each sandwich with about ½ cup of the slaw.

**TIP:** This recipe works best with extra-firm tofu that has been frozen and squeeze-dried so the tofu retains its shape and absorbs the barbecue sauce well. See Kung Pao Chicken or Tofu (page 179) for instructions.

v v v v v v v v v v v v v v v v v v v v v v v v v v v v v v v v v v v v v v v

**VEGAN VARIATION:** Be sure to read the ketchup label. Most are sweetened with corn syrup, but if it is sweetened with sugar or honey, find another brand. Substitute agave syrup for honey in the barbecue sauce.

## Sweet and Sour Slaw

*Serves 6 as a side*

Tossing the cabbage and carrots in a bit of salt helps draw out the liquid that would otherwise make the slaw watery. Make the slaw while the pork is in the oven to allow ample time for the flavors to meld.

> 1 pound green cabbage
> 1 large carrot
> ½ teaspoon salt
> ⅓ cup apple cider vinegar
> ⅓ cup sugar
> ¼ teaspoon celery seeds
> 2 green onions, finely chopped

1. Halve the cabbage; cut out the hard white core and discard. Finely chop or shred the cabbage and place it in a colander set in the sink. Julienne the carrot with a sharp chef's knife or grate it and add it to the colander. Toss with the salt and let the mixture drain for 30 minutes. Pat the vegetables dry with paper towels and transfer to a bowl.

2. In a small microwave-safe measuring cup, combine the vinegar, sugar, and celery seeds. Microwave until hot and stir to dissolve the sugar. (Alternatively, heat in a small saucepan over medium heat.)

3. Combine the warm dressing with the cabbage, carrots, and green onions. Cover with plastic wrap, and set aside. Toss again before serving.

# SHREDDED CHICKEN OR BLACK BEAN TAMALES

*Makes 9 black bean and 12 chicken tamales*

Tamale dough traditionally contains lard and chicken stock, and the filling is often made of shredded chicken or pork. Part of this version of tamales is vegetarian: I use Spectrum's trans-fat-free shortening instead of lard, packaged corn soup instead of chicken stock, and the filling is a simple canned bean-and-salsa affair. Since tamales freeze well, you may want to double the recipe so you can have tamales anytime.

1 tablespoon vegetable oil

1 cup finely chopped onions

1 teaspoon finely chopped garlic

One 15-ounce can black beans, rinsed and drained

½ cup jarred medium salsa, plus additional for serving

1 tablespoon chopped cilantro

Salt and black pepper

1½ cups crumbled *queso fresco* (see Glossary) or shredded
    Monterey Jack cheese, plus additional

12 ounces cooked boneless, skinless chicken breasts or
    store-bought rotisserie chicken, shredded

2 tablespoons chopped cilantro

30 dried cornhusks, soaked in hot water for 1 hour

4 cups masa harina (dry masa flour)

1½ teaspoons baking powder

1½ teaspoons salt

3 cups packaged corn soup (I use Pacific Natural Food's Buttery
    Sweet Corn Soup)

⅔ cup non-hydrogenated shortening, room temperature

1. **VEGETARIAN: Heat the oil in a sauté pan over medium-high heat. Add the onions and sauté until translucent, about 5 minutes. Add the garlic and sauté until fragrant, about 30 seconds. Add the beans and ¼ cup of the salsa. Bring to a simmer and mash with a potato masher until you have a thick, chunky mixture. Simmer gently for**

**10 minutes. Stir in the cilantro, season with salt and pepper, and set aside.**

**2.** In a medium bowl, combine the chicken, remaining ¼ cup of salsa, ¾ cup of the cheese, and cilantro. Season with the salt and pepper to taste.

**3.** Rinse the cornhusks well and drain in a colander. In a large bowl, whisk together the masa harina, baking powder, and salt. With a wooden spoon, slowly stir in the corn soup and stir until combined; set aside. Using the whip attachment of a stand mixer, beat the shortening for 1 minute on medium speed. Switch to the paddle attachment. With the mixer on medium speed, slowly add golf-ball-size pieces of the masa harina mixture until all of it has been added to the mixing bowl. (Don't rush this process; it should take about 5 minutes for adequate air to be beaten into the dough.)

**4.** To make the tamales, put on some good music (David Byrne's Latin-influenced album *Rei Momo* always puts me in a tamale-folding mood). Set the ingredients on a table. Open a cornhusk with the smooth side up and tapered end toward you. With your fingers, spread about ⅓ cup of the masa dough in a 6-inch-long horizontal strip over the center of the husk, leaving ¼ inch of uncovered husk at the top end and about 4 inches at the bottom (tapered) end. Put about 2 heaping tablespoons of the chicken filling in the center of the dough. Top with a bit of the cheese. Fold in the left side first and then the right side of the husk so the dough makes an overlapping seam in the center. Fold the bottom (tapered) end of the cornhusk up to meet the top end of the tamale. (Leave the top end open.) Repeat to make 12 chicken tamales.

**5. VEGETARIAN: Repeat process with the remaining dough, bean filling, and cheese. Tie the tamales around the middle using a long, thin strip of cornhusk or string to differentiate them from the omnivore tamales. Repeat to make 9 bean tamales.**

**6.** Put 2 pennies in a large pot. Place a metal steaming rack in the pot and fill the pot with water to just below the bottom of the steamer. Place the vegetarian tamales open end up on one side of the steamer; place a few cornhusks beside the tamales. Place the chicken tamales open end up on the other side of the cornhusks in the same way.

7. Top the tamales with a few layers of cornhusks, cover with a tight-fitting lid, and place over high heat. When the water begins to boil (you will hear the pennies rattling vigorously), reduce the heat to medium and simmer until the dough no longer sticks to the cornhusk when a tamale is opened, about 50 minutes. Monitor the water level by listening carefully. If the coins stop rattling, all the water has likely evaporated or the water is no longer simmering. Pour a few cups of boiling water against the inside of the pot if you suspect your water level is low. (Alternatively, cook the tamales on a steaming rack in a pressure cooker on highest pressure for 40 minutes.)

8. Carefully remove the tamales and place them on 2 separate platters. Serve with additional salsa on the side. (Steamed and cooled tamales can be wrapped in plastic wrap, stacked in a resealable freezer bag, and frozen for up to 3 months. Thaw overnight in the refrigerator and reheat in a micro-wave or steamer set over simmering water.)

∨ ∨ ∨ ∨ ∨ ∨ ∨ ∨ ∨ ∨ ∨ ∨ ∨ ∨ ∨ ∨ ∨ ∨ ∨ ∨ ∨ ∨ ∨ ∨ ∨ ∨ ∨ ∨ ∨ ∨ ∨ ∨ ∨ ∨ ∨ ∨ ∨

**VEGAN VARIATION:** Omit the cheese in the black bean tamale filling.

# TAGLIATELLE BOLOGNESE FOR ALL

*Serves 1 vegetarian and 3 omnivores*

Pasta with rich, meaty tomato sauce is as familiar as apple pie, but its real roots are in Bologna, Italy, where the sauce is far more than just a spaghetti sauce with browned hamburger in it. In Italy this long-simmered sauce often calls for beef, pork, and veal. Sounds delicious, but what about vegetarians at the table?

This Bolognese sauce recipe includes a vegetarian portion flavored with dried porcini mushroom powder to give it a rich, savory flavor. The omnivore's sauce gets its meaty flavor thanks to boneless beef ribs and their simmering liquid. This step takes a few hours of unattended simmering; a slow cooker works well. Be sure to serve the pasta with plenty of warm baguette pieces so you can sop up excess sauce off your plate.

4 tablespoons olive oil

1 pound boneless country beef ribs, or chuck roast cut into large chunks

2 cups finely chopped onion

2 large carrots, finely chopped

2 stalks celery, finely chopped

2 bay leaves

4 ounces cremini mushrooms (about 12 medium), finely chopped

2 tablespoons tomato paste

1 cup dry red wine, such as a good-quality Chianti or Nebbiolo

One 28-ounce can tomatoes in purée, chopped

1 teaspoon porcini mushroom powder (see **TIP**)

Two 2-inch pieces Parmigiano-Reggiano cheese rind

3 tablespoons water

1 tablespoon salt, plus additional

Freshly ground black pepper

12 ounces fresh tagliatelle or other pasta

1 cup grated Parmigiano-Reggiano cheese

1. Heat 1 tablespoon of the oil in a medium saucepan over medium-high heat until hot. Add the beef in batches and brown on all sides. Add ½ cup

of the chopped onion, half the carrots, half the celery, 1 bay leaf, and enough water to cover. Bring to a boil; reduce the heat and simmer until tender, about 2 hours (or 4 hours on low in a slow cooker), skimming off any foam that surfaces. Top off with additional water to keep the meat covered. Remove the beef from the cooking liquid and set aside. Strain cooking liquid and reserve.

2. Heat 2 tablespoons of the oil in a heavy-bottomed saucepan over medium heat. Add the remaining 1½ cups of onion, carrot, celery, and cremini mushrooms; sauté until tender and beginning to brown, about 10 minutes. Add the tomato paste and cook for 1 minute. Add the wine, bring to a simmer, and scrape up browned bits on the bottom of the pan; cook until the wine is almost evaporated, about 4 minutes. Stir in the tomatoes.

3. **VEGETARIAN: Transfer 2 cups of the tomato mixture to a small saucepan; add the porcini powder, 1 cheese rind, and the water. Bring to a gentle simmer, cover, and cook over medium-low heat.**

4. Skim off the fat that has risen to the top of the beef cooking liquid. Finely chop the beef and add it and 1 cup of the liquid to the remaining tomato sauce. Reserve any remaining broth for another use. Add the remaining cheese rind, bring to a gentle simmer, and cover.

5. Simmer both sauces for 45 minutes, stirring occasionally. Season both sauces with the salt and pepper to taste. (The sauces can be made up to this point and refrigerated in airtight containers for up to 3 days or frozen for up to 3 months.)

6. Bring a large pot of water to a boil. Add the 1 tablespoon of salt and pasta and cook, stirring frequently, until the pasta is al dente, about 2 minutes. Drain, toss with the remaining 1 tablespoon of oil, and serve with the sauces and the cheese on the side.

> **TIP:** Porcini mushroom powder can be found at gourmet stores and online (see Resources). You can make your own by pulsing dried porcinis in a clean spice grinder.

v v v v v v v v v v v v v v v v v v v v v v v v v v v v v v v v v v v v v v v v
**VEGAN VARIATION:** Omit the cheese rind from sauce and serve on egg-free pasta.

# SHEPHERD'S PIE

*Serves 1 to 2 vegetarians and 4 omnivores*

This easy recipe is just the thing for blustery winter weather when a casserole and a pint of Guinness stout is in order. Everything is better when it is topped with home-made mashed potatoes and cheddar cheese, but if you don't have time to make your own, you can use good-quality boxed mashed potatoes to top the stew instead. You will need two 4-ounce packages.

**TOPPING:** 4 large Yukon Gold potatoes (1½ pounds), peeled and quartered
2 teaspoons salt, plus additional
⅔ cup milk
2 tablespoons butter
¼ teaspoon ground nutmeg
1 pinch cayenne
Freshly ground black pepper

**STEW:** 3 tablespoons olive oil
1½ cups finely chopped onion
1 large carrot, finely chopped
1 stalk celery, finely chopped
6 ounces cremini mushrooms, sliced (2 cups)
2 tablespoons all-purpose flour
1 heaping tablespoon tomato paste
1 teaspoon fresh thyme leaves, or ¼ teaspoon dried thyme
2 tablespoons dry sherry
2½ cups Roasted Mushroom Stock (page 226) or packaged mushroom stock (see Resources)
Salt and freshly ground black pepper

**ASSEMBLY:** 3 ounces (about 1 cup) soy crumbles (I use Yves Meatless Ground crumbles)
1 pound ground lamb
1 cup grated sharp cheddar cheese

1. Put the potatoes in a 4-quart saucepan; add 2 teaspoons of the salt and cold water to cover by 2 inches. Bring to a boil and cook until the potatoes are tender when pierced with a fork, about 20 minutes. Drain; return to the saucepan and mash with a potato masher until almost smooth. Add the milk, butter, nutmeg, and cayenne and mash until completely smooth. Season with the salt and pepper to taste and set aside.

2. Preheat the oven to 375 degrees F. Heat the oil in a large sauté pan over medium heat. Add the onions, carrots, celery, and mushrooms; sauté, stirring occasionally, until the onions are translucent and the vegetables are tender, about 10 minutes. Add the flour, stir until it has been absorbed, and cook for 1 minute. Add the tomato paste, thyme, sherry, and stock; bring to a simmer over medium-high heat. Adjust the heat to maintain a gentle simmer and cook until the stew is thick and bubbly, about 15 minutes.

3. **VEGETARIAN: Put the soy crumbles in a 1½ cup baking dish, stir in ⅔ cup of the vegetable stew, spoon mashed potatoes on top in a 1-inch-thick layer, and set aside.**

4. Pour the remaining stew into a 2-quart baking dish. Wipe out the sauté pan and return it to medium heat. Add the lamb and cook, stirring to break it up, until it is browned and cooked through. Drain off the fat and stir the lamb into the larger baking dish. Top with the remaining mashed potatoes.

5. Sprinkle the cheese over both dishes, place them on a baking sheet on the center rack of the oven, and bake until the stews are bubbly, about 15 minutes. Turn on the broiler and broil until the cheese is bubbly and browned in places, about 2 minutes. Cool at room temperature for 10 minutes before serving; the pies will be atomic-hot.

v v v v v v v v v v v v v v v v v v v v v v v v v v v v v v v v v v v

**VEGAN VARIATION:** Replace the butter and milk in the mashed potatoes with vegan margarine and unsweetened soy milk. Omit the cheese on the vegetarian pie.

# CASSOULET FOR THE WHOLE CROWD

*Serves 2 vegetarians and 4 omnivores*

Cassoulet is a classic French dish that can take up to three days to make, what with the duck confit, homemade sausages, and cooking the flageolet beans. I've made the dish a lot easier; it's less about the meat and more about the beans and wonderful root vegetables. I use flageolet beans because they have a delicate flavor and keep their shape without becoming mushy. You can find them at some grocery stores or order them online (see Resources). Cannellini beans will work if you can't find flageolets. Don't try this recipe with canned beans; they will get far too mushy in the oven.

1½ cups dried flageolet (see Resources) or cannellini beans

1 large head garlic

3 tablespoons plus 1 teaspoon olive oil

¼ cup hot water

¾ cup coarsely chopped onion, plus 1 cup finely chopped onion

1 bay leaf

8 cups cold water

2 carrots cut into 2-inch-long by ½-inch-thick sticks

2 stalks celery, chopped

1 parsnip, peeled and roughly chopped (½ cup)

2 teaspoons fresh thyme leaves, chopped

2 tablespoons tomato paste

1 cup dry white wine

½ ounce dried porcini mushrooms, reconstituted in
   ½ cup boiling water

½ to ¾ cup vegetable stock

2 links (4 ounces) vegetarian sausage, cut into ½-inch-thick slices

3 cups coarsely chopped fresh bread crumbs

2 tablespoons butter, melted

1 pound (4 links) mild pork sausage

2 cups chicken stock

1. At least 8 hours before cooking, soak the dried beans with water to cover by 2 inches.

2. Preheat the oven to 400 degrees F. Slice ¼ inch off the top of the garlic and discard. Place the garlic in a small oven-safe baking dish and drizzle with 1 teaspoon of the oil. Cover with foil and bake until the garlic is tender when squeezed, about 1 hour. Remove from oven, pour the hot water into the baking dish, and cover again with the foil; set aside. Reduce the oven temperature to 350 degrees F.

3. Drain the beans and rinse well with cold water. In a soup pot, combine the beans, coarsely chopped onion, bay leaf, and cold water. Bring to a boil, reduce the heat, and simmer until the beans are just tender, about 35 minutes, skimming off the white foam that surfaces. Drain the beans and discard the bay leaf.

4. In a large oven-safe sauté pan, heat 2 tablespoons of the oil over medium-high heat. Add the finely chopped onion, carrot, celery, parsnip, and thyme and sauté, stirring occasionally, until the vegetables begin to brown, about 5 minutes. Stir in the tomato paste and cook for 30 seconds. Deglaze the pan with the wine, scraping up any browned bits on the bottom of the pan, and simmer until the wine has almost evaporated, about 1 minute.

5. **VEGETARIAN: Transfer 1 cup of the vegetable mixture and 1¼ cups of the beans to a 3-cup baking dish. Drain the mushrooms and reserve the soaking liquid. Chop and add the mushrooms to the baking dish. Slowly pour the soaking liquid into the baking dish, stopping before you get to the sediment at the bottom of the bowl. Squeeze the garlic out of its papery skin and add 1 scant tablespoon to the baking dish. Add enough vegetable stock to come up level with the beans. Nestle the vegetarian sausage into the beans. Toss the bread crumbs and butter together in a bowl and sprinkle 1 cup over the beans. Transfer the dish to the oven.**

6. Scrape the remaining vegetable mixture into a small bowl with a rubber spatula. Return the sauté pan to the stove over medium heat. Put in the remaining 1 tablespoon of oil and pork sausages and cook, turning occasionally, until they are evenly browned, about 8 minutes. Add the remaining roasted garlic, beans, vegetable mixture, and enough chicken stock to just cover the beans, about 2 cups. Top the beans with the remaining bread crumbs and transfer the pan to the oven.

7. Bake the cassoulets until the bread crumbs are golden brown and the sauce is bubbly around the edges, about 1 hour. Remove the pans and let cool for 10 minutes before serving (or you will irrevocably burn the roof of your mouth!).

**VEGAN VARIATION:** For the vegetarian cassoulet, toss 1 cup of the bread crumbs with extra-virgin olive oil instead of butter.

# FRESH PEA AND FENNEL RISOTTO WITH SPICE-CRUSTED SEARED SCALLOPS

*Serves 1 vegetarian and 3 omnivores*

This vegetarian risotto is best when fresh peas are in season—late spring and early summer. The creamy, subtly anise-flavored risotto pairs nicely with the spice-dusted scallops for omnivores, but it is a meal all by itself without the seafood. The risotto takes about 18 minutes of absentminded stirring, but you get to stand by a warm stove, sip wine, and space out while you are doing it, so it's really more of a mini-vacation than cooking.

1 pound fresh English peas (1 cup shelled) or 1 cup frozen peas

6 ounces fennel (about ½ medium bulb)

5 cups No-Chicken Stock (page 225) or mild packaged vegetable stock

2 tablespoons olive oil

1½ cups finely chopped onion

1½ cups Arborio rice

½ cup dry vermouth or dry white wine

½ cup grated Parmigiano-Reggiano cheese, plus additional for garnish

Salt and freshly ground black pepper

1 teaspoon fennel seeds

½ teaspoon coriander seeds

10 to 12 large (about 1 pound) "dry pack" scallops (see **TIP**)

½ teaspoon ground white pepper

1 tablespoon vegetable oil

2 tablespoons minced Italian parsley

1. Shell the peas and set aside. Cut the hard core out of the base of the fennel and discard. Finely chop the fennel and feathery leaves, keeping the leaves separate. In a medium pot, bring the stock to a low simmer.

2. Heat the oil in a medium saucepan over medium-high heat. Add the onion and fennel and sauté until the onion is tender, about 5 minutes. Reduce the

heat to medium; add the rice and cook, stirring constantly for 1 minute. Add the vermouth and cook, stirring constantly, until it is absorbed. Add 1 ladle (about 8 ounces) of the hot stock and bring to a simmer, stirring constantly until the liquid is absorbed. Continue adding stock in intervals until almost all the stock is used, about 15 minutes. Bite into a grain of rice; if it has an opaque white center the diameter of a pin and has just a hint of chewiness, it is perfectly cooked.

3. Add the peas and the remaining stock. Reduce the heat to low, stir in ½ cup of the cheese, and season with the salt and pepper to taste. Cover and keep warm over very low heat.

4. Grind the fennel seeds and coriander seeds to a powder in a mortar and pestle or clean spice grinder. Pat the scallops dry; sprinkle both sides with the spice mixture, white pepper, and a few pinches of salt. Heat the vegetable oil in a sauté pan over high heat until the oil is very hot but not smoking. Add the scallops and sear without moving them until they are golden brown on 1 side, about 2 minutes. Turn with a thin spatula and sear on the other side until they are just opaque white in the center, 1 to 2 minutes depending on their thickness.

5. **VEGETARIAN: Put a bit more than a quarter of the risotto in 1 bowl and sprinkle with some of the parsley and fennel leaves.**

6. Divide the remaining risotto among 3 bowls, top them with the scallops, and sprinkle with the remaining parsley and fennel leaves. Serve.

TIP: Be sure to buy scallops that have not been treated with tripolyphosphate, a food additive that makes scallops retain moisture. These "wet pack" scallops will exude moisture when they hit a hot pan and will swim in liquid instead of sear to crispy perfection. If you're not sure about the scallops you are buying, ask your fishmonger for "dry pack" scallops. They are generally more expensive, but they are well worth the price for their flavor and texture.

# PRIMAVERA POTPIES

*Serves 1 vegetarian and 3 omnivores*

What better way to celebrate spring's best vegetables than to cook them in a dill-infused gravy (with chicken or not) and tuck them under a crisp, flaky crust? This recipe easily adapts to the seasons: add zucchini and fresh corn shaved off the cob in summer, sautéed mushrooms in fall, and root vegetables sautéed along with the carrots in winter. If you don't have time to make your own crust, use packaged pie dough instead. Be sure to read the label; some contain lard or other animal products.

CRUST: 1⅓ cups all-purpose flour

¼ teaspoon salt

½ cup unsalted butter, cut into ½-inch pieces

2 to 3 tablespoons ice water

FILLING: ½ cup all-purpose flour

4 cups Roasted Vegetable Stock (page 227) or mild packaged vegetable stock

2 tablespoons olive oil

1 cup finely chopped onion

2 teaspoons minced garlic

2 medium carrots, cut into ¼-inch-thick rounds

2 stalks celery, finely chopped

¼ cup dry white wine

1 large red new potato, cut into ½-inch dice (about 1 cup)

½ cup heavy cream

6 ounces asparagus (about 8 stalks), tough ends snapped off and discarded, spears cut into 1-inch-thick pieces

½ cup fresh-shelled peas or frozen shelled edamame

2 tablespoons chopped fresh dill

Salt and freshly ground black pepper

1½ pounds boneless, skinless chicken breasts, fat trimmed, cut into bite-size pieces

1 chicken bouillon cube, crumbled (I like Knorr)

1 egg, lightly beaten

1 tablespoon water

1. Combine the flour, salt, and butter in a food processor or large mixing bowl. Pulse or work in the butter with a pastry blender until the mixture resembles granola, with blobs of butter no larger than lentils. Add the water, 1 tablespoon at a time, and toss with a silicone spatula until the mixture just comes together (you may not need all the water). Gather the dough into a disk, wrap tightly in plastic wrap, and refrigerate for at least 30 minutes. (The dough can be made up to 2 days in advance. Let it sit at room temperature for 15 minutes before rolling it out.)

2. Preheat the oven to 425 degrees F. To make the filling, put the flour in a small bowl and gradually whisk in 1 cup of the stock; set aside. Heat the oil in a medium saucepan over medium heat. Add the onion and sauté for 2 minutes. Add the garlic and sauté for 30 seconds. Add the carrots and celery and sauté for 4 minutes. Pour in the wine and simmer for 1 minute. Add the potatoes, flour-stock mixture, and remaining stock and bring to a simmer. Cover, reduce the heat to medium low, and simmer gently until the sauce is bubbly and the potatoes are just fork tender, about 10 minutes. (If the sauce begins to stick to the bottom, reduce the heat.) Stir in the cream and reduce the heat to low.

3. **VEGETARIAN: Ladle 1½ cups of the sauce into a 2-cup baking dish. Add a quarter of the asparagus and peas and 1½ teaspoons of the dill and stir to combine. Season to taste with the salt and pepper and set aside on a rimmed baking sheet.**

4. Stir the chicken and bouillon cube into the remaining sauce and bring to a simmer over medium heat. Cook, stirring occasionally, until the chicken is cooked through, about 8 minutes. Stir in the remaining asparagus, peas, and dill. Divide the mixture among three 2-cup baking dishes and set on the rimmed baking sheet, making sure to note which potpie is vegetarian.

5. Divide the dough into 4 equal balls. Roll out on a lightly floured surface until they are about ⅛ inch thick and are at least 1 inch larger than the diameter of the top of the baking dishes. Place the rounds on a baking sheet and freeze for 10 minutes.

6. Top the chicken pies with chilled dough circles and fold dough around edges of baking dishes. Pinch the dough together in places so that it is

slightly pleated around the edges. With the tip of a paring knife, cut a few 1-inch slashes in the crust.

**7. VEGETARIAN: Top the vegetarian pie with dough in the same way. With the tip of a clean knife, cut a "V" in the crust.**

**8.** Combine the egg and water and brush crusts with the egg wash. Bake until the crusts are golden brown, 25 to 30 minutes.

ᵛᵛᵛᵛᵛᵛᵛᵛᵛᵛᵛᵛᵛᵛᵛᵛᵛᵛᵛᵛᵛᵛᵛᵛᵛᵛᵛᵛᵛᵛᵛᵛᵛᵛᵛᵛᵛᵛᵛᵛᵛᵛᵛ

**VEGAN VARIATION:** Substitute nonhydrogenated vegetable shortening for the butter in the pie dough. Omit the cream in the filling.

# GOOEY MACARONI AND CHEESE
# WITH TOMATOES AND HAM

*Serves 1 vegetarian and 4 to 5 omnivores*

I had to include this recipe because it has received rave reviews from readers of my column in *The Oregonian*'s "FoodDay" section, cooking class students, *and* my husband. This homemade macaroni and cheese recipe gets the luxury treatment with a layer of ripe heirloom tomatoes, plus a bit of chopped ham for the omnivores' portion. A little bit wicked, very creamy, and quite different from the bright orange stuff that comes in a box, this comfy dish is bound to draw rave reviews for you, too.

1 garlic clove, smashed

1 bay leaf

3 sprigs fresh thyme

6 peppercorns

4 cups 2-percent milk

3 tablespoons butter

⅓ cup flour

1 teaspoon mustard powder

¼ teaspoon ground nutmeg

⅛ teaspoon cayenne

2 cups grated sharp cheddar cheese

1 tablespoon salt, plus additional

Freshly ground black pepper

1 pound penne or other short tubular pasta

6 ounces ham, roughly chopped

2 medium ripe tomatoes (12 ounces), cut into ¼-inch-thick slices

1 cup grated aged cheese such as Gruyère, Manchego, or Parmigiano-Reggiano

1. Combine the garlic, bay leaf, thyme, peppercorns, and milk in a 2-quart saucepan over medium heat. Cook until the milk is hot and small bubbles appear around the edges of the pan, about 8 minutes. Remove from the heat and let mixture steep for 10 minutes. Discard the garlic, bay leaf, thyme, and peppercorns.

**2.** Wash the pan and return it to medium heat. Melt the butter in the pan, whisk in the flour, and cook, stirring constantly for 1 minute. Gradually whisk in the milk and cook until thickened, about 5 minutes. Monitor the sauce carefully and reduce the heat if it begins to stick to the bottom while cooking. Remove from the heat; whisk in the mustard powder, nutmeg, cayenne, and 1½ cups of the grated cheddar cheese. Season with the salt and pepper and set aside.

**3.** Preheat the broiler. Spray a 2-cup baking dish and an 8-cup baking dish with nonstick cooking spray. Bring a large pot of water to a boil. Add 1 tablespoon of the salt and the pasta and boil until al dente, about 8 minutes. Drain and return the pasta to the pot. Stir in the cheese sauce.

**4. VEGETARIAN: Put 1½ cups of the pasta-sauce mixture into the small baking dish.**

**5.** Stir the ham into the remaining pasta mixture; pour into the large baking dish.

**6.** Lay tomato slices on top of the pasta in both baking dishes and sprinkle with the remaining cheddar and the grated aged cheese. Place the baking dishes 4 inches below the broiling element and broil until the cheese is bubbly and crisp in places, about 5 minutes. Serve immediately.

# 5

## FOODS FROM AFAR

Living in a mixed-diet family is a great opportunity to expand your culinary repertoire to include dishes from other lands. In many countries meat is expensive and much more scarce than here; thus, their cuisines use meat more as a seasoning or a condiment, or they eat vegetable-based meals almost exclusively. Indian cuisine has a long history of vegetarian cuisine, thanks to the Hindu influence; Chinese cooking often uses just a bit of meat to accent fresh vegetables, with tofu taking an equally important role. Thai food focuses on a balance of hot, sour, sweet, and salty flavors rather than on meat proteins. Pickled vegetables and rice star in Korean dishes, with fish and meat playing supporting roles.

Since the focus of the following recipes is on the delicious mingling of spices, herbs, and other strong flavors, it's a breeze to substitute seitan, tofu, nuts, and other meat alternatives without sacrificing flavor. So make a foray to the international grocery stores in your area or visit them when you are in larger cities. At these small markets, a world of new foods, flavors, and cooking methods will help you jump-start your pantry and cooking to include global influences whether you eat meat or not.

# TWO-WAY LO MEIN EXPRESS

*Serves 1 vegetarian and 3 omnivores*

This simple noodle recipe is endlessly adaptable. Add whatever tender vegetable you have on hand—frozen shelled edamame, water chestnuts, fresh pea pods—they're all good in this pantry put-together. If you don't have seitan, substitute extra-firm tofu; if you have neither, add some chopped cashews or almonds to provide protein for the non–steak eater.

I use the wheat-based egg noodles labeled *chuka soba* or Filipino *pansit* noodles because their starchiness holds onto the tasty black bean–garlic sauce so well, but ramen noodles (without the seasoning packet) will work in a pinch.

**BEEF:** 2 teaspoons packed brown sugar

2 tablespoons soy sauce

2 teaspoons chile paste such as sambal oelek

6 to 8 ounces strip steak, trimmed of fat, partially frozen

**NOODLES:** 6 dried shiitake mushrooms, reconstituted in 2 cups boiling water for 30 minutes

1½ tablespoons sliced garlic

½ cup thinly sliced green bell pepper, red bell pepper, or both

1 large carrot, thinly sliced

1 cup chopped green cabbage

3 chopped green onions

2 ounces Homemade Seitan (page 229) or packaged, thinly sliced

1½ tablespoons soy sauce

1½ tablespoons rice wine or dry sherry

1½ teaspoons sugar

2 tablespoons black bean–garlic sauce (see Glossary)

12 ounces *chuka soba* noodles

4 tablespoons vegetable oil

1. Combine the brown sugar, soy sauce, and chile paste in a small bowl. Cut the steak into ¼-inch-thick slices and toss with the soy mixture; set aside.

2. Stem the mushrooms, and thinly slice the caps. Assemble the garlic; mushrooms, bell pepper, carrot, cabbage, and green onions; and seitan in 3 bowls near the stove. In a small measuring cup, combine the soy sauce, rice wine, sugar, and black bean–garlic sauce.

3. Bring a large pot of water to a boil. Add the noodles and cook until they are tender when bitten into, 3 to 4 minutes (2 to 3 minutes if using ramen noodles). Drain and set aside.

4. Heat a large wok over high heat. Place 2 tablespoons of the oil in the wok and swirl. Add the garlic, combined vegetables, and seitan; stir-fry until the carrots are crisp-tender, about 3 minutes, pressing the seitan on the sides of the wok with a spatula to sear it.

5. While the vegetables cook, heat 1 tablespoon of the oil in a small sauté pan over medium-high heat. Remove the steak from the marinade, discard the marinade, and add the meat to the pan. Cook without stirring until the meat is browned on one side, about 1 minute. Turn the slices with tongs and remove the pan from the heat (the slices will finish cooking in the hot pan).

6. Push the vegetables up the sides of the wok and add the remaining 1 tablespoon of oil. Add the noodles and soy sauce mixture; stir-fry for 1 minute. Toss noodles with vegetables and remove from heat.

7. **VEGETARIAN: Place a quarter of the noodles and vegetables and most of the seitan in 1 bowl.**

8. Toss the remaining noodles with the steak and any accumulated juices and divide among 3 bowls. Serve.

v v v v v v v v v v v v v v v v v v v v v v v v v v v v v v v v v v v v v v

**VEGAN VARIATION:** Use vegan pasta instead of egg noodles.

# HUNT AND PECK MEDITERRANEAN GRILLED MEZZE

*Serves 6, with enough lamb for 4 omnivores*

When the weather is warm, I love to throw casual dinner parties on our patio. A favorite menu is this selection of mezze (Mediterranean appetizers) with lots of little bowls of goodies—hummus, salad, warm marinated olives, grilled lamb, vegetables and puffy grilled bread. The wide array of easy dishes means omnivores, vegetarians, and vegan guests can linger and nibble for hours over bottles of good chilled rosé wine, as people do in the Mediterranean.

If you like, substitute the homemade Greek salad and pizza dough with store-bought salad and packaged pizza dough. One pound of dough will make enough grilled bread for four to six people.

**DOUGH:**  ¾ teaspoon active dry yeast

1 cup warm water

1 tablespoon plus 1 teaspoon olive oil

2 cups all-purpose flour

½ cup whole-wheat flour

½ teaspoon salt

**SALADS:**  1 teaspoon minced garlic

1 tablespoon red wine vinegar

3 tablespoons extra-virgin olive oil

1 large (8 ounces) cucumber, halved, seeded, and thinly sliced

8 ounces (2 medium) ripe heirloom tomatoes, chopped

2 green onions, finely chopped

¼ cup Italian parsley, chopped

¼ cup fresh mint leaves, chopped

Salt and freshly ground black pepper

2 ounces feta cheese, crumbled

One 8-ounce package prepared hummus

**OLIVES:**  12 ounces mixed olives

½ teaspoon fennel seeds

1 large garlic clove, peeled and halved lengthwise

1 pinch hot chile flakes

1 strip lemon peel, peeled with a sharp vegetable peeler

1 sprig fresh thyme

½ cup olive oil

LAMB AND
VEGETABLES: 4 teaspoons ground cumin

4 teaspoons ground Aleppo pepper (see Glossary)

½ teaspoon ground cinnamon

1 teaspoon salt

½ teaspoon freshly ground black pepper

2 tablespoons plus 2 teaspoons extra-virgin olive oil

2 Japanese eggplants (8 ounces), halved lengthwise

1 medium zucchini (8 ounces), cut lengthwise into ¾-inch slices

2 pounds lamb loin chops, 1 to 1½ inches thick

1. Combine the yeast, water, and 1 tablespoon of the oil in the bowl of a stand mixer; set aside for 10 minutes. Add the all-purpose flour, whole-wheat flour, and salt to the bowl and knead with the dough hook for 6 minutes, until the dough is smooth and elastic. (Alternatively, knead the dough for 10 minutes on a lightly floured surface.) Rub a large mixing bowl with 1 teaspoon of the oil, place dough in bowl and cover. Let the dough rise in a warm, draft-free place until doubled in volume, 1½ to 2 hours. (The dough can be made up to 2 days in advance and refrigerated in a plastic bag. Let sit at room temperature for 30 minutes before rolling out.)

2. In a medium serving bowl, whisk together the garlic, vinegar, and 2 table-spoons of oil. Add the cucumbers, tomatoes, green onions, parsley, and mint and toss to combine. Season with the salt and pepper to taste, sprinkle with the cheese, and set aside. Put the hummus in a small serving bowl, drizzle with remaining tablespoon of oil; set aside. Combine the olives, fennel seeds, garlic, chile flakes, lemon peel, thyme, and the ½ cup oil in a small oven-proof pan, cover with foil and set aside.

3. Combine the cumin, Aleppo pepper, cinnamon, salt, and black pepper in a small bowl. Brush the eggplant and zucchini with 2 tablespoons of the oil and sprinkle with half the spice mixture. Brush the lamb chops with the remaining 2 teaspoons of oil and rub the remaining spice mixture into the meat.

4. Preheat a gas grill or start charcoal briquettes. Place the olives over the coolest part of the grill. Divide the dough into 4 equal balls. Roll out each ball on a lightly floured surface into 8-inch-long, ¼-inch-thick oblongs; they don't have to be perfect. Stack the dough between sheets of parchment paper dusted with flour and place them on a baking sheet.

5. When the grill is ready or the briquettes just begin to ash over, place the eggplant and zucchini on one side of the grill and cook until the edges of the eggplant are sizzling, about 3 minutes. Flip the vegetables with tongs and continue to grill until they are tender when pierced with tongs, about 3 minutes. Arrange the vegetables on a platter, cover with foil. Meanwhile, on the other side of the grill, cook the lamb until an instant-read thermometer inserted in the center of a chop registers 140 degrees F for medium-rare, 3 to 4 minutes per side. Place the lamb on another serving platter and cover with foil. Remove olives from the grill.

6. Brush the grill with a wire brush or wad of foil. Place 2 of the pieces of dough on the grill and cook until bubbles begin to rise on the uncooked side, about 1 minute. Flip with clean tongs and continue to grill until the bread is crisp and browned on the bottom, about 1 minute. Cut into wedges and put in a basket lined with a cloth napkin. Repeat with the remaining dough.

7. **VEGETARIAN: As you serve the food, notify guests that all plates are vegetarian aside from the grilled lamb.**

8. Set the lamb aside for the omnivores. Set serving platters on the dining table, letting guests dish up their own plates and nibble for hours.

˅ ˅ ˅ ˅ ˅ ˅ ˅ ˅ ˅ ˅ ˅ ˅ ˅ ˅ ˅ ˅ ˅ ˅ ˅ ˅ ˅ ˅ ˅ ˅ ˅ ˅ ˅ ˅ ˅ ˅ ˅ ˅ ˅ ˅ ˅ ˅ ˅ ˅

**VEGAN VARIATION:** Make the salad without the feta cheese. All other plates, aside from the grilled lamb, are vegan.

# PAD THAI WITH SHRIMP OR TOFU

*Serves 1 to 2 vegetarians and 3 omnivores*

Thais take their noodles very seriously. I remember watching in amazement as street vendors in Bangkok made dozens of orders of pad thai all at once in separate woks as patrons shouted out their specific orders—some with extra chiles, some with pickled cabbage, others with only a sprinkle of dried shrimp. This recipe follows the Thai vendors' lead: the noodles are made with vegan fish sauce and tofu and a portion is set aside for vegetarians, then the noodles are finished with shrimp and "real" fish sauce for omnivores, so all your "customers" are satisfied.

8 ounces dry rice noodles, soaked in very hot water until pliable (about 30 minutes)

2 tablespoons brown sugar

1 tablespoon white sugar

1 tablespoon tamarind concentrate (see Glossary)

1 tablespoon hot water

3 tablespoons Vegan Fish Sauce (page 228)

2 tablespoons plus 1 teaspoon vegetable oil

½ cup sliced shallots

1 tablespoon minced garlic

2 eggs, lightly beaten

2 ounces fried tofu (see page xviii), diced (1 cup)

3 tablespoons salted pickled radish, rinsed and chopped (see Glossary), optional

1 cup Roma tomatoes (about 2 medium), chopped

½ to 1 teaspoon dried chile flakes

2 cups bean sprouts

10 ounces shrimp, shelled, deveined, and chopped

2 tablespoons fish sauce

2 green onions, chopped

3 tablespoons roasted peanuts, chopped

2 limes cut into wedges

1. Drain the noodles and set aside. Combine the brown sugar, sugar, tamarind concentrate, water, and vegan fish sauce in a measuring cup and stir until the sugars dissolve. Set aside.

2. Line up all the ingredients next to the stove. Heat 1 tablespoon of the oil in a wok over medium-high heat. Add the shallots and fry, stirring with 2 spatulas until they begin to brown, about 1 minute. Add the garlic and stir-fry for 20 seconds. Add the eggs and stir vigorously with a spatula. When they are just set, push them aside and add the tofu, pickled radish, tomatoes, and chile flakes and stir-fry for 2 minutes until the tomato pieces begin to soften and collapse. Push everything up the side of the wok.

3. Heat 1 tablespoon of the oil in the wok, add the noodles, toss them with the 2 spatulas, and push them against the sides of the wok so they sear, about 1 minute. Add the sugar-tamarind mixture and bean sprouts; cook and toss for 1 minute.

4. **VEGETARIAN: Place a quarter of the noodles and most of the tofu in a small serving bowl, cover, and set aside.**

5. Put the remaining noodle mixture in a large serving bowl and quickly return the wok to high heat. Add the remaining teaspoon of oil to the wok. Add the shrimp and stir-fry until they are pink and cooked through, about 1 minute. Add the fish sauce and stir to coat the shrimp. Add to the large bowl of noodles and toss to combine.

6. Sprinkle both bowls of noodles with the green onions and peanuts; serve with lime wedges on the side.

vvvvvvvvvvvvvvvvvvvvvvvvvvvvvvvvvvvvvvvvvvv

**VEGAN VARIATION:** Omit the eggs.

# JAMAICAN JERK SEITAN AND PORK LOIN WITH COCONUT RICE AND BEANS

*Serves 1 to 2 vegetarians and 3 omnivores*

Wherever I travel, I ask cab drivers where I should eat. Cabbies know the off-the-beaten-path joints where the food is great, the people are real, and the prices aren't jacked up for tourists. Rocky, a cab driver in Montego Bay, Jamaica, was one such culinary expert who brought me to Roy's Hideaway, a repurposed chicken shack where I ate phenomenal jerk chicken that was grilled over allspice branches. After several visits, I convinced the cook to give me an approximate recipe for their jerk marinade; a slightly less atomic version is the basis of this recipe.

Seitan holds up well on the grill and absorbs the flavors of the jerk marinade famously; the pork, of course, does the same. Be sure to buy chops that haven't been injected with "flavor enhancers" or saline; they have an artificial flavor and are usually quite dry once cooked.

**SEITAN AND PORK:**

6 ounces Homemade Seitan (page 229) or packaged, drained and cut into 1-inch pieces

3 boneless center-cut or rib pork chops (about 1¼ pounds), 1½ inches thick

2 tablespoons soy sauce

¼ cup warm water

Zest and juice of 1 lime

3 chopped green onions

½ small habañero chile, chopped (wear gloves when handling hot chiles)

2 teaspoons chopped garlic

1 tablespoon brown sugar

1 tablespoon peeled, minced ginger

½ teaspoon dried thyme

1½ teaspoons ground allspice

½ teaspoon ground nutmeg

½ teaspoon mace

3 tablespoons olive oil

RICE AND
BEANS:

4 bamboo skewers, soaked in cold water for 1 hour

½ small sweet onion, cut into 1-inch pieces

⅓ small red bell pepper, cut into 1-inch pieces

2 tablespoons olive oil

1 cup chopped onion

½ cup chopped red bell pepper

2 teaspoons peeled, minced ginger

1 teaspoon paprika

¼ teaspoon ground nutmeg

¼ teaspoon turmeric

1 cup long grain white rice, uncooked

1 cup coconut milk

1 cup warm water

¾ teaspoon salt

One 15-ounce can red beans, rinsed and drained

½ cup chopped fresh tomatoes

1 tablespoon hot sauce (optional)

1. A few hours or up to 2 days before grilling, marinate the seitan and pork. Combine the ketchup, soy sauce, water, lime zest and juice, green onions, chile, garlic, sugar, ginger, thyme, allspice, nutmeg, mace, and oil in a blender; blend until smooth.

2. **VEGETARIAN: In a small bowl, combine ¾ cup of the ketchup mixture with the seitan. Cover with plastic wrap and refrigerate.**

3. In a medium bowl, rub the remaining ketchup mixture all over the pork. Cover with plastic wrap and refrigerate. Let pork sit at room temperature for 20 minutes before grilling to ensure even cooking.

4. **VEGETARIAN: Thread the seitan onto the bamboo skewers, alternating with all the pieces of onion and pepper; set aside. Reserve excess marinade.**

5. Preheat the grill over high heat, or until charcoal briquettes have just ashed over but are still very hot. Let the pork chops sit at room temperature while making the rice and beans. In a large sauté pan with a cover, heat the oil

over medium-high heat until hot. Add the onion, bell pepper, and ginger and sauté until they are tender, about 5 minutes. Add the paprika, nutmeg, turmeric, and rice; stir to coat the rice with the spices. Add the coconut milk, water, and salt and bring to a simmer. Reduce the heat to medium low, cover, and cook until most of the liquid is absorbed and the rice is almost tender, about 15 minutes. Add the beans, tomatoes, and hot sauce and stir gently with a rubber spatula. Cover and keep warm over low heat.

6. Remove the pork chops from the marinade, discard the marinade, and place the chops on one side of the grill. Grill for 4 minutes, turn with tongs, and continue to grill until an instant-read thermometer registers 140 degrees F when inserted in the thickest chop, about 5 minutes. Place on a serving platter, loosely tent with foil, and set aside.

7. **VEGETARIAN: While the pork is grilling, place the seitan skewers on the other side of the grill. Grill on 1 side until the seitan and vegetables are sizzling, about 3 minutes. With clean tongs, flip the skewers, brush with the reserved marinade, and grill on the other side for 3 minutes. Place skewers on a serving platter.**

8. Transfer the rice and beans to a large bowl and serve alongside the skewers and pork chops.

# WHICH CAME FIRST CURRY

*Serves 1 vegetarian and 3 omnivores*

This simple yet authentic tomato-based chicken and egg curry is a great way to use up extra hard-boiled Easter eggs. It's also a great pantry-staple dish since most of the ingredients are probably in your spice drawer and cupboard. It's crucial to slowly caramelize the onions when starting this recipe; they thicken the sauce and add a savory sweetness that is a good foil for the acidic tomato sauce. The onions are sautéed in clarified butter, which will not burn as regular butter does. I've included instructions on how to clarify butter at the end of the recipe. If you don't want to make the dish with butter, vegetable oil will also work, though the flavor isn't quite as, well, buttery.

3 tablespoons clarified butter (see **TIP**), or vegetable oil

1½ cups minced onion

1 tablespoon peeled, minced ginger

1 tablespoon minced garlic

2 teaspoons ground coriander

2 teaspoons ground cumin

3 green cardamom pods

1 bay leaf

One 3-inch cinnamon stick

1½ teaspoons turmeric

One 15-ounce can tomato sauce

1 cup water

1 small Serrano chile, minced (wear gloves when handling hot chiles)

Salt and freshly ground black pepper

2 hard-boiled eggs, peeled and quartered

3 boneless, skinless chicken thighs cut into bite-size pieces

1 small ripe tomato (4 to 6 ounces), cut into wedges

½ cup minced cilantro

5 cups steamed basmati rice

1. Heat the clarified butter in a large sauté pan over medium heat until hot. Add the onions and sauté, stirring occasionally, until they are soft and begin to take on a deep brown color, about 15 minutes. (Lower the heat to medium low if they begin to burn.) Add the ginger, garlic, coriander, cumin, cardamom, bay leaf, and cinnamon stick. Sauté, stirring constantly, until the garlic is fragrant, about 1 minute. Add the turmeric, tomato sauce, water, and chile. Increase the heat to bring the sauce to a gentle simmer, cover, and cook for 30 minutes, stirring occasionally. Season with the salt and pepper to taste.

2. **VEGETARIAN: Transfer 1¼ cups of the tomato sauce mixture to a small sauté pan and place over low heat. Gently nestle the eggs into the sauce and spoon a little of the sauce over them; do not stir or the eggs will break apart. Cover.**

3. Stir the chicken into the remaining sauce, increase the heat to medium high, cover, and simmer until the chicken is cooked through, about 6 minutes.

4. **VEGETARIAN: With a large serving spoon, gently transfer the egg quarters and sauce onto 1 dinner plate. Garnish with the tomato wedges.**

5. Put the chicken mixture in a serving bowl. Sprinkle both dishes with the cilantro and serve with the rice on the side.

TIP: To make 3 tablespoons of clarified butter, microwave ¼ cup of butter in a measuring cup, or melt it in a small saucepan and pour into a measuring cup. Let the melted butter sit for a few minutes. Skim the white foam off the top and discard. Spoon out and use the golden liquid, discarding any milky liquid at bottom of cup.

# LAMB AND DATE TAGINE WITH SEVEN-VEGETABLE TAGINE AND COUSCOUS

*Serves 2 vegetarians and 4 omnivores*

Moroccan cuisine is one of the most romantic cuisines on Earth. It's full of heady exotic spices and subtle combinations of sweet and savory elements that are both unexpected and comforting at the same time. At the center of Moroccan cuisine are *tagines*, savory stews that are cooked in dome-lidded earthenware dishes of the same name.

In this dual-tagine recipe, dates and tender bits of lamb are simmered until rich and velvety for one tagine, while an array of farmers market–fresh vegetables are cooked in a golden saffron stock for the other. It's the perfect mixed-diet dinner party option: it holds well, can be made up to two days in advance, and it can feed vegans, vegetarians, and omnivores.

**LAMB TAGINE:**
- 1½ pounds boneless leg of lamb or blade chops, fat trimmed, cut into bite-size pieces
- 1 tablespoon Ras Al Hanout (recipe follows)
- 1 pinch saffron
- ½ teaspoon freshly ground black pepper
- 2 tablespoons olive oil, plus additional as needed
- 2 tablespoons all-purpose flour
- 8 small shallots (6 ounces), peeled and halved through the root end into large chunks
- ⅓ cup pitted dates, chopped
- 2 tablespoons (3 to 4) sundried tomatoes packed in oil, finely chopped
- 2 cups chicken or beef stock
- 1 generous pinch chile flakes
- 1 bay leaf
- Salt and freshly ground black pepper

**VEGETABLE TAGINE:**
- 2 pinches saffron
- 2 tablespoons hot water
- 2 tablespoons olive oil

2 large carrots, cut into 2-inch sticks

8 ounces winter squash (butternut or kabocha squash works
well), peeled and cut into 1-inch pieces

1 cup finely chopped onion

1 medium stalk celery, roughly chopped

1 tablespoon Ras Al Hanout (recipe follows)

2 teaspoons minced garlic

1 medium Yukon Gold potato (6 ounces), cut into wedges

One 15-ounce can garbanzo beans, rinsed and drained

1 cup chopped canned tomatoes, without juice

2 tablespoons sundried tomatoes packed in oil (3 to 4),
finely chopped

1 medium zucchini, cut into 2-inch sticks

2 cinnamon sticks

2 cups Roasted Vegetable Stock (page 227) or packaged
vegetable stock

1 bay leaf

Salt and freshly ground black pepper

SERVING: ½ cup finely chopped cilantro leaves

4 cups cooked couscous (or double the recipe on page 95)

1. Combine the lamb, Ras Al Hanout, saffron, pepper, and 1 tablespoon of the
oil. Cover and refrigerate at least 1 hour or up to 2 days. Remove from the
refrigerator and toss with the flour. In a small saucepan or Dutch oven, heat
1 tablespoon of the oil over medium-high heat. Add the lamb and brown in
3 to 4 batches, adding more oil if needed. Return all the lamb to the pan,
add the shallots, dates, tomatoes, stock, chile flakes, and bay leaf; bring to
a simmer. Cover partially and cook, stirring occasionally, until just tender,
about 1 hour 15 minutes.

2. **VEGETARIAN: Combine the saffron with the water; set aside. Heat the
oil in a large pot over medium-high heat. Add the carrots, squash,
onion, celery, and Ras Al Hanout; sauté, stirring frequently, until the
onion begins to brown, about 5 minutes. Add the garlic and sauté
until fragrant, about 30 seconds. Stir in the potatoes, beans, canned
tomatoes, sundried tomatoes, zucchini, cinnamon sticks, stock, and**

**bay leaf; bring to a simmer. Cook until the vegetables are tender, about 20 minutes.**

3. Remove the bay leaves and cinnamon sticks from tagines. Season both tagines with the salt and pepper. Sprinkle with the cilantro and serve with hot couscous.

## Ras Al Hanout
*Makes about ½ cup*

*Ras al hanout* means "top of the shop," as in the top shelf of the spice shop. There's a little bit of everything in this mysterious blend—I've seen ancient recipes that even called for belladonna leaves and Spanish fly! I've pared down my recipe to the essential spices you are likely to have on hand. Rosebuds can be found where bulk tea is sold; it's fine to leave them out if you can't find them.

> 2½ teaspoons cumin seeds
> ½-inch piece cinnamon stick
> 2 teaspoons peppercorns
> 2 rosebuds
> 1 clove
> 2 teaspoons paprika
> ½ teaspoon cayenne
> ½ teaspoon ground ginger
> ½ teaspoon turmeric
> ¼ teaspoon ground allspice
> ½ teaspoon ground nutmeg

1. Toast the cumin seeds in a dry sauté pan over medium heat until fragrant. Combine with the cinnamon stick, peppercorns, rose buds, and clove in a clean spice grinder or mortar and pestle and grind them to a fine powder. Combine with paprika, cayenne, ginger, turmeric, allspice, and nutmeg. (Keeps well in an airtight container in a cool, dry place for up to 6 months.)

# STEAK OR SEITAN AND PEPPER STIR-FRY

*Serves 1 vegetarian and 3 omnivores*

This Chinese-inspired dish relies on an agreeably garlicky black bean sauce for an authentic-tasting stir-fry that comes together in minutes. If you don't eat red meat, use boneless, skinless chicken thighs cut into bite-size pieces instead of steak.

1½ teaspoons cornstarch

2 tablespoons soy sauce

4 teaspoons Chinese rice wine or dry sherry

1 teaspoon chili oil

5 ounces Homemade Seitan (page 229) or packaged, cut into thin strips

12 ounces sirloin steak, frozen until semi-firm, cut into ¼-inch-thick strips

2 heaping tablespoons black bean–garlic sauce (see Glossary)

1 teaspoon sugar

3 tablespoons vegetable stock or water

1 tablespoon Chinese rice wine or dry sherry

2 tablespoons plus 1 teaspoon vegetable oil

1 tablespoon peeled, minced ginger

1 tablespoon finely chopped garlic

1 medium onion, halved and thinly sliced through root end

1 large green pepper, thinly sliced

1 large red pepper, thinly sliced

2 green onions, chopped

5 cups steamed rice

1. Combine the cornstarch and soy sauce in a medium bowl. Stir in the rice wine and chili oil.

2. **VEGETARIAN: Transfer 1 tablespoon of the rice wine mixture to a small bowl and toss with the seitan; set aside.**

3. Toss the meat in the remaining rice wine mixture and set aside.

**4.** In a small bowl or measuring cup, combine the black bean–garlic sauce, sugar, stock, and rice wine; stir until the sugar is dissolved.

**5. VEGETARIAN: Heat 2 teaspoons of the oil in a small sauté pan until hot. Add the seitan and sauté until it is crisped around the edges, about 2 minutes. Remove the pan from the heat and set aside.**

**6.** Heat 1 tablespoon of the oil in a wok over medium-high heat, add the ginger and garlic, and stir-fry until fragrant, about 10 seconds. Add the onion and peppers and stir-fry until they are just singed, about 1 minute. Add the black bean–garlic sauce and stir-fry for 1 minute.

**7. VEGETARIAN: Transfer one quarter of the vegetables in black bean–garlic sauce to the sauté pan containing the seitan and stir to combine. Keep warm over medium-low heat.**

**8.** Transfer the remaining vegetables in black bean–garlic sauce to a serving bowl. Return the wok to medium-high heat. Heat the remaining 2 teaspoons of oil, add the meat, and stir-fry until it is just cooked through, about 2 minutes. Return the reserved vegetables in black bean–garlic sauce to the wok, toss with the meat, and cook until the sauce is bubbly, about 1 minute.

**9.** Sprinkle both stir-fries with the green onions and serve with the steamed rice.

# MOUSSAKA WITH LAMB OR FRENCH LENTILS

*Serves 2 vegetarians and 4 to 6 omnivores*

Despina Kritharalis, my host during a home-stay in the far north of Greece, taught me to make this timeless Greek dish. Despina didn't speak English, and I knew only a few words of Greek, but we found a common language in the kitchen. Despina extended her lamb filling with lentils du Puy when her budget was tight, and I'm using lentils to replace the lamb entirely in the vegetarian moussaka. Though this recipe takes a bit of puttering in the kitchen, you can prepare all the components up to a day ahead and assemble and bake the moussakas when you are ready.

½ cup plus 3 tablespoons olive oil

One 2-pound globe eggplant

¼ teaspoon salt, plus additional

Freshly ground black pepper

2 cups water

¼ cup lentils du Puy (see Glossary and Resources)

1 cup finely chopped onion

1 cup finely chopped green pepper

½ cup finely chopped celery (about 1 stalk)

2 tablespoons garlic, chopped

One 28-ounce can diced tomatoes

½ cup dry red wine

½ teaspoon dried oregano

¼ to ½ teaspoon ground cinnamon

2 pinches ground cloves

¼ cup vegetable stock or water

2 cups 2-percent milk

1 bay leaf

1 garlic clove, slightly smashed

4 tablespoons all-purpose flour

½ teaspoon ground nutmeg

1 pinch cayenne

1 cup (4 ounces) crumbled *mizithra* cheese (see Glossary)

3 eggs, beaten

10 ounces ground lamb, browned and drained

1. Preheat the broiler and brush 2 rimmed baking sheets with olive oil. Cut the stem off the eggplant and discard. Halve eggplant lengthwise and cut the halves crosswise into ½ inch slices. Brush both sides of the slices with the oil (you'll need about ⅓ to ½ cup), place on the baking sheets without overlapping, and season with the salt and pepper. Broil until they are browned on one side and tender, about 3 minutes. Turn with a fork and broil for 2 to 3 minutes on the opposite side. Remove from the oven and set aside.

2. In a small saucepan, bring the water, ¼ teaspoon of the salt, and the lentils to a boil. Cook until they are tender, about 30 minutes. Drain and set aside.

3. Heat 2 tablespoons of the oil in a medium saucepan over medium-high heat. Add the onion, green pepper, and celery and sauté until the onions are translucent, about 5 minutes. Add the chopped garlic, tomatoes, wine, oregano, cinnamon, and cloves; bring to a simmer. Reduce the heat, cover, and simmer for 30 minutes, adding the stock if the sauce becomes too dry. Season with the salt and pepper and keep warm over low heat.

4. In a medium saucepan, heat the milk, bay leaf, and garlic clove over medium heat until the milk is just hot. Put the flour into a medium mixing bowl and gradually whisk 1 cup of the hot milk into the flour to make a slurry. Return the slurry mixture to the saucepan and cook, whisking frequently, until the sauce is smooth and bubbly, about 15 minutes. Remove the pan from the heat and remove the garlic and bay leaf. Whisk in the nutmeg, cayenne, cheese, and salt and pepper to taste. Let the sauce cool for 10 minutes. Whisk the eggs into the sauce and set aside. Preheat the oven to 350 degrees F.

5. **VEGETARIAN: Spray a 3-cup baking dish with nonstick cooking spray. In a small bowl, combine 1½ cups of the tomato sauce with the lentils. Spoon half the mixture into the baking dish and top with a layer of eggplant. Repeat with a layer of the remaining tomato-lentil sauce and top with a second layer of eggplant.**

6. Spray an 8-inch-square baking dish with nonstick cooking spray. Stir the lamb into the remaining tomato sauce and spoon half into the baking dish. Top with a single layer of eggplant, the remaining lamb-tomato sauce, and the remaining eggplant.

7. Spoon the white sauce over both casseroles and transfer them to a baking sheet. Bake until the tops are puffed and golden brown around the edges, about 50 minutes for the vegetarian and 1 hour 10 minutes for the omnivore moussaka. Let the moussakas sit for at least 10 and up to 30 minutes before serving.

# THAI RED CURRY WITH GREEN BEANS
# AND CHICKEN OR TOFU

*Serves 1 to 2 vegetarians and 4 omnivores*

In this Thai "dry curry," no coconut milk is used; instead, the curry paste is wok-fried and the vegetables and proteins absorb its flavor with the help of Vegan Fish Sauce and a little palm sugar. Using homemade curry paste makes this dish really pop with flavor, but you can use canned red curry paste if you like. If you use canned curry, reduce the amount called for in the recipe—they tend to be more fiery than home-made curry paste.

¼ cup Vegan Fish Sauce (page 228)

2 tablespoons palm sugar (see Glossary) or loosely packed brown sugar

4 tablespoons vegetable oil

4 to 5 tablespoons Malaysian Curry Paste (page 36), or 3 to 4 tablespoons canned red curry paste

5 ounces extra-firm tofu, cut into 1-inch cubes

1 pound green beans, trimmed and cut into 1-inch pieces

1 medium red bell pepper, sliced

10 kaffir lime leaves

1 pound boneless, skinless chicken breasts or thighs, cut into bite-size pieces

1 tablespoon fish sauce (optional)

1 cup Thai basil leaves, roughly chopped (see **TIP**)

5 cups steamed jasmine rice

1. Stir the vegan fish sauce and palm sugar together in a small bowl until the sugar is dissolved; set aside.

2. Heat 3 tablespoons of the oil in a wok over medium-high heat. Add the curry paste and stir-fry, stirring constantly, for 30 seconds. Add the tofu and stir-fry until it becomes coated with the curry paste and the edges become crisp, about 1½ minutes. Add the green beans, bell pepper, and kaffir lime

leaves and stir-fry for 2 minutes. Add the palm sugar–vegan fish sauce mixture and stir-fry for another 2 minutes, until the beans are crisp-tender.

3. **VEGETARIAN: Transfer a quarter of the mixture, including most of the tofu, to a small serving bowl, cover, and keep in a warm place.**

4. Transfer the remaining vegetable-sauce mixture to a large serving bowl and cover.

5. Return the wok to medium-high heat and heat the remaining tablespoon of oil. Add the chicken and stir-fry until the chicken is cooked through, about 4 minutes. Add the vegetable mixture from the large serving bowl. Add the fish sauce, toss to combine, and cook 1 minute. Return mixture to the large serving bowl.

6. Top both curries with the basil and serve with the rice.

   **TIP:** Thai basil has an anise-meets-basil flavor that adds a mildly spicy punch to curries. Look for it at Asian markets, or use standard fresh basil leaves.

# NASI GORENG (INDONESIAN FRIED RICE) WITH SHRIMP, TOFU, AND SHRIMP CHIPS

*Serves 1 vegetarian and 3 omnivores*

In Indonesian, *nasi goreng* means "fried rice," but the literal name only tells part of the story. *Nasi goreng* does feature stir-fried rice, but the kaffir lime leaves, lemongrass, and crisp shrimp chips in this dish help make it a masterpiece compared to the sometimes greasy, soy-doused takeout fried rice you may have eaten. The key to success here is to cook the rice in advance and chill it for at least three hours before proceeding to prevent the rice from becoming mushy when it is stir-fried.

2 cups long-grain rice

4 cups water

1 lemongrass stalk

3 kaffir lime leaves

1 teaspoon turmeric

1 cup plus 2 tablespoons vegetable oil

6 ounces shrimp chips (see Glossary)

3 tablespoons *kecap manis* (see **TIP**)

1 tablespoon soy sauce

1 tablespoon sweet chili sauce such as Mae Ploy brand

1 teaspoon vinegary chili sauce such as sambal oelek

2 eggs, lightly beaten

1 small onion, thinly sliced

1 tablespoon minced garlic

1 carrot, finely chopped

4 ounces fried tofu (see page xviii), cut into bite-size pieces

3 green onions, thinly sliced

3 cups finely shredded napa cabbage

1 cucumber, peeled in strips, halved, seeded, and thinly sliced

8 ounces shrimp, peeled, deveined, and roughly chopped

1. Rinse the rice well in several bowls of cool water. Drain well and place in a medium saucepan with the 4 cups of water. Smack the lemongrass with a pestle or meat tenderizer to bruise it, tie it into a rough knot, and add it to the saucepan with the kaffir lime leaves and turmeric; bring to a boil over medium-high heat. Reduce the heat to a simmer, cover, and cook until the rice is just tender, about 18 minutes. (Alternatively, cook in a rice cooker.) Pour onto a rimmed baking sheet and let cool in the refrigerator for at least 3 hours or up to 2 days. Remove lime leaves and lemongrass before using.

2. Line a baking sheet with crumpled paper towels. Heat 1 cup of the oil in a small, heavy saucepan over high heat. Add 1 shrimp chip and fry until it is puffed, about 15 seconds. Transfer it to the prepared baking sheet to drain and repeat with the remaining chips, reducing the heat if they begin to burn. Set aside.

3. Combine the *kecap manis*, soy sauce, and both chili sauces in a measuring cup. Set aside. Heat a wok over high heat, swirl 1 teaspoon of the oil to coat, pour in the eggs, and cook without stirring until the they are just set into an omelet-like round, about 40 seconds. Flip over and cook on the other side for 10 seconds; transfer to a cutting board. Roll the omelet into a tight roll and julienne. Set aside.

4. Return the wok to high heat, add 1 tablespoon of the oil, onion, garlic, carrot, and tofu. Stir-fry until the onion begins to brown, about 3 minutes. Crumble the rice into the wok; add the chili sauce mixture, green onions, and cabbage. Stir-fry until the rice is hot and the cabbage is wilted, about 3 minutes. Add the omelet strips and toss to combine.

5. **VEGETARIAN: Place one quarter of the mixture, including most of the tofu, on a small serving platter. Decorate the edges of the platter with one quarter of the cucumber, cover, and set aside.**

6. Place the remaining fried rice mixture on a large platter and decorate with the remaining cucumber; cover and set aside. Return the wok to high heat and add the remaining 2 teaspoons of oil. Add the shrimp and stir-fry until pink and cooked through, about 1 minute. Arrange shrimp over the fried

rice mixture. Serve with shrimp chips on the side, instructing omnivores to crumble them over their rice.

TIP: *Kecap manis* (Indonesian sweet soy sauce) adds a sweet caramel-like flavor to the rice. You can find it at Asian markets. Thick soy sauce is a suitable substitute; reduce the quantity to 2 tablespoons.

vvvvvvvvvvvvvvvvvvvvvvvvvvvvvvvvvvvvvvvvvv

VEGAN VARIATION: Omit the egg from the vegetarian portion.

# VEGETABLE AND CHICKEN KORMA WITH CASHEWS

*Serves 1 vegetarian and 3 omnivores*

The term *korma* refers to a long-braised Indian dish, often using mild spices and yogurt as both the marinade and the braising liquid. In this recipe, the same mix of finely chopped onions and spices serves as a base for both the vegetarian and the omnivore dishes, but the results are quite different. The vegetables absorb the yogurt in the former; while the chicken dish is quite saucy. This recipe makes enough vegetable korma so both omnivores and vegetarians get a portion.

2 cups plus 3 tablespoons plain full-fat yogurt

4 teaspoons minced garlic

½ teaspoon salt, plus additional

2 teaspoons turmeric

2 teaspoons New Mexican chile powder

3 chicken legs, skin removed

2 tablespoons vegetable oil

2 cups finely chopped onions (see **TIP**)

1 cinnamon stick, broken into 2 pieces

6 whole cloves

4 green cardamom pods

1 teaspoon coriander seeds

1 tablespoon peeled, minced ginger

3 large Yukon Gold potatoes, peeled and cut into ½-inch chunks

1 medium carrot, cut into ½-inch chunks

¼ cup shelled edamame

Freshly ground black pepper

½ cup toasted cashews

3 tablespoons finely chopped cilantro

Butter and Spice Basmati Rice (recipe follows)

1. At least 4 hours or up to 2 days before serving, combine 1 cup of the yogurt, 2 teaspoons of the garlic, ½ teaspoon of the salt, 1 teaspoon of the turmeric, and 1 teaspoon of the chile powder in a nonreactive bowl. Cut

the chicken legs through the joint, separating the drumstick and thigh. Add the pieces to the yogurt mixture and turn to coat. Cover and refrigerate.

2. About 1 hour before serving, transfer the chicken and marinade to a medium saucepan and bring to a simmer over medium heat. Cover; reduce the heat to medium low, and cook for 30 minutes, turning the chicken occasionally with tongs.

3. Heat the oil in a large sauté pan over medium heat. Add the onions, cinnamon stick pieces, cloves, cardamom pods, and coriander seeds and sauté until the onions begin to brown, 10 to 15 minutes. Add the remaining 2 teaspoons of the garlic and the ginger and cook, stirring constantly until fragrant, about 1 minute.

4. Scrape half the onion and spice mixture and 1 piece of the cinnamon stick into the chicken and marinade in saucepan. Add a third of the potatoes, stir to combine, cover, and continue to cook over medium-low heat.

5. **VEGETARIAN: Add 1 cup of the yogurt to the remaining onion and spice mixture. Stir in the remaining 1 teaspoon chile powder, 1 teaspoon of the turmeric, and potatoes, plus the carrots and edamame. Bring to a simmer, cover, and cook, stirring occasionally until the potatoes are tender, about 25 minutes. (Add a few tablespoons of water if the mixture becomes too dry.) Stir in the remaining 3 tablespoons of yogurt and remove from the heat.**

6. Season both kormas with the salt and pepper to taste, transfer to separate serving dishes, sprinkle with the cashews and cilantro, and serve with the rice.

TIP: The onions must be very finely chopped, almost to a purée, since they act as a thickener to the sauce. I use a mini-chopper to get the onions finely minced. (Alternatively, use a regular-size food processor or blender, stopping frequently to scrape down the sides; or grate the onions, perhaps while wearing goggles.)

# Butter and Spice Basmati Rice

*Serves 4*

After a brief soaking period, the delicate, needlelike grains of basmati rice cook quickly in this uncovered cooking method. The rice turns out fluffy, buttery, and a brilliant yellow color thanks to the saffron threads. Be sure to warn everyone at the table that the rice contains whole cloves and cardamom pods that are not meant to be eaten and should be removed from the rice.

> ¼ teaspoon saffron threads
> 1 tablespoon boiling water
> 2 cups basmati rice
> Cool water, for rinsing rice
> 4 cups water
> 2 tablespoons butter
> 2 cloves
> 4 whole green cardamom pods
> ½ teaspoon cumin seeds
> 1 teaspoon salt

1. Combine the saffron with the boiling water in a small measuring cup; set aside. Put the rice in a large bowl and add enough cool water to cover by 2 inches. Swirl with your hand and drain. Repeat with 2 more changes of cool water to rinse away excess starch. Drain and add enough cool water to cover by a few inches; let rice soak for 30 minutes. Drain well in a fine-mesh sieve.

2. Bring the 4 cups of water to a boil in a teakettle or small saucepan. Heat the butter in a large saucepan over medium-low heat. Add the cloves, cardamom pods, and cumin seeds and cook, stirring constantly, until the spices smell toasty, about 2 minutes. Add the drained rice and stir to coat with the butter. Stir in the saffron and its soaking liquid, the boiling water, and salt; bring to a simmer. Lower the heat to maintain a gentle simmer. Cook uncovered until the rice is tender, 15 to 20 minutes.

# BIBIMBAP

*Serves 1 vegetarian and 3 omnivores*

My Korean friend Cathy taught me to make *bibimbap*, the quintessential Korean comfort food that is fun to say and even more fun to eat, and I will be forever grateful. Essentially it is rice decorated with a wide array of pickled vegetables, sweet-salty marinated grilled steak, and spicy kimchi, and it is one of the most delicious foods I have ever put in my mouth.

The soy mixture used to marinate the beef also works well for tofu, so vegetarians can join in the build-your-own-bowl fun. For added protein and richness, you can top each rice bowl with a fried egg. The list of ingredients may look long, but the salads are very easy to put together and can be done up to two days in advance. (Alternatively, look for premade boxes of similar salads for *bibimbap* and thinly sliced beef at Korean grocery stores.)

½ cup low-sodium soy sauce

2 tablespoons plus 1½ teaspoons dark sesame oil

1 tablespoon brown sugar

1 tablespoon minced garlic

2 tablespoons plus ½ teaspoon rice vinegar

½ teaspoon freshly ground black pepper

1 finely chopped green onion

6 ounces firm tofu, cut into 1-inch-thick slabs

12 ounces beef rib eye, trimmed of fat, frozen until semi-firm and very thinly sliced

1 large cucumber (12 ounces), halved lengthwise and seeded

1 tablespoon plus ¾ teaspoon kosher salt

2½ teaspoons toasted sesame seeds

¼ pound bean sprouts

2 large carrots, thinly sliced

One 12-ounce bag fresh baby spinach leaves

8 cups hot steamed medium-grain rice, such as CalRose

4 eggs

Korean red chili sauce (such as Daesang *bibimbap* sauce) or
Sriracha chile paste
Prepared kimchi for garnish (see **TIP**)

1. For the marinade, whisk together the soy sauce, 1 tablespoon of the oil,
sugar, garlic, 1 tablespoon of the vinegar, pepper, and green onion in a small
bowl until the sugar is dissolved.

2. **VEGETARIAN: Put the tofu in a small bowl and spoon 3 tablespoons of
the marinade over it, turning to coat.**

3. Toss the meat with the remaining marinade. Marinate the proteins for at
least 30 minutes, or cover and refrigerate for up to 24 hours.

4. For the salad, cut the cucumber into ⅛-inch-thick slices. Toss with 1 tablespoon of the salt in a medium bowl and set aside for 10 minutes. Rinse
well, drain in a colander, and press firmly to squeeze out the excess liquid.
Transfer to a clean serving bowl and toss with 1½ teaspoons of the oil, 1½
teaspoons of the vinegar, and 1 teaspoon of the sesame seeds; set aside.

5. For the bean sprouts, bring a large pot of water to a boil. Add the sprouts
and cook until they are slightly wilted but still crisp, 5 seconds. Remove
with a small sieve, rinse with cold water, and drain well. Transfer to a bowl
and toss with 1 teaspoon of the oil, 1 teaspoon of the vinegar, and ½ teaspoon of the sesame seeds. For the carrot and spinach salads, repeat blanch-
ing process as with the bean sprouts, boiling them for 3 minutes and 1
minute, respectively. Toss carrots in a bowl with ½ teaspoon of the salt and
1 teaspoon of the vinegar, and set aside. Toss spinach in another bowl with
remaining 2 teaspoons of oil, the remaining ¼ teaspoon of salt and remaining teaspoon of sesame seeds.

6. **VEGETARIAN: Preheat a nonstick grill pan or cast iron skillet over
medium-high heat. Shake the excess marinade off the tofu and
discard. Grill the tofu until it is seared and heated through, about
2 minutes per side. Put 2 cups of rice in 1 bowl, top with the tofu,
cover, and set aside.**

7. Shake the excess marinade off the meat and discard. In the same pan, cook
the steak in batches until the meat is seared on both sides, 30 seconds to

1 minute per side, depending on the thickness of the slices. Do not overcook. Divide the remaining rice among 3 bowls, top with the meat, and set aside.

8. Spray a nonstick skillet with cooking spray. Heat over medium-high heat, add the eggs, and fry until the whites are set and yolks are still runny, about 4 minutes. Top each bowl with 1 egg. Serve, allowing diners to add salads, chili sauce, and kim chee to their bowls. (Leftover vegetables can be stored in the refrigerator in airtight containers for up to 1 week, with the exception of the spinach, which must be used within 2 days of cooking.)

TIP: Kimchi is a spicy napa-cabbage pickle available in jars at Asian markets. It keeps in the refrigerator for up to 4 weeks.

v v v v v v v v v v v v v v v v v v v v v v v v v v v v v v v v v v v v v v

VEGAN VARIATION: Omit the egg from the tofu portion.

# KUNG PAO CHICKEN OR TOFU

*Serves 1 vegetarian and 3 omnivores*

This Chinese takeout favorite traditionally gets its kick from Szechwan peppercorns, a spice that comes from the prickly ash tree. I use easier-to-find small dried red chiles, (available in the Asian or Mexican section of well-stocked supermarkets) to add a smoky, moderate heat to this stir-fry.

**MARINADE AND PROTEINS:**
- 3 tablespoons soy sauce
- 3 tablespoons Chinese rice wine (see Glossary)
- 2 teaspoons cornstarch
- 1 pound chicken breast, thinly sliced
- 8 ounces firm nigari tofu, frozen and thawed (see **TIP**), cut into 1-inch cubes

**SAUCE:**
- 1 tablespoon cornstarch
- 2 tablespoons brown sugar
- 2 tablespoons soy sauce
- 2 tablespoons apple cider vinegar
- 2 teaspoons toasted sesame oil
- ¼ cup Asian-Style Stock (page 224), packaged vegetable stock, or water
- 1 tablespoon Asian chili sauce, such as sambal oelek

**STIR-FRY AND SERVING:**
- 3 tablespoons vegetable oil
- 10 to 12 small dried red chiles
- 1 tablespoon peeled, minced ginger
- 1 tablespoon minced garlic
- 4 chopped green onions
- 2 celery stalks, thinly sliced on the bias
- One 8-ounce can sliced water chestnuts, drained
- ½ cup roasted peanuts
- 5 cups hot cooked rice
- Chili sauce to pass, such as sambal oelek (optional)

1. Make the marinade. Whisk together the 3 tablespoons soy sauce, rice wine, and 2 teaspoons cornstarch in a medium bowl until smooth. Spoon

4 tablespoons of the mixture into a small bowl, add the chicken, and toss to combine.

2. VEGETARIAN: **Toss the tofu with the remaining marinade.**

3. Marinate the tofu and chicken while preparing the remaining ingredients, or cover and marinate in refrigerator for up to 3 hours.

4. Make the sauce. Combine the 1 tablespoon of cornstarch, brown sugar, the 2 tablespoons of soy sauce, vinegar, sesame oil, stock, and chile sauce in a small measuring cup; set aside.

5. Heat 1 tablespoon of the vegetable oil in a wok over high heat. Add the chicken and stir-fry until it is cooked through and lightly singed in areas, about 4 minutes. Transfer to a clean bowl and set aside.

6. Wash out the wok thoroughly and put it over medium-high heat. Add the remaining 2 tablespoons of vegetable oil and chiles and stir-fry until they begin to brown, about 30 seconds. Remove the chiles and reserve, leaving the flavored oil in the wok. Add the tofu and fry without stirring until it is golden brown on 1 side, about 2 minutes. Add the ginger and garlic and stir-fry until fragrant, 10 seconds. Add the green onions, celery, water chestnuts, and peanuts and stir-fry until the vegetables are crisp-tender, about 2 minutes. Stir the sauce mixture and add it to the wok. Return the reserved chiles and stir-fry until the sauce is thickened and bubbly, about 2 minutes.

7. VEGETARIAN: **Put a quarter of the stir-fry (including most of the tofu) into a bowl; cover and set aside.**

8. Return the chicken to the wok with the remaining vegetables and sauce and stir-fry for 30 seconds to reheat. Put in a serving bowl.

9. Serve with the rice and chili sauce.

TIP: To render tofu wok-ready and firm, freeze it overnight (or longer). Let it thaw on a paper towel–lined plate, weighting the top of the tofu with a few heavy cans set on top of a dinner plate. The excess moisture in the tofu will melt away, leaving the tofu firmer and spongelike so it will absorb marinades and sauces more effectively.

# 6

## SPECIAL OCCASIONS

The scenario is the same in many homes: a holiday or special occasion is approaching and you have a beautiful meal planned. Big-ticket roast? Check. The traditional gravy, vegetable side dishes, and starches? Check. The perfect dessert finale? Check. But at the last minute, or perhaps because you didn't know what to do about it earlier, you finally come to terms with the fact that vegetarians or vegans will be coming to dinner. It's a special occasion for them, too, but besides serving them a plate of mashed potatoes and brussels sprouts, what will you cook so they feel they are part of the celebration?

Whether it is St. Patrick's Day and one of your clan won't touch the corned beef, or Christmastime and you are hosting a vegan who would rather eat snow than dig into prime rib, every recipe in this chapter will help you provide vegetarian and vegan meals that are quick or can be made ahead, *and* that are special enough to make them feel welcome and well fed.

# SWEETHEART MUSHROOM RAVIOLI
# WITH BEURRE ROUGE SAUCE

*Makes 24 ravioli; serves 4 as a first course or 2 as a main course*

These heart-shaped ravioli stuffed with truffled mushroom filling are perfect for St. Valentine's Day, and they are much more romantic than a store-bought box of chocolates. The burgundy-hued butter sauce adds to the romance.

The ravioli and most of the sauce can be made in advance and cooked right before serving, so you can wear something tantalizing without worrying about getting flour all over you. This dish is quite substantial by itself, but if your significant other happens to see the plate as half empty without meat on it, seared lamb chops or a simple grilled tenderloin steak make a fine accompaniment.

**DOUGH:** 1½ cups all-purpose flour

2 eggs, beaten

1 tablespoon plus 1 teaspoon salt

**FILLING:** ½ ounce dried wild mushrooms (I use a mix of porcini and morels)

1 medium Yukon Gold potato (5 ounces), unpeeled

½ cup plus 4 tablespoons grated Parmigiano-Reggiano cheese

1 tablespoon finely chopped Italian parsley

1 teaspoon white truffle oil (see Resources)

Freshly ground black pepper

**SAUCE:** 1 cup dry red wine

1 tablespoon red wine vinegar

1 bay leaf

¼ cup thinly sliced shallots (1 large)

3 tablespoons cream

½ cup cold unsalted butter, cut into ½-inch pieces

Salt and ground white pepper

1. For the pasta dough, combine the flour, eggs, and a pinch of salt in a stand-mixer bowl. Blend with a wooden spoon, adding 1 to 2 tablespoons of water if necessary until the dough comes together. Attach the dough hook

and knead on medium speed for 3 minutes. (Alternatively, knead the dough by hand on a lightly floured surface for 10 minutes.) Cover with plastic wrap and let the dough rest for 30 minutes. (The dough can be made up to 2 days in advance; wrap tightly in plastic wrap and refrigerate. Bring to room temperature before using.)

2. For the filling, bring 2 cups of water to a boil. Place the mushrooms in a small bowl, pour the water over them, cover, and let them soak for 30 minutes. Put the potato in a small saucepan with 1 teaspoon of the salt; cover with cold water. Boil until a paring knife pierces the potato easily, about 25 minutes. Slip the skin off with your fingers and cut the potato into ¼-inch cubes. Drain the mushrooms, finely chop them, and combine with the potato, 4 tablespoons of the Parmigiano-Reggiano, parsley, and truffle oil, mashing the potatoes lightly with a fork. Season to taste with the salt and pepper.

3. Lightly sprinkle a baking sheet with flour and set aside. Divide the pasta dough into 4 pieces. Slightly flatten 1 piece and feed it through the pasta maker on the thickest setting. Fold the dough in half and feed it through again on the first setting. Dust with the flour and continue to feed through the rollers, turning to the next-thinnest setting each time through until you reach the second-thinnest setting (number 6 on most pasta machines). Cut the sheets into 1-foot lengths.

4. Lay 1 sheet on a lightly floured surface. Place a 3-inch heart-shaped cookie cutter on the dough as a guide. Place a scant tablespoon of the mushroom mixture in the center of the heart. Move the cutter a few inches to the right and continue to use it as a guide, spacing mounds of filling in a row. (You will be able to make 3 to 4 ravioli on a 1-foot length of dough.) Brush water around each mound of filling and carefully lay another sheet of pasta over the first. Press down around the fillings, sealing the pasta sheets together and pushing out any air bubbles. Using the cookie cutter, cut the ravioli into heart shapes and place them on the prepared baking sheet. Repeat, using the remaining dough and filling (you can re-roll pasta scraps), to make 24 ravioli. Cover with plastic wrap and refrigerate until ready to cook. (The ravioli can be made up to 3 days ahead. You can also freeze the ravioli on a baking sheet until solid and then

transfer them to an airtight container and freeze them for up to 3 months. Simmer frozen ravioli for 5 to 6 minutes, or until the pasta is tender.)

5. For the sauce, in a small saucepan combine the wine, vinegar, bay leaf, and shallots. Bring to a boil and cook until the mixture is reduced to about 2 tablespoons of liquid, about 10 minutes. (The sauce can be prepared to this point up to 3 hours in advance; keep at room temperature.) Stir in the cream and bring to a simmer. Reduce the heat to very low and gradually whisk in the butter, adding more butter only when the previous addition has melted, creating a creamy sauce. If the sauce begins to look oily instead of creamy, take the pan off the heat and continue to whisk in the butter. Season with salt and white pepper; remove from burner and keep warm.

6. Bring a large pot of water to a simmer and add the 1 tablespoon salt. Cook the ravioli until tender, about 4 minutes. (Do not bring to a boil or the ravioli may burst.) With a slotted spoon, carefully scoop out the ravioli and divide among the plates. Blot any excess moisture from the plates with paper towels. Drizzle the sauce around the ravioli and serve with the remaining ½ cup Parmigiano-Reggiano, passed separately.

v v v v v v v v v v v v v v v v v v v v v v v v v v v v v v v v v v

**VEGAN VARIATION:** Use egg-free wonton wrappers instead of pasta and serve with marinara sauce.

# EASTER GREENS AND RISOTTO TART

*Serves 4 to 6*

A traditional dish in late winter and spring in Piedmont, Italy, this baked vegetable and rice tart is a lovely vegetarian alternative to the usual Easter ham. The rice, full of spring greens and herbs, makes a nice side dish to ham, too, so it's a win-win recipe for every bunny. Another plus: It can be served hot or at room temperature, making it ideal for a buffet meal.

12 ounces day-old focaccia bread or French bread, torn into pieces

4 cups No-Chicken Stock (page 225) or mild vegetable stock

2 tablespoons butter

1 leek, white and light green parts only, thinly sliced

1 medium carrot, finely chopped

1 medium stalk celery, finely chopped

1 cup Arborio rice

½ cup white wine

2 cups dandelion greens or watercress leaves, torn into bite-size pieces

½ cup fresh shelled peas (about ½ pound in the pod)

3 tablespoons minced fresh basil

2 tablespoons minced chives

½ teaspoon ground nutmeg

4 ounces creamy cow's milk cheese such as fontina or Crescenza, diced

Salt and freshly ground black pepper

3 eggs, beaten

1. Preheat the oven to 350 degrees F. Spray an 8-inch springform pan with nonstick cooking spray. Line the bottom with parchment paper and spray it with nonstick cooking spray. Pulse the focaccia in a food processor until you have coarse crumbs, or finely chop with a chef's knife. Sprinkle 1 cup of the crumbs over the bottom of the pan and set aside.

2. Heat the stock in a small saucepan over medium heat until hot, reduce the heat, and keep warm. Melt the butter in a 3-quart saucepan over medium heat. Add the leek, carrot, and celery and sauté until the leek is tender, about 4 minutes. Add the rice and cook for 1 minute, stirring constantly. Add the wine and simmer, stirring frequently until the liquid is absorbed. Add 1 ladle (about 8 ounces) of the stock and bring to a simmer, stirring constantly until the liquid is absorbed. Continue adding stock in intervals until almost all the stock is used, 15 to 18 minutes. Bite into a grain of rice; if it has an opaque white center the diameter of a pin and is slightly chewy, it is perfectly cooked.

3. Remove the rice from the heat and stir in the greens, peas, basil, chives, nutmeg, and cheese. Season with the salt and pepper and let the mixture cool for 10 minutes. Add the eggs 1 at a time, stirring after each addition. Transfer the mixture to the prepared pan, top with the remaining crumbs, and place the pan on a baking sheet. Bake for 45 minutes or until a knife inserted in the center comes out with moist crumbs attached but with no liquid egg clinging to it. Let the tart cool for 15 minutes. Run a thin knife around the edges of the pan, remove the sides and bottom of the pan, cut the tart into wedges, and serve.

# SPINACH ROULADE WITH RED PEPPERS AND RICOTTA

*Serves 4*

I love serving this impressive roulade to the vegetarians in my clan, slicing it at the dining table as I would a special roast. The green spinach soufflé roll with the red and white filling make it a festive choice for the Christmas season. You can prepare it up to 2 days in advance and bake it right before mealtime.

1 tablespoon olive oil

2 teaspoons minced garlic

10 ounces frozen chopped spinach, thawed

4 eggs, separated (see **TIP** on page 211)

¾ cup grated Parmigiano-Reggiano cheese

½ teaspoon salt, plus additional

½ teaspoon ground nutmeg

1 heaping cup (10 ounces) full-fat ricotta cheese

2 tablespoons minced fresh basil

2 tablespoons minced Italian parsley

½ teaspoon lemon zest

Freshly ground black pepper

½ cup Roasted Red Peppers (page 232), or jarred,
   cut into thin strips

4 cups warm store-bought or homemade marinara sauce
   (optional)

1. Preheat the oven to 425 degrees F. Line a 9- by 13-inch rimmed baking sheet with parchment paper and spray with nonstick cooking spray.

2. Heat the olive oil over medium heat in a large sauté pan or wok. Add the garlic and sauté until fragrant, about 30 seconds. Add the spinach and cook until all of the liquid has evaporated, about 3 minutes. Drain the spinach in a fine-mesh sieve and squeeze to remove excess moisture. Combine the spinach, egg yolks, ½ cup of the Parmigiano-Reggiano, ½ teaspoon salt, and nutmeg in a food processor and pulse until combined. Transfer the mixture to a large mixing bowl and set aside.

**3.** In a medium bowl, whip the egg whites with a pinch of salt until soft peaks form. Gently fold a quarter of the egg whites into the spinach mixture, then fold in the remaining egg whites. Spoon the mixture gently into the prepared baking sheet and smooth it with a rubber spatula. Bake until the roulade base feels firm when touched, 12 to 15 minutes. Invert onto a parchment paper–lined cutting board, remove the pan, and allow the roulade to cool for 30 minutes.

**4.** Pour off any excess liquid from the ricotta and discard. Combine the ricotta, basil, parsley, lemon zest, and the remaining ¼ cup of Parmigiano-Reggiano in a medium bowl. Season with salt and pepper to taste.

**5.** Reduce the oven temperature to 350 degrees F. Carefully peel the top layer of parchment paper from the roulade and discard. Spread the cheese mixture evenly over the roulade, leaving a ½-inch border on the sides. Blot the peppers dry with paper towels and distribute them evenly over the cheese mixture. With the long end facing you, use the bottom piece of parchment paper as a guide to tightly roll up the roulade as you would a jelly roll. Carefully place the roulade seam side down on a baking sheet. (The unbaked roulade can be stored in the refrigerator, wrapped tightly in parchment paper, for up to 1 day. Unwrap it and allow it to sit at room temperature for 40 minutes before baking.)

**6.** Bake the roulade until heated through, about 25 minutes. Slice into 1½-inch-thick slices with a sharp serrated knife, and serve with the warm marinara, if desired.

# TWICE-BAKED POTATOES WITH EDAMAME

*Serves 4 as a light entrée or side dish*

St. Patrick's Day can be a rather bleak dining day for vegetarians. If you don't partake of lamb-filled Irish stew or corned beef, you're often left to celebrate with a meager pint of stout and a slab of soda bread. These twice-baked spuds keep with the spirit of things, and they contain a good dose of protein thanks to the buttery edamame in the cheesy mashed potato stuffing.

> 4 large russet potatoes (8 to 10 ounces each)
>
> ½ teaspoon olive oil
>
> 4 tablespoons butter (I like Kerrygold Pure Irish Butter; see Resources)
>
> ½ cup finely chopped onion
>
> 2 cups chopped green cabbage
>
> ½ cup frozen shelled edamame, thawed
>
> ¾ cup buttermilk or half-and-half
>
> 1 teaspoon nutritional yeast (see Glossary)
>
> Salt and freshly ground black pepper
>
> 1 cup grated sharp cheddar cheese (I like Kerrygold Vintage Cheddar; see Resources)

1. Preheat the oven to 400 degrees F. Scrub the potatoes with a stiff-bristled brush under running water. Pat them dry and rub them all over with the oil. Place the potatoes directly on the center rack of the oven. Bake until they give easily when gently squeezed, 45 minutes to 1 hour. Use a serrated knife to cut off the top quarter of the potatoes and set aside. Let the steam escape from the potatoes while preparing the other ingredients.

2. Reduce the oven temperature to 350 degrees F. Heat 2 tablespoons of the butter in a large sauté pan over medium heat. Add the onion and cabbage and cook, stirring frequently until they begin to brown, about 10 minutes. Add the edamame, stir to combine, and remove from the heat.

3. Use a soup spoon to scoop out the potato flesh from the potato tops and discard the skin. Scoop out the flesh from the center of the potatoes,

leaving a ¼-inch-thick shell on the bottom and sides. Mash the potato flesh with the remaining 2 tablespoons of butter, buttermilk, and nutritional yeast. Gently fold the onion-cabbage mixture into the mashed potatoes and season with the salt and pepper to taste.

4. Mound the mashed potato mixture into the potato shells and sprinkle the tops with the cheese. (The potatoes can be made up to 2 days ahead. Cool, wrap in plastic wrap, and refrigerate. Add 10 minutes to baking time.)

5. Place the potatoes on a baking sheet. Bake until the cheese is melted and bubbly, about 20 minutes.

**VEGAN VARIATION:** Substitute vegan margarine or olive oil when sautéing the vegetables. Separate a quarter of the potato flesh and mash with unsweetened soy milk and vegan cheese instead of butter and buttermilk. Omit the cheese topping.

# GRILLED VEGETABLE WEDGES

*Serves 4*

"Wedge" is just another name for a well-stuffed submarine sandwich. In this case, the sandwich is a round loaf of bread filled with grilled vegetables, cheese, and pesto sauce that is pressed for a few hours so the slices stay attractively compact after slicing. The resulting sandwiches are sophisticated, substantial, and meat free—the perfect thing for vegetarians who are on a midsummer picnic with omnivores who might be enjoying cold fried chicken or other meaty picnic fare.

> 1 large Japanese eggplant (6 ounces), cut into ¾-inch-thick slices
>
> 4 tablespoons olive oil
>
> Salt and freshly ground black pepper
>
> 1 medium zucchini (8 ounces), cut into ½-inch-thick slices
>
> 1 small yellow summer squash (6 ounces), cut into ½-inch-thick slices
>
> 2 large portobello mushrooms (6 ounces), stemmed
>
> 1 tablespoon balsamic vinegar
>
> 2 small roasted red or yellow bell peppers (see Roasted Red Peppers on page 232), or jarred
>
> One 1-pound loaf of crusty bread, preferably round
>
> 4 to 5 slices provolone cheese
>
> ¼ cup Blender Pesto (page 231) or jarred pesto sauce

1. Heat a grill pan or gas grill over medium-high heat. Brush the eggplant with 2 tablespoons of the oil and season with the salt and pepper. Grill until the edges begin to sizzle, about 3 minutes. Turn with tongs and grill on the other side until the eggplant is tender when pierced with tongs, about 4 minutes. Place a large rack over a baking sheet and cool the eggplant on the rack. Brush the zucchini and squash with 1 tablespoon of the oil, season with the salt and pepper, and grill until tender, about 4 minutes per side. Transfer to the rack.

2. Scrape the black gills off the underside of the mushrooms and discard. Brush both sides with the remaining 1 tablespoon of oil and vinegar. Reduce the heat to medium and grill the mushrooms until they are tender,

about 3 minutes per side. Quarter and place them on the rack. (The vegetables can be prepared to this point up to 2 days ahead. Cool completely and refrigerate in an airtight container; blot excess moisture with paper towels before using.)

3. Cut off the top third of the bread and set aside. Pull the spongy bread out of the center of the loaf to create a ½-inch-thick shell all around. (Process the excess bread in a food processor or finely chop it to make fresh bread crumbs. Freeze in a resealable freezer bag for another use.) Lay the cheese evenly over the bottom and sides of the bread shell, reserving 2 slices for the lid. Spread most of the pesto over the cheese in the bread shell. Blot the mushrooms, zucchini, squash, and peppers with paper towels to absorb excess moisture and layer them in the bread shell. Put the 2 remaining cheese slices on the cut side of the bread lid, spread with the remaining pesto, and place the lid on top of bread shell to make a sandwich.

4. Wrap the bread tightly in paper towels and then in plastic wrap and place on a plate. Place another plate on top of the bread and weight it down with a few heavy cans. Refrigerate and let the sandwich compress for 2 hours.

5. Unwrap the bread, slice into 4 wedges with a sharp serrated knife, and serve.

∨ ∨ ∨ ∨ ∨ ∨ ∨ ∨ ∨ ∨ ∨ ∨ ∨ ∨ ∨ ∨ ∨ ∨ ∨ ∨ ∨ ∨ ∨ ∨ ∨ ∨ ∨ ∨ ∨ ∨ ∨ ∨ ∨ ∨ ∨ ∨ ∨ ∨

**VEGAN VARIATION:** Omit the provolone cheese and make the pesto without cheese as well.

# QUINOA-STUFFED HEIRLOOM TOMATOES
# WITH ROMESCO SAUCE

*Serves 4 as a main course, 8 as a side dish*

This Middle Eastern take on stuffed tomatoes is just the thing to serve in the dog days of summer, when tomatoes are at their best. The nutrient-rich quinoa in the stuffing makes this a great entrée for vegetarians and vegans. The smoky red pepper–based *romesco* sauce pairs particularly well with lamb and beef, so these stuffed jewels are a great side dish for "steak night" too.

**ROMESCO SAUCE:**
1 pound red bell peppers, roasted (for instructions, see page 232)
1 ounce stale bread, toasted and torn into small pieces
(a scant ½ cup)
¼ cup slivered blanched almonds, toasted
2 teaspoons chopped garlic
2 tablespoons chopped and seeded tomato
½ teaspoon smoked paprika (see Glossary)
1 tablespoon red wine vinegar
2 tablespoons extra–virgin olive oil
Salt and freshly ground black pepper

**QUINOA AND TOMATOES:**
½ cup lentils du Puy (see Glossary and Resources)
½ bay leaf
2 cups water
8 large ripe tomatoes
½ teaspoon salt, plus additional
Freshly ground black pepper
½ cup quinoa (see Glossary)
1 tablespoon olive oil
¼ cup thinly sliced onion
1 teaspoon minced garlic
1 teaspoon peeled, minced ginger
½ teaspoon ground cinnamon
1 pinch ground cloves

1 cup Roasted Vegetable Stock (page 227) or packaged
   vegetable stock
2 tablespoons minced Italian parsley
1 tablespoon minced dill

1. Make the *romesco* sauce. Remove the seeds and stems from the bell peppers. Blend the peppers, bread, almonds, garlic, tomato, paprika, vinegar, and oil in a blender until smooth. Season with salt and pepper to taste. (The sauce can be made ahead and refrigerated in an airtight container for up to 4 days.)

2. In a small saucepan, combine the lentils, bay leaf, and water. Bring to a boil; reduce to a simmer, cover, and cook until the lentils are tender but not mushy, about 30 minutes. Drain in a fine-mesh sieve and discard the bay leaf.

3. With a sharp paring knife, cut off the tops of the tomatoes to create little lids and set aside. Scoop out the seeds and discard. Cut out the flesh in the center of the tomato, finely chop, and set aside. Season the tomato shells with salt and pepper.

4. Preheat the oven to 375 degrees F. Put the quinoa in the sieve, stir, and rinse under cold running water to remove the bitter coating (called *saponin*) that coats the grain; drain well. In a medium sauté pan, heat the oil over medium-high heat. Add the onions and sauté until they begin to brown, about 8 minutes. Add the garlic and ginger; sauté for 30 seconds. Stir in the quinoa, tomato flesh, the ½ teaspoon of the salt, cinnamon, cloves, and stock. Bring to a boil, reduce to a simmer, and cook until the quinoa is tender and the stock has been absorbed, about 20 minutes.

5. Spray a baking dish with nonstick cooking spray. In a medium bowl, combine the lentils and quinoa, parsley, dill, and salt and pepper to taste. Spoon the mixture into the tomatoes, replace their tops, and place in the baking dish. (The tomatoes can be made up to this point, covered with plastic wrap, and refrigerated for up to 1 day. Add 15 minutes to the baking time.)

6. Bake for 20 to 30 minutes or until the tomatoes are tender and the skins have wrinkled. Transfer to a serving plate, spoon the *romesco* sauce around them, and serve hot or at room temperature.

# ROASTED GREEK VEGETABLE PHYLLO ROLLS

*Serves 2 as an entrée, plus 4 as a side dish*

Though it's not really a special occasion, almost every Sunday I season a free-range chicken with garlic and herbs, stuff it with lemons, and roast it for dinner. The aroma of lemony roast chicken fills every room and makes loafing about the house all the more comforting. But, there is always the question of what to serve my vegetarian. These simple phyllo rolls filled with roasted vegetables and feta cheese are one of my favorite vegetarian quick fixes. I usually double the roasted vegetables and use some as a side dish for the chicken; it's hard to resist the lure of a baking sheet full of roasted veggies.

½ cup sliced red onion

6 ounces zucchini, halved lengthwise and cut into ¼-inch-thick slices (3 cups)

1 Roma tomato, thickly sliced

½ cup jarred artichoke hearts, drained and quartered

1 teaspoon chopped garlic

½ teaspoon dried oregano

1 tablespoon olive oil

Salt and freshly ground black pepper

½ cup sliced Roasted Red Peppers (page 232) or jarred

½ cup feta cheese, crumbled

8 sheets phyllo dough, thawed

3 tablespoons melted butter

1. Preheat the oven to 400 degrees F. On a rimmed baking sheet, toss the onion, zucchini, tomato, artichoke hearts, garlic, oregano, and oil. Season with the salt and pepper and roast until the zucchini is tender, about 20 minutes.

2. Place the vegetables in a medium mixing bowl and gently fold in the red pepper and cheese. Tilt the bowl to the side and let the excess liquid gather in the lowest part of the bowl for 5 minutes. Spoon off any accumulated liquid and discard (it will make the rolls soggy).

3. Line a baking sheet with parchment paper. Place a sheet of phyllo dough on a cutting board, short end facing you. (Cover the remaining sheets with a clean towel as you work to prevent them from drying out.) Brush the first sheet with the melted butter (see **TIP**). Top with another sheet, butter it, and repeat twice more to make a stack of 4 sheets. Spoon half the vegetable mixture across the short end of the stacked phyllo, leaving a 1-inch border on the sides. Starting with the end closest to you, roll up into a cylinder and place it seam side down on the prepared baking sheet. Repeat with the 4 remaining sheets of phyllo dough, butter, and filling to make 1 more roll. (The rolls can be baked up to 1 day in advance. Cover with foil and refrigerate once cool. Reheat in the oven at 350 degrees F for 10 minutes.)

4. Brush the rolls with the remaining butter and bake until the phyllo is golden brown, about 20 minutes. Cool for 10 minutes, cut each roll in half, and serve.

> **TIP:** Brushing phyllo with butter without tearing the sheet or having it flop all over the counter can be tricky. Instead, dip the pastry brush in butter and drizzle the butter over the entire sheet. Hold the sheet steady at one corner and lightly brush the drizzled butter evenly over the sheet.

ˇ ˇ ˇ ˇ ˇ ˇ ˇ ˇ ˇ ˇ ˇ ˇ ˇ ˇ ˇ ˇ ˇ ˇ ˇ ˇ ˇ ˇ ˇ ˇ ˇ ˇ ˇ ˇ ˇ ˇ ˇ ˇ ˇ ˇ ˇ ˇ

**VEGAN VARIATION:** Omit the cheese and use oil instead of butter to brush the phyllo dough.

# CARAMELIZED ONION, OLIVE, AND RICOTTA TART

*Serves 6*

This elegant tart is a cross between an eggy quiche and oniony *pissaladière*, the classic French onion tart. It's a wonderful dish when you have company coming for lunch or supper—it's light but satisfying and can be made up to a day ahead and reheated right before slicing. Serve it with a green salad dressed with lemon and your best olive oil.

1½ cups all-purpose flour

1 teaspoon salt

6 tablespoons cold butter, cut into ½-inch dice

4 tablespoons ice water

2 tablespoons olive oil

1½ pounds onions (about 2 large), thinly sliced through the root ends

Salt and freshly ground black pepper

½ cup water

15 ounces part-skim ricotta cheese

1 tablespoon minced parsley

1 tablespoon minced fresh herbs (I use a mix of thyme, sage, and rosemary)

2 eggs

¼ teaspoon ground nutmeg

¼ cup niçoise olives

1. Combine the flour, ½ teaspoon of the salt, and butter in a food processor. Pulse until the butter is in lentil-size pieces. Sprinkle the water over the flour mixture and pulse until the dough comes together. (Alternatively, work the butter into the flour with a pastry blender or your fingers and stir in the water with a plastic spatula until the dough comes together.) Transfer the dough to a sheet of plastic wrap and press into a 1-inch-thick disk. Wrap with the plastic wrap and chill for at least 1 hour or up to 2 days.

2. Set aside an 8-inch tart pan with a removable bottom. On a lightly floured work surface, roll the dough into a 12-inch round, lifting the dough and

rotating it a quarter turn after every stroke to make sure the dough isn't sticking. Transfer to the tart pan. Gently press the dough into the scalloped sides of the pan. With scissors or a paring knife, cut any of the excess dough to within ¼ inch of the edge of the pan. Push the dough out over the edge of the pan to create a small, even rim; this will prevent the crust from shrinking back into the pan. Place in the freezer for 30 minutes.

3. Preheat the oven to 400 degrees F. Place the tart shell on a baking sheet. Spray a piece of foil with nonstick cooking spray. With the sprayed side down, press the foil into the tart shell and fill the bottom with pie weights or dried beans. Bake until the crust is dry and the edges are light golden, about 20 minutes. (The tart shell can be baked up to 1 day in advance. When cool, wrap in plastic wrap and keep at room temperature.)

4. Heat the oil in a large sauté pan over medium-high heat. Add the onions and a sprinkle of salt and pepper. Cook, stirring frequently, until the onions begin to brown, about 10 minutes. Deglaze with the water, scraping up the browned bits on the bottom of the pan. Reduce the heat to medium low, cover, and cook, stirring occasionally, until the onions are deep brown and softened to a marmalade-like consistency, about 20 minutes.

5. In a medium bowl, combine the ricotta, parsley, mixed herbs, eggs, nutmeg, and the remaining ½ teaspoon of salt. Reduce the oven temperature to 375 degrees F. Remove the pie weights and foil from the tart shell. Fill the shell with the ricotta mixture and top with the onions and olives. Bake in the center of the oven until the crust is golden brown and a paring knife inserted into the center comes out with no liquid egg clinging to it, 45 to 50 minutes. Let the tart cool for 20 minutes, remove the tart pan ring, and slice into wedges. Serve, alerting diners that the olives contain pits.

# SWEET-POTATO GNOCCHI WITH SAGE AND WALNUT BROWN BUTTER

*Serves 4*

These gorgeous little sweet potato dumplings get extra protein and autumnal flavor from a toasty walnut–brown butter sauce and crispy sage. The cooked gnocchi keep well in the fridge for a few days and can be reheated in the butter sauce right before serving, so I use this recipe frequently when I'm throwing a dinner party and I aim to impress. Serve it with seared artisanal sausages or an herbed roast pork loin if you want a bit of meat for the omnivores.

1½ pounds garnet yams (or other orange-fleshed sweet potato)

1 egg yolk

1 tablespoon plus ½ teaspoon salt, plus additional

¼ teaspoon ground nutmeg

1 pinch cayenne

1½ cups all-purpose flour

Ice water, for cooling the gnocchi

2 teaspoons olive oil

¼ cup unsalted butter

15 to 20 fresh sage leaves, washed and patted dry

½ cup toasted walnuts, roughly chopped

Freshly ground black pepper

1 cup grated Parmigiano-Reggiano cheese

1. Preheat the oven to 350 degrees F. Spray a small baking dish with nonstick cooking spray. Prick the yams all over with a fork. Bake until the yams are tender when pierced with a fork, about 1 hour and 15 minutes. Transfer to a cutting board, split them open to allow steam to escape, and let cool for 1 hour. Peel the skins and discard.

2. Lightly sprinkle a baking sheet with flour and set aside. Place the yams in a medium mixing bowl and mash them with a potato masher until smooth; you should have about 2 cups. Add the egg yolk, ½ teaspoon of the salt, nutmeg, and cayenne and stir until well combined. Add 1 cup of

the flour and stir gently until you have a moist dough. Place the dough on a clean surface and gently fold and knead for 1 minute, gradually adding the remaining ½ cup of flour until you have a workable dough that is only slightly sticky. Dust the work surface with flour, divide the dough into 4 pieces, and roll the pieces into ½-inch-diameter logs. Cut each log into ¾-inch pieces and place them on the prepared baking sheet. You should have about 100 pieces. (The gnocchi can be made up to this point and frozen until firm. Transfer to 2 resealable freezer bags and freeze for up to 3 months. Simmer frozen, adding a few minutes to the cooking time.)

3. Fill a large bowl with the ice water. Line a baking sheet with parchment paper. Bring a large pot of water and the remaining 1 tablespoon of salt to a boil. Carefully drop half of the gnocchi into the boiling water, stir gently, and return to a simmer. (Make sure the water does not boil again or the gnocchi may come apart.) When the gnocchi float to the surface, cook for 1 minute. With a slotted spoon, take a piece out of the water, cut it in half, and bite into it. It should be firm but light and no longer gummy in the center. If needed, cook for 1 minute more and test again. Larger gnocchi can take up to 3 minutes to cook. Use a small sieve or slotted spoon to quickly transfer the gnocchi to the ice water. Cook the remaining gnocchi in the same way, and transfer them to the ice water. Remove all of the gnocchi from the ice water, place them on the prepared baking sheet, and toss with the oil. (Gnocchi can be prepared up to 2 days ahead. Cover with plastic wrap and refrigerate until ready to use.)

4. Melt the butter over medium heat in a large skillet or sauté pan. Add the sage leaves and cook until crisp, about 2 minutes per side. (Do not let the butter burn; reduce the heat if necessary.) Remove sage with a slotted spoon, place on a plate, and set aside. Place the gnocchi and walnuts in the pan, and cook without stirring until the gnocchi are crisped on 1 side, about 2 minutes. Toss gently and sauté until the gnocchi are lightly browned on the second side, about 2 minutes more. Season with the salt and pepper, transfer to pasta bowls, top with the sage leaves, and serve with the cheese on the side.

# QUICK-BUT-ELEGANT PESTO TARTLETS

*Serves 4 as a main course with a green salad*

My husband is a self-professed "pestophile"—put pesto in it and he'll eat it with gusto. With that in mind, I came up with these simple cottage cheese–based tartlets with ingredients I always have on hand. They're visually and texturally appealing thanks to their showy phyllo crusts, but they are a cinch to put together. They are perfect for a Mother's Day lunch or a light dinner entrée served with a nice salad.

16 ounces cottage cheese
1 tablespoon olive oil
½ cup finely chopped shallots or red onion
¼ cup sundried tomatoes packed in oil
3 tablespoons Blender Pesto (page 231), or jarred pesto
2 eggs, beaten
¼ teaspoon freshly ground black pepper
8 sheets phyllo pastry, thawed
3 tablespoons melted butter
½ cup walnuts, roughly chopped

1. Preheat the oven to 350 degrees F. Spray four 1-cup ovenproof ramekins with nonstick cooking spray; set aside. Put the cottage cheese in a fine-mesh sieve and drain off the milky liquid for 10 minutes.

2. Heat the oil in a small sauté pan over medium heat. Add the shallots and sauté until tender but not browned, 2 to 3 minutes. In a medium bowl, combine the shallots, cottage cheese, sundried tomatoes, pesto, eggs, and pepper and stir gently to combine.

3. Stack 8 sheets of phyllo dough on a work surface, the long edge facing you. (Refreeze the remaining dough for another use.) Cut the stack in half crosswise. Transfer 4 half-sheets to a clean work surface and cover the remaining sheets with a clean towel. Brush the bottom-most piece with butter, lay another piece on top at a slight angle, brush with butter, and continue with the 2 remaining pieces until you have a multipointed stack.

Gently ease the stack into a prepared ramekin, pushing downward with your knuckles so the dough rests in the ramekin and the excess dough drapes over the edges. Repeat with the remaining sheets and ramekins.

4. Place the ramekins on a rimmed baking sheet and divide the cottage cheese mixture among them. Sprinkle the tops with the walnuts and bake until the cheese mixture is set when jiggled and the dough is golden brown, about 45 minutes. Serve hot or warm. (Leftover tartlets keep for up 2 days loosely covered with plastic wrap and refrigerated. They reheat well in the microwave without sacrificing their crisp texture.)

# INDIAN SPAGHETTI SQUASH CAKES
# WITH YOGURT RAITA

*Makes 10 cakes; serves 4 as a light entrée*

These crispy, flavorful cakes are a fun alternative to traditional potato latkes during Hanukkah. Spaghetti squash cooks into spaghetti-like strands, so the painstaking grating necessary for potato latkes is eliminated. I've added Indian spices for flavor and coated the cakes in panko (coarse bread crumbs available at supermarkets and Asian groceries) to help make them extra crisp. These make a great vegetarian main course when served with the cucumber-yogurt sauce called *raita*, or you can serve them as an appetizer, perhaps with smoked salmon on the side for omnivores.

**SQUASH CAKES:**
- 1 spaghetti squash (about 2½ pounds)
- 1¼ teaspoons salt
- 1 cup warm water
- 3 tablespoons vegetable oil, plus additional for frying
- 2 teaspoons brown mustard seeds
- 1 cup finely chopped onion
- 2 tablespoons peeled, minced ginger
- 1 tablespoon minced garlic
- 1½ teaspoons ground cumin
- 1 to 1½ teaspoons minced serrano or jalapeño chile
- 3 tablespoons chopped cilantro
- ½ teaspoon freshly ground black pepper
- 1 egg, beaten
- 1½ cups panko

**RAITA:**
- 1 cup plain yogurt
- 1 tablespoon chopped cilantro
- 1 small cucumber, seeded and finely chopped
- ¼ teaspoon New Mexican chile powder
- Salt and freshly ground black pepper

1. Preheat the oven to 350 degrees F. Halve the squash lengthwise and scoop out the seeds with a sturdy spoon. Set the squash cut side up in a

9- by 13-inch baking dish and sprinkle with ½ teaspoon of the salt. Pour the water into the bottom of the pan and cover the dish tightly with foil. Bake until the squash is tender and the strands of flesh separate easily when "combed" with a fork, 35 to 45 minutes. (Alternatively, place the halves in a microwave-safe dish, add the water, cover the dish with plastic wrap, and microwave until tender, 12 to 15 minutes.) Remove the squash from the baking dish and set aside to cool. Use a fork to rake the cooked squash flesh into strands and place in a large bowl; you will need 4 cups. (The cooked squash can be stored, loosely wrapped in plastic, in the refrigerator for up 2 days.)

2. Reduce the oven temperature to 200 degrees F. Heat 1 tablespoon of the oil in a large sauté pan over medium heat. Add the mustard seeds, cover, and cook until they have popped, about 1 minute. Add the onion, ginger, garlic, cumin, and chile; sauté until the onions are beginning to brown, about 10 minutes. Add the mixture to the spaghetti squash. Stir in the cilantro, the remaining ¾ teaspoon of salt, pepper, egg, and ½ cup of the panko. Using a ⅓-cup measure, form the squash mixture into ten 3-inch cakes. Spread the remaining cup of panko on a large plate and coat the cakes with it.

3. Wipe out the sauté pan and heat 2 tablespoons of the oil over medium-high heat. Fry 4 to 5 cakes until golden and crisp, about 3 minutes per side. Transfer to a baking sheet and keep warm in the oven while frying the remaining cakes, adding more oil if necessary. (The cakes can be made up to 1 hour in advance and kept warm in the oven.)

4. Make the *raita*. Combine the yogurt, cilantro, cucumber, and chile powder in a small serving bowl. Season with the salt and pepper and serve alongside the hot squash cakes.

v v v v v v v v v v v v v v v v v v v v v v v v v v v v v v v v v v v v

**VEGAN VARIATION:** Make the *raita* with soy-based yogurt.

# BROCCOLI AND GOUDA SOUFFLÉS

*Makes four 8-ounce soufflés*

Soufflés aren't actually as difficult to make as they may seem, but don't tell your guests that! While the rest of your family is celebrating the holidays or a special occasion with a meaty roast, why not break out these easy, cheesy soufflés for the vegetarians in the clan?

I like the nutty flavor of Gouda cheese, but you could use whatever fancy cheese you have leftover from the holiday cheese board, such as Stilton, Gorgonzola, or goat cheese.

The base for the soufflés (before the addition of the egg whites) can be prepared up to a day in advance, and the soufflés themselves can be assembled up to an hour ahead and popped in the oven while the roast rests.

2½ tablespoons unsalted butter at room temperature

¼ cup grated Parmigiano-Reggiano cheese

8 ounces broccoli florets (about 3 cups)

2 tablespoons finely chopped shallots

1½ tablespoons all-purpose flour

½ cup warm milk

¾ cup (2 ounces) Gouda or other full-flavored cheese, grated

1 generous pinch freshly grated nutmeg

1 generous pinch cayenne

½ teaspoon Dijon mustard

¼ teaspoons salt

2 egg yolks

3 egg whites (see **TIP**)

⅛ teaspoon cream of tartar

1. Preheat the oven to 400 degrees F. Generously butter four 8-ounce ramekins with 1 tablespoon of the butter. Add 1 tablespoon of the Parmigiano-Reggiano to each ramekin; tap them so the cheese coats the insides.

2. Steam the broccoli until tender, about 10 minutes. Finely chop and set aside. Melt the remaining 1½ tablespoons of butter in a small saucepan

over medium heat. Add the shallots and cook until tender, about 2 minutes. Add the flour and cook for 1 minute, stirring constantly. Reduce the heat to medium low; gradually whisk in the milk and cook until very thick and bubbly, about 1 minute.

3. Take the pan off the heat and stir in the broccoli, Gouda cheese, remaining Parmigiano-Reggiano, nutmeg, cayenne, mustard, and salt. Let the mixture cool for 5 minutes. Whisk in the egg yolks, one at a time. (The soufflé base can be made up to 1 day ahead, covered with plastic wrap, and refrigerated. Let it come to room temperature before proceeding.)

4. In a large bowl, whip the egg whites with a hand mixer until frothy, about 5 seconds. Add the cream of tartar and continue to beat until soft peaks form, about 2 minutes. Gently fold a quarter of the egg whites into the broccoli-cheese mixture. Gently fold in the remaining egg whites and spoon into the prepared ramekins. Run your thumb along the inside of the rim of each ramekin, which will help the soufflés rise. (The soufflés can be kept at room temperature in a draft-free area for up to 1 hour.)

5. Place the ramekins on a heavy baking sheet and then on the center rack of the oven. Reduce the oven temperature to 375 degrees F and bake until puffed and golden, 30 to 35 minutes. Serve immediately.

TIP: It is crucial that the eggs whites are devoid of any traces of egg yolk. Any presence of yolk or oil will prevent the whites from whipping to their full volume, which, in turn, prevents the soufflés from puffing up in the oven. The best method to ensure clean whites is to break the eggs on a flat surface; over a small bowl transfer the yolk back and forth between the shell halves so the whites drip into the bowl. Transfer the clean egg white to a large mixing bowl. Repeat with the additional eggs, adding the whites one at a time to the large bowl. If a bit of yolk gets into one of the whites while you are separating it over the small bowl, you can just throw away that egg white; the others in the large bowl won't be contaminated.

# DELICATA SQUASH STUFFED WITH APPLE CORNBREAD DRESSING

*Serves 4 as a main course, with enough dressing
for 4 omnivores as a side dish*

This recipe is a great answer to the "Oh dear, vegetarians are coming to Thanksgiving dinner, what am I going to do?" question. Delicata squash filled with the same cornbread and apple dressing you serve the turkey eaters makes a special centerpiece for the vegetarians' plates without a lot of extra work. The squash is tender enough to be eaten (skin and all) with a knife and fork, and the buttery corn-like flavor marries perfectly with the cornbread and apples in the rich dressing.

I use homemade cornbread, but when time is tight store-bought cornbread works fine. Just be sure to first dry it in the oven, as explained in the recipe. The addition of chopped vegetarian sausage adds some protein and texture to the dressing, but it can be left out of the omnivores' portion if they are suspicious of anything involving tofu. The recipe for Shiitake–Red Wine Sauce (page 103) is a nice accompaniment.

**CORNBREAD:** ⅓ cup butter

1 cup cornmeal

1 cup all-purpose flour or whole-wheat pastry flour

¼ cup sugar

1 tablespoon baking powder

½ teaspoon salt

1 cup buttermilk

2 eggs

**DRESSING:** 3 tablespoons unsalted butter

1½ cups minced onion

2 stalks celery, chopped

1 tablespoon minced garlic

2 tablespoons poultry seasoning

3 cups Roasted Vegetable Stock (page 227) or packaged vegetable stock

2 vegetarian sausages (4 ounces), finely chopped (such as Field Roast Grain Meat Company's Italian sausages; see Resources)

3 tablespoons finely chopped Italian parsley

8 ounces Granny Smith apples (2 large), peeled, cored, and cut into ½-inch chunks

Salt and freshly ground black pepper

2 medium delicata squash

1 tablespoon extra-virgin olive oil

1 cup warm water or stock

1. Make the cornbread several hours or up to 3 days before making the dressing. Preheat the oven to 350 degrees F. Spray a 9- by 13-inch baking pan with nonstick cooking spray. Melt the butter and set aside to cool. In a large bowl, whisk together the cornmeal, flour, sugar, baking powder, and salt. In a medium bowl, whisk together the buttermilk, eggs, and melted butter. With a wooden spoon, stir the buttermilk mixture into the flour mixture until combined. Pour the batter into the prepared pan and bake for 30 minutes or until the top is golden and a knife inserted in the middle comes out clean. Reduce the temperature to 250 degrees F.

2. Cut the cornbread into ½-inch squares and spread them evenly on 2 rimmed baking sheets. Bake until the cubes are golden brown and dry, about 1 hour, stirring once while baking. (The toasted cornbread cubes can be made up to 2 days in advance, covered loosely with paper towels, and set aside in a cool place. Or, freeze in freezer bags for up to 2 months.)

3. Preheat the oven to 350 degrees F. For the dressing, melt 2 tablespoons of the butter in a large sauté pan over medium-high heat, add the onion and celery, and cook until the onion is translucent, about 5 minutes. Add the garlic and poultry seasoning and sauté until fragrant, about 30 seconds. Add 2 cups of the stock and bring to a simmer, scraping up browned bits on the bottom of the pan. Place the mixture in a large bowl.

4. Return the pan to medium heat. Place the remaining 1 tablespoon of butter and the vegetarian sausages in the pan and sauté until golden brown, about 3 minutes, stirring constantly. Add the vegetarian sausage, parsley, cornbread cubes, and apples to the onion-celery mixture in the bowl and toss gently to combine. Season with the salt and pepper to taste and let stand for 10 minutes. Add additional stock to moisten the dressing if necessary.

**5.** Halve the squash lengthwise and scrape out the seeds and stringy bits with a spoon. Brush the cut sides with the olive oil, season with the salt and pepper, and place them cut side up in a medium baking dish. Mound about 1 cup of dressing into each squash boat. Add the 1 cup warm water to the bottom of the dish and cover tightly with foil. Spray a medium baking dish with nonstick cooking spray, place the remaining dressing in the dish, and cover tightly with foil. (The squash and dressing can be made up to this point and refrigerated for up to 2 days. Bring to room temperature before baking.)

**6.** Bake the stuffed squash and extra dressing until the squash is tender when pierced with a fork, about 35 minutes. Uncover the stuffing and bake until crisped, about 10 minutes.

˅ ˅ ˅ ˅ ˅ ˅ ˅ ˅ ˅ ˅ ˅ ˅ ˅ ˅ ˅ ˅ ˅ ˅ ˅ ˅ ˅ ˅ ˅ ˅ ˅ ˅ ˅ ˅ ˅ ˅ ˅ ˅ ˅ ˅ ˅ ˅ ˅ ˅

**VEGAN VARIATION:** Substitute 6 cups of dry, day-old whole-wheat bread cubes for the cornbread and olive oil for butter when sautéing the onions and celery.

# SWISS CHARD GALETTES WITH GOAT CHEESE AND SOY NUTS

*Makes four 6-inch galettes*

These little rustic tarts are a great go-to menu option when you are entertaining veg-etarians. Though these ingredients give a nod to how greens are typically prepared in southern Italy, other seasonal vegetable fillings like roasted squash, roasted toma-toes, zucchini, or mashed roasted eggplant are equally tasty when tucked into this buttery crust.

CRUST: ½ cup all-purpose flour

½ cup whole-wheat flour

¼ cup fine cornmeal

1 teaspoon sugar

½ teaspoon salt

7 tablespoons cold unsalted butter, cut into small pieces

2 tablespoons plain yogurt

¼ cup cold water

FILLING: ¼ cup golden raisins

½ cup boiling water

2 bunches Swiss chard (1 pound), tough stems removed

2 tablespoons olive oil

2 cups finely chopped onions

1 tablespoon finely chopped garlic

1 teaspoon fresh thyme leaves, or ¼ teaspoon dried thyme

1 generous pinch red pepper flakes

Salt and freshly ground black pepper

4 tablespoons grated Parmigiano-Reggiano cheese

4 ounces goat or feta cheese, crumbled

¼ cup soy nuts

1 egg

1 tablespoon cold water

1. Combine the all-purpose flour, whole-wheat flour, cornmeal, sugar, and salt in the bowl of a food processor. Add the butter and pulse on and off until the mixture resembles coarse granola, about twelve 1-second pulses. (Alternatively, combine the ingredients with a pastry blender or your fingers.)

2. Whisk together the yogurt and water in a 1-cup measuring cup. Gradually add to the flour mixture with on and off pulses until the mixture starts to come together in a ball (or add the yogurt mixture and toss with a silicone spatula until the dough comes together). Gently knead the dough on a lightly floured surface until it just comes together (you should still be able to see little blobs of butter). Divide the dough into 4 equal disks, wrap them in plastic wrap, and chill for 1 hour. (If you want to prep the dough in advance, wrap the dough tightly in plastic wrap and refrigerate for up to 2 days or freeze for up to 1 month. Thaw in refrigerator completely before rolling out.)

3. Put the raisins in a small bowl, pour the boiling water over them, and let them plump for 10 minutes. In a large bowl, wash the chard leaves in 2 changes of cold water. Spin the leaves dry in a salad spinner or pat dry with paper towels; roughly chop them.

4. Heat the oil in a large sauté pan or wok over medium heat. Add the onions and sauté, stirring frequently until they are evenly caramelized, about 12 minutes. (Add a few tablespoons of water if they begin to burn.) Add the garlic, thyme, and red pepper flakes and cook for 30 seconds. Drain the raisins and discard soaking liquid. Add the raisins to the pan along with the chard; toss with tongs. Cook until the chard is wilted and tender, about 5 minutes. Remove from the heat and season with the salt and pepper to taste. Transfer to a colander and let drain until mixture is at room temperature, about 20 minutes.

5. Preheat the oven to 375 degrees F and line a baking sheet with parchment paper or foil. On a lightly floured surface, roll 1 disk of dough into an 8-inch round. Transfer to the prepared baking sheet, sprinkle the center of the round with 1 tablespoon of the Parmigiano-Reggiano, and top with a quarter of the chard mixture, leaving a 1- to 1½-inch border around the edges. Sprinkle a quarter of the goat cheese and soy nuts over the chard. Bring the edges of the dough up and over the outer edges of the filling,

gently pleating the dough wherever the edges meet. (The galettes are meant to be rustic-looking, so don't worry if they aren't perfectly round.) Repeat with the remaining dough and filling to make 4 galettes. Whisk together the egg and water and brush lightly over the galettes. Bake until the crusts are golden brown, about 35 minutes. Serve warm or at room temperature. (The galettes can be made up to 1 day in advance. Cool completely, wrap loosely in plastic wrap, and refrigerate. Let stand at room temperature for 20 minutes and reheat in moderate oven until heated through, about 15 minutes.)

ᵛ ᵛ ᵛ ᵛ ᵛ ᵛ ᵛ ᵛ ᵛ ᵛ ᵛ ᵛ ᵛ ᵛ ᵛ ᵛ ᵛ ᵛ ᵛ ᵛ ᵛ ᵛ ᵛ ᵛ ᵛ ᵛ ᵛ ᵛ ᵛ ᵛ ᵛ ᵛ ᵛ ᵛ ᵛ ᵛ ᵛ ᵛ ᵛ ᵛ

**VEGAN VARIATION:** Use chilled nonhydrogenated shortening and soy sour cream or plain soy yogurt instead of butter and yogurt in the crust. Omit the cheeses and the egg wash.

# VEGAN CHOCOLATE BIRTHDAY CAKE WITH DREAMY VANILLA FROSTING

*Serves 8 to 12*

All vegans have birthdays, and most vegans love chocolate, so there is no reason that they shouldn't be served a rich, chocolaty birthday cake just because they don't eat butter or eggs. Lisa Higgins, the owner of the wildly popular Sweetpea Baking Company in Portland, Oregon, kindly shared this recipe with me for just such occasions. This cake, like all her creations, is moist, dense, and delicious—no one will notice that this cake is vegan. It's so good, in fact, it has become my go-to birthday cake recipe, whether I'm baking for vegans or omnivores.

This recipe can also be used to make about 18 chocolate cupcakes. Halve the frosting recipe if you decide to bake cupcakes, and decorate the tops with crushed vegan sandwich cookies such as Newman-O's for a fun touch. The recipe can be made wheat-free by using spelt flour instead of wheat flour.

2⅔ cups unbleached all-purpose flour, or 3 cups spelt flour

1¾ cups sugar

1 cup cocoa powder

2 teaspoons baking powder

1¾ teaspoons baking soda

¾ teaspoon salt

2¼ cups plain (unsweetened) soy milk

½ cup canola oil

2 teaspoons pure vanilla extract

Dreamy Vanilla Frosting (recipe follows)

1. Preheat the oven to 350 degrees F. Spray two 9-inch cake pans with non-stick cooking spray. Sift the flour, sugar, cocoa, baking powder, baking soda, and salt into a large bowl.

2. In a small bowl, whisk together the soy milk, canola oil, and vanilla. Add to the flour mixture and whisk until smooth. Divide the batter evenly between the prepared cake pans and bake until a toothpick inserted into the center of the cakes comes out clean, 35 to 40 minutes.

3. Transfer the cakes to a wire rack and let them cool for 30 minutes. Invert the cakes onto 2 parchment paper–lined dinner plates and let them stand until completely cool, 2 hours. (The cake can be made up to 2 days in advance. Wrap tightly in foil or plastic wrap and store in a cool place.)

4. To frost the cake, cut a piece of cardboard into a 9-inch round and place 1 cake layer top side down on it. Hold the cake up at eye level and put 1 cup of the frosting on the top of the cake. Using an offset spatula spread the frosting over the top of the cake, moving the spatula forward in smooth movements. Repeat with enough frosting to cover the sides. Place the cake on a cake stand or serving plate. Place the second layer top side down on the frosted layer. Repeat with another frosting layer, smoothing and applying frosting until about two thirds of the frosting has been used. Place the cake in the refrigerator for 30 minutes; this will help "set" the frosting and seal in any crumbs.

5. Spread the remaining frosting over the cake, smoothing with a spatula dipped in hot water to make the frosting completely smooth. Serve at room temperature with soy- or rice milk–based ice cream.

## Dreamy Vanilla Frosting

*Frosting for one 9-inch 2-layer cake*

Only vegan *stick* margarine like Earth Balance Vegan Buttery Sticks works in this recipe. Tub margarine contains much more liquid and will not whip to the correct consistency.

> 4 sticks (2 cups) Earth Balance Natural Buttery Sticks
> 1 tablespoon pure vanilla extract
> ¼ cup soy milk
> 7 cups powdered sugar, sifted

1. With an electric mixer, beat the margarine sticks with the vanilla until fluffy, about 2 minutes. Scrape down the sides of the bowl and add the soy milk and 1 cup of the powdered sugar. Mix on low speed until combined. Scrape down the sides of the bowl again and add the remaining powdered sugar, cup by cup, until all the sugar has been added. (The frosting can be made up to 1 day ahead and refrigerated in an airtight container. Bring to room temperature before using.)

# 7

## BASICS

Here is a collection of vegetarian and vegan basic flavor anchors I turn to time and again to add "oomph" to recipes. Think of them as little insurance policies for your mixed-diet kitchen. Most of the recipes can be doubled or even tripled and kept frozen, flat, in resealable freezer bags until you need them.

# ASIAN-STYLE STOCK

*Makes 2 quarts*

This rich brown vegetable stock is a great base for Asian-flavored soups like Savory Springtime Wonton Soup (page 44), and it adds a helpful boost for stir-fries or provides a springboard for a simple vegetable soup.

1 tablespoon vegetable oil

6 green onions, roughly chopped

4 medium carrots, finely chopped (2 heaping cups)

2 stalks celery, finely chopped (1 cup)

Six ¼-inch-thick slices ginger (about 1 inch in diameter)

8 dried shiitake mushrooms

2 garlic cloves, peeled

8 cups cold water

2 tablespoons soy sauce, or to taste

1. Heat the oil in a 3-quart stock pot over medium heat. Add the green onions, carrots, celery, and ginger and sauté, stirring occasionally, until the vegetables begin to soften, about 3 minutes. Increase the heat to high and add the mushrooms, garlic, and water; bring to a boil. Reduce the heat and simmer gently for 30 minutes. Strain the stock through a fine-mesh sieve and add the soy sauce to taste. Cool completely. (Cover and refrigerate for up to 1 week or store in an airtight container or resealable freezer bag for up to 3 months.)

# NO-CHICKEN STOCK

*Makes 2 quarts*

This light-colored stock is a good alternative to chicken stock. Whenever you need a bit of stock to make a soup, risotto, or sauce but don't want to overpower the other ingredients, this quick stock will come in handy. Its flavor is full but neutral—a quality difficult to find in store-bought vegetable stocks, which tend to be very salty and taste heavily of onion.

1 large leek, white and light green parts only
1 tablespoon mild olive oil
2 large onions, peeled and roughly chopped
4 large carrots, roughly chopped
4 celery stalks, roughly chopped
5 sprigs parsley, roughly chopped (about ½ cup)
1 bay leaf
10 black peppercorns
12 cups cold water
2 tablespoons soy sauce or Bragg Liquid Aminos All Purpose Seasoning (see Glossary)

1. Remove the root end of the leek. Halve the leek lengthwise and rinse it well between the layers under cold water to remove grit; thinly slice.

2. Heat the oil in a medium soup pot over medium heat. Add the leek, onions, carrots, and celery and sauté, stirring frequently, until the onions are translucent but not browning, about 10 minutes. Add the parsley, bay leaf, peppercorns, and water. Bring to a boil over high heat, reduce to a simmer, and cook for 1 hour. Add the soy sauce to taste.

3. Strain the stock through a fine-mesh sieve. Cool completely. (Refrigerate in an airtight container for up to 1 week or freeze in resealable freezer bags for up to 3 months.)

# ROASTED MUSHROOM STOCK

*Makes 1 quart*

This stock is good for rich sauces like the brown gravy in the Hanger Steak and Crisp Polenta Triangles with Shiitake–Red Wine Sauce recipe (page 103) and rich soups that normally use beef stock, like French Onion Soup (page 31). The rich flavor comes from roasting the mushrooms to concentrate their flavor. The recipe can easily be doubled; use two baking sheets to roast the mushrooms instead of just one.

1½ pounds mushrooms (a mix of cremini, wild mushrooms, and mushroom stems and trimmings)
1 large shallot, roughly chopped (about ½ cup)
1 large carrot, chopped
2 large unpeeled garlic cloves
1 tablespoon olive oil
Salt and freshly ground black pepper
1 stalk celery, chopped
8 cups cold water
6 peppercorns
1 bay leaf

1. Preheat the oven to 400 degrees F. Wash the mushrooms in 2 changes of water; drain and spin dry in a salad spinner or pat dry with a clean dish towel. Combine the mushrooms, shallot, carrot, and garlic on a rimmed baking sheet. Toss with the oil and season with the salt and pepper. Roast, stirring once with a spatula, until the garlic has softened and the mushrooms have released their moisture and have begun to brown, about 35 minutes.

2. Transfer vegetables to a 4-quart pot; add the celery, 7½ cups of the water, peppercorns, and bay leaf. Spoon the remaining ½ cup of water onto the baking sheet and scrape the pan to get up the browned bits; pour the liquid into the pot.

3. Bring the stock to a boil, reduce the heat, and simmer gently for 45 minutes. Strain through a fine-mesh sieve, pressing on the mushrooms to extract as much liquid as possible. Cool completely. (Refrigerate the stock for up to 1 week or freeze in resealable freezer bags for up to 3 months.)

# ROASTED VEGETABLE STOCK

*Makes 1 quart*

This stock is darker and richer than the all-purpose No-Chicken Stock (page 225), but it isn't dominated by mushroom flavor as is the Roasted Mushroom Stock (opposite page). Roasting the vegetables adds another dimension of flavor; it's the best base for rich soups like the Roasted Squash or Shrimp Bisque (page 53) and for gravies used in recipes like the Primavera Potpies (page 137).

1 leek, white and light green parts only
1 large onion, peeled and cut into large chunks
3 large carrots, cut into 1-inch-thick slices
1 parsnip, peeled and cut into 1-inch-thick slices
3 stalks celery, roughly chopped
1 tablespoon olive oil
1 teaspoon tomato paste
3 tablespoons chopped parsley stems
¼ teaspoon black peppercorns
1 bay leaf
1 sprig fresh thyme
10 cups cold water

1. Preheat the oven to 400 degrees F. Halve the leek lengthwise and rinse it well between the layers under cold running water to remove any grit. Cut it into 2-inch pieces and place them on a rimmed baking sheet. Add the onion, carrots, celery, and parsnip, drizzle with the oil, and transfer the baking sheet to the center rack of the oven. Bake for 20 minutes, stir vegetables with a spatula, and continue to roast until the vegetables are beginning to brown, about 20 minutes.

2. Transfer the vegetables to a large pot; add the tomato paste, parsley stems, peppercorns, bay leaf, thyme, and water. Bring to a boil, then reduce the heat and simmer for 45 minutes. Strain through a fine-mesh sieve. Cool completely. (The stock keeps well refrigerated for up to 1 week or frozen in resealable freezer bags for up to 3 months.)

# VEGAN FISH SAUCE

*Makes about ½ cup*

Thai cooking is based on the concept of balance; nearly every dish has equal parts spicy, sour, sweet, and salty. The result is a vibrant food that jumps around on your palate. Instead of using salt or soy sauce to attain the salty part in their cuisine, Thais usually use *nam pla*, literally "fish water," or fish sauce. Fish sauce is made by salting and fermenting small fish like anchovies and draining the resulting amber liquid to use in cooking. Although it may not be that pleasant by itself, it adds a distinct flavor to Thai and Vietnamese food that is difficult to replicate for vegetarians and vegans.

You can find several vegetarian or vegan fish sauces at markets specializing in Thai and Vietnamese food, but from my experience, they try a little *too* hard to achieve the funkiness of fish sauce and miss the mark completely.

This recipe reasonably replicates the saltiness and complexity of fish sauce without the fish, and it is really tasty. If you cook a lot of Southeast Asian food, you may want to make a quadruple batch so you'll always have it at the ready in your refrigerator.

> 3 tablespoons light soy sauce
> 5 teaspoons Bragg Liquid Aminos All Purpose Seasoning (see Resources)
> 1 tablespoon sugar
> 4 teaspoons lime juice

1. Combine the soy sauce, liquid aminos, sugar, and lime juice in a small airtight container. (Keeps refrigerated for several weeks.)

# HOMEMADE SEITAN

*Makes 1 pound*

Seitan (pronounced *SAY-tan*), also called "wheat meat," is a firm, slightly chewy vegetarian protein source made from gluten, the natural protein in wheat. It's one of my favorite vegetarian protein choices because it's so versatile—it can be added to stir-fries, simmered in soup, or slathered with barbecue sauce and baked, and you never have to worry about it falling apart as you do with tofu.

Seitan comes prepackaged, though it is rather expensive (about eight dollars per pound), and the steep sodium content makes it strictly a convenience food in my kitchen. I prefer to make my own and freeze it in 5-ounce portions.

The basis for seitan is vital wheat gluten flour, a high-protein wheat flour available at health food stores (see Resources). When liquid is added, it comes together quickly into an oddly springy mass that you must knead for a few minutes. It then gets simmered in stock until it becomes a firm, some people even say meat-like, loaf.

The seasoning for this recipe is very basic; you could certainly add curry powder, Italian herbs, or Cajun seasoning for pizzazz, but keep in mind that this recipe will make enough for at least four or five servings. I normally keep the flavor neutral and let the seitan pick up the flavors of the dish I am making.

> 1½ cups vital wheat gluten flour (see **TIP**)
>
> 9 cups plus 1 tablespoon vegetable stock
>
> 1 teaspoon soy sauce or Bragg Liquid Aminos All Purpose Seasoning (see Resources)
>
> 2 tablespoons soy sauce

1. Combine the flour, 1 cup plus 1 tablespoon of the stock, and liquid aminos in the bowl of a stand mixer until the flour is moistened. Attach the dough hook and knead on medium speed for 3 minutes. (Alternatively, lightly dust a work surface with vital wheat gluten flour and knead the dough by hand for 6 minutes. Use some elbow grease; it is very springy stuff.) Wrap the dough in plastic and let it rest for 30 minutes.

2. Divide the dough into 3 balls and stretch and shape each ball into 3 strips. Cover the strips loosely with plastic and let them rest for 10 minutes. Bring

the remaining 8 cups stock and soy sauce to a simmer, add the dough strips, and cook for 45 minutes to 1 hour, flipping them once with tongs while cooking.

3. To test for doneness, remove 1 dough strip and cut it in half. Slice a thin piece from the center and taste it; if you would like the texture to be firmer, return the strip to the stock and simmer for a bit longer. When the texture is to your liking, remove the dough strips from the liquid and let them cool for 30 minutes. When they are cool enough to handle, cut into 4- to 5-ounce portions. (Refrigerate in an airtight container for up to 1 week or freeze in resealable freezer bags for up to 3 months.)

TIP: If you prefer a spongier texture, add ½ teaspoon baking powder to the flour before mixing in the liquid. Be aware that the seitan dough with baking powder will expand quite a bit while cooking, so simmer it in a large pot.

# BLENDER PESTO

*Makes about 2 cups*

The Parmigiano-Reggiano and Pecorino Romano cheeses in this pesto help balance the sweetness of the basil and the richness of the nuts. I freeze the pesto in flat sheets so I can break off just what I need without thawing a whole batch.

> 2 packed cups fresh basil leaves (about 1 ounce), stemmed
> 1 pinch sea salt
> ½ teaspoon fresh lemon juice
> 1 large garlic clove, peeled
> ¼ cup toasted pine nuts or walnuts
> 6 tablespoons extra-virgin olive oil
> ½ cup grated Parmigiano-Reggiano cheese
> ¼ cup grated Pecorino Romano cheese
> Salt and freshly ground black pepper

1. If necessary, wipe the basil with a moistened paper towel to remove any dirt. (Rinsing the leaves can wash away their aromatic oils.) Tear leaves into small pieces.

2. Put the basil in a blender with the salt and lemon juice. Halve the garlic lengthwise and discard the green sprout in the center, if present (it imparts too sharp a flavor when eaten raw). Add the garlic and nuts to the blender.

3. With the blender running and the lid slightly ajar, slowly add the oil, stopping a few times to scrape down the sides with a rubber spatula. Blend until smooth. Transfer the mixture to a bowl, stir in the cheeses, and season to taste with the salt and pepper. (Refrigerate for up to 5 days in an airtight container or freeze for up to 3 months in resealable freezer bags.)

# ROASTED RED PEPPERS

*Makes 2 cups*

Whenever red and yellow peppers come down in price even a tad, I buy a lot, roast and peel them, and store them in the fridge submerged in olive oil. These silky, smoky beauties find their way into sauces like the smoky Spanish-inspired *romesco* sauce in the Quinoa-Stuffed Heirloom Tomatoes with Romesco Sauce (page 196), sandwiches like Grilled Vegetable Wedges (page 193), and just about everything else!

> 2 pounds red and/or yellow bell peppers (about 4 medium)
> 1 medium, clean, resealable glass jar
> Olive oil

1. Preheat the broiler and adjust the rack 4 inches below the broiling element. Place the peppers on a baking sheet and broil until their skins are blackened on 1 side, about 3 minutes. With tongs, turn the peppers and continue to broil until they are blackened all over, about 10 minutes total. Place them in a large bowl, cover with a plate, and let them steam for 30 minutes. Peel off the skin and discard. Carefully open the peppers and remove the seeds and stems.

2. Pack the whole peppers snugly in the jar. Add enough of the oil to cover them completely, cover with the lid, and refrigerate until ready to use. When the peppers are gone, the oil can be used in vinaigrettes or drizzled over pasta. (As long as the peppers are refrigerated and completely submerged in oil, they will keep for up to 1 month. Or freeze them without the oil in resealable freezer bags for up to 3 months.)

# GLOSSARY

**AGAVE NECTAR:** Agave nectar is syrup made from several species of the agave plant. It is lighter in color and viscosity than honey but is quite a bit sweeter. It is vegan and therefore a good substitute for honey in most recipes.

**ALEPPO PEPPER:** An Aleppo pepper is a mild red pepper from the Middle East with a smoky, earthy flavor similar to ancho chiles (see Resources). You can substitute ancho chile powder or mild New Mexican chile powder for ground Aleppo pepper.

**BRAGG LIQUID AMINOS ALL PURPOSE SEASONING:** "Bragg's Aminos," as it is commonly called, is a liquid made from unfermented soybeans that adds a salty, savory flavor to foods. Use it as you would soy sauce to add "oomph" to marinades and sauces, but keep in mind that it is higher in sodium than soy sauce. Though it contains amino acids, it should not be considered a protein supplement. Find it at grocery and health food stores or order online (see Resources).

**BONITO FLAKES:** Also called *katsuobushi*, bonito flakes are made from dried, thinly shaved tuna. They add a rich, smoky flavor to Japanese soups. You can buy them in small plastic bags at Asian markets, especially those that cater to Japanese patrons.

**CHAYOTE SQUASH:** Chayote are a light-green pear-shaped squash with a firm texture and mild flavor. They are available at well-stocked grocery stores. Substitute peeled, diced butternut squash if chayote is unavailable.

**CHINESE BARBECUED PORK:** Chinese barbecued pork, which is coated with a bright red marinade, is sold in whole pieces or thinly sliced, often with a packet of hot mustard. It is used in soups, steamed buns, and salad rolls. Find it in the meat department at grocery stores and Asian markets, or buy it directly from Chinese restaurants that specialize in quality takeout food.

**CHINESE BLACK BEAN–GARLIC SAUCE:** This sweet-salty condiment is a kissing cousin to the more traditional fermented black beans found in some stores. Whereas fermented black beans are so salty they need to be rinsed first, black bean–garlic sauce can be added directly to stir-fries. I prefer the Lee Kum Kee brand with the red label. Fnd it in well-stocked grocery stores and Asian markets.

**CHINESE BROCCOLI:** Chinese broccoli has deep green relatively thin stalks, large deep green leaves, and tiny yellow flower buds. It has a slightly bitter, earthy flavor that pairs well with sweeter sauces like oyster sauce. It is often sold in Asian groceries as *gai lan*. Long-stemmed broccolini or standard broccoli florets can be used as substitutes.

**CHINESE RICE WINE:** This seasoning gives dishes the elusive, savory flavor present in good Chinese restaurant meals. A bottle of clear, aromatic Chinese rice wine will cost you a few dollars, last you forever, and transform all your stir-fries into authentic-tasting works of art. If you can't find rice wine, try using dry sherry instead.

**GALANGAL:** Galangal is a tough rhizome related to ginger. It has a fresh, lemon and eucalyptus-like flavor that adds great depth to soups like Tom Kha Gai or Tofu (page 37) and brightness to homemade curry pastes. It keeps well for up to 3 months in the freezer in a resealable freezer bag. Though available in dried form, the desiccated version of the rhizome doesn't have much flavor.

**GARAM MASALA:** Garam masala is an Indian spice blend made from toasted black peppercorns, cumin seeds, coriander seeds, cloves, cinnamon, and green cardamom pods. You can make your own blend by dry-toasting equal amounts of the spices and grinding them in a clean spice grinder or mortar and pestle. Premade garam masala is available at grocery stores, Indian markets, and online (see Resources).

**HARVEST 2000 VEGETARIAN BOUILLON MIX (CHICKEN FLAVOR):** This vegetarian bouillon mix makes a savory, golden stock. Though I wouldn't base a simple soup on this convenience food, it is handy in a mixed-diet kitchen when a recipe calls for small amounts of "no-chicken" stock. Find it at Asian markets or order online (see Resources).

**KOMBU:** Sheets of dried sea kelp called kombu are used to add a savory flavor to soups in Japan and other Asian countries. The sheets are deep green, almost black, when dried and have a naturally occurring white powder on them. Once they impart a soup with their savory flavor they are removed, as they are too tough to eat. Find kombu in long packages where nori and other sea vegetables are sold.

**LENTILS DU PUY:** Lentils du Puy, sometimes labeled "French lentils," are small dark green legumes that hold their shape when cooked, unlike regular brown lentils.

Find them in the bulk section of natural food stores, in precious bags in gourmet stores, or online (see Resources).

**MEXICAN OREGANO:** Mexican oregano has a stronger, less sweet flavor than Mediterranean oregano and suits spicy dishes flavored with cumin. You can find it in small packets at Latin markets or by mail order (see Resources). Mediterranean oregano will work in a pinch.

**MIZITHRA CHEESE:** *Mizithra* is a creamy, crumbly sheep's milk cheese of Greek origin. Find it at grocery stores with good cheese selections or substitute feta cheese.

**NUTRITIONAL YEAST:** Nutritional yeast is a deactivated yeast that comes in flake and powder forms. It is used in cooking to add a cheesy flavor to foods. Nutritional yeast has the added benefit of being high in B-complex vitamins. Some brands are further fortified with vitamin B-12. Find it at health food and grocery stores in the bulk foods department.

**PALM SUGAR:** A sweet, syrupy sugar made from the sap of palm trees, palm sugar is a common ingredient in Southeast Asian cuisine. It is available in Asian grocery stores and online (see Resources) in a rock-hard cake form or in jars in a softer, easier-to-measure form. Brown sugar can be substituted.

**QUESO FRESCO:** *Queso fresco* is a soft, slightly salty cow's milk cheese used in Mexican cuisine. Find it at Latin markets and grocery stores. Monterey Jack cheese will do in a pinch.

**QUINOA:** Quinoa is a grain native to South America that contains more protein than any other grain. Quinoa looks something like a tiny sesame seed, cooks in water in about 15 minutes, and tastes slightly nutty. You must rinse the grain thoroughly before cooking.

**SALTED PICKLED RADISH:** Available at Asian markets in clear packets, often refrigerated. Rinse the radish briefly and add it to Thai dishes for a salty crunch that helps replace the funky saltiness usually derived from traditional fish sauce. See Resources for mail order options.

**SAN MARZANO TOMATOES:** San Marzano tomatoes are an heirloom variety of tomato imported from Italy. They yield delicious, ripe tomato flavor and few seeds. You can buy them at grocery stores and online (see Resources).

**SHRIMP CHIPS:** Shrimp chips are a tapioca-based snack made with dried shrimp for a subtle seafood flavor. The chips puff and expand when fried, creating a lovely melt-in-your mouth snack. Find Indonesian shrimp chips (*krupuk udang*) at Asian markets; you can use the smaller, round Vietnamese shrimp chips (*bánh phồng tôm*) in their place, but they tend to be less flavorful.

**SMOKED PAPRIKA:** Made from peppers that are smoked slowly over oakwood fires for several weeks, smoked paprika adds a pungent smoky flavor to Mediterranean dishes with no spicy overtones. It typically comes packaged from Spain in lovely square tins and can be found at some grocery stores or by mail order from Penzey's Spices (see Resources).

**TAMARIND CONCENTRATE:** Made from the pulp of tamarind pods, tamarind concentrate adds a sour flavor to Indian and Southeast Asian curries, soups, dips, and chutneys. I like the Indian Tamicon brand, but Thai varieties work well, too. It is available at Asian grocery stores and online (see Resources).

**TRUFFLE OIL:** White and black truffle oils are made from olive oil that is infused with the aromatic truffle fungus and, in most cases, augmented with artificial truffle flavors. It is available at gourmet shops, grocery stores, and online (see Resources). Store in a cool, dark place and use within a few months of opening, as the flavors fade with time.

**VITAL WHEAT GLUTEN FLOUR:** Vital wheat gluten flour is made from gluten, the natural protein found in wheat. Small amounts are added to breads in commercial bakeries to add elasticity to the dough. It is also used to make homemade seitan, a chewy meat alternative used by vegetarians and vegans. Store the flour in resealable bags in the freezer; it's high protein content makes it very attractive to moths and other pantry pests. Find it at health food shops, grocery stores, and online (see Resources).

# RESOURCES

## BACON
Nueske's Applewood Smoked Meats
800-392-2266
www.nueskes.com

## BOUILLON CUBES, DEMI-GLACE BASE, STOCKS
*Vegetarian Bouillon Mix*
Harvest 2000 International, Inc.
www.amazon.com

*Chicken, Beef, and Chipotle Bouillon Cubes*
Knorr
www.letsmakeknorr.com

*Demi-Glace Gold*
More Than Gourmet
800-860-9385
www.morethangourmet.com

*Mushroom Stock*
Pacific Natural Foods
www.pacificfoods.com

*Veal Demi-Glace*
Williams-Sonoma
877-812-6235
www.williams-sonoma.com

## CHEESE AND DAIRY
*Kerrygold Vintage Cheddar and Kerrygold Pure Irish Butter*
igourmet.com
877-446-8763
www.igourmet.com

*Parmigiano-Reggiano Cheese*
igourmet.com
877-446-8763
www.igourmet.com

*Smokey Blue Cheese*
The Rogue Creamery
866-396-4704
www.roguecreamery.com

## FIELD ROAST ITALIAN SAUSAGES
Field Roast Grain Meat Company
www.fieldroast.com/wheretobuy.htm

## LIQUID AMINOS
Bragg Live Foods, Inc.
800-446-1990
www.bragg.com

## PANTRY ITEMS
*Petite French Green Lentils (Lentils du Puy), TVP, and Vital Wheat Gluten Flour*
Bob's Red Mill
800-349-2173
www.bobsredmill.com

*San Marzano Tomatoes*
CyberCucina
800-796-0116
www.cybercucina.com

*Spanish Chorizo, Truffle Oil, Porcini Mushroom Powder, and Flageolet Beans*
igourmet.com
877-446-8763
www.igourmet.com

## SPICES AND CONDIMENTS

*Curry Powder, Garam Masala, Mexican Oregano, Salt-Free Cajun Seasoning, and Smoked Paprika*
Penzey's Spices
800-741-7787
www.penzeys.com

*Tamarind Concentrate, Pickled Radish, and Palm Sugar*
Temple of Thai
877-811-8773
www.templeofthai.com

## VEGAN SUGAR

*The following is a list of suppliers and producers of vegan sugar. When in doubt about any brand of sugar, call the company and ask if the sugar is refined through active carbon, or if it is beet sugar, which is vegan.*

Florida Crystals
407-996-9072
www.floridacrystals.com

*Organic Powdered Sugar*
Hain Pure Foods
800-434-4246
www.hainpurefoods.com

*365 Everyday Value Vegan Cane Sugar*
Whole Foods Market
512-477-4455
www.wholefoodsmarket.com

# BIBLIOGRAPHY

**W**hile developing my mixed-diet method of cooking, I consulted many books, articles, and reports. The following resources have proven invaluable:

*Dietary Reference Intakes: Recommended Intakes for Individuals.* Food and Nutrition Board, Institute of Medicine, National Academy of Sciences, 2005.

Hassell, Mea and Miles, M.D. *Good Food, Great Medicine—A Homemade Cookbook: Recipes and Ruminations from a Medical Practice.* www.goodfoodgreatmedicine.com.

Kasabian, Anna and David. *The Fifth Taste: Cooking with Umami.* New York: Universe Publishing, 2005.

Nestle, Marion. *What to Eat: An Aisle-by-Aisle Guide to Savvy Food Choices and Good Eating.* New York: North Point Press, 2006.

Willet, Walter C., M.D., with Patrick J. Skerrett. *Eat, Drink, and Be Healthy: The Harvard Medical School Guide to Healthy Eating.* New York: Free Press, 2001.

# RECOMMENDED READING AND MEDIA

The following books, Web sites, and media provide useful information on sustainably raised meats and seafood and on vegetarian and vegan diets and lifestyles. A few of them may inspire your cooking as well.

*Anna Karenina*, by Leo Tolstoy (Translated by Richard Pevear and Larissa Volokhonsky). New York: Penguin Books, 2002. Enjoy with borscht or anytime.

The Monterey Bay Aquarium Seafood Watch (www.mbayaq.org) is a program that provides information on which fish and shellfish are good choices to eat, environmentally speaking. The Web site provides a handy printable wallet-size chart that recommends fish sustainably caught from healthy fisheries, helping you be a responsible seafood consumer.

PETA (People for the Ethical Treatment of Animals, www.peta.org) has an extensive fact sheet ("Animal Ingredients and Their Alternatives") listing more than 200 animal-derived ingredients that are therefore not vegan. Download it from www.caringconsumer.com/resources_ingredients_list.asp.

*Rei Momo*, recorded by David Byrne. Sire/London/Rhino: 1989. Compact disc. Recommended listing while making tamales.

The Sustainable Table (www.sustainabletable.org) features a searchable database and pointers on how consumers can find locally produced food and sustainably raised meats within their zip-codes.

Toronto Vegetarian Association (www.veg.ca) offers excellent downloadable articles on vegetarian nutrition.

The Vegetarian Resource Group (www.vrg.org) offers valuable information on nutrition, ethics, and even recipes for vegetarians and vegans.

*VegNews* magazine (www.vegnews.com) is a great resource for those interested in vegan cooking and lifestyle issues.

*Vegetarian Cooking for Everyone, 10th Anniversary Edition*, by Deborah Madison. New York: Broadway Books, 2007. Truly a great cookbook for all.

# INDEX

## M

mayonnaise, xxi

meal portions, x

meat alternatives

    alternative protein primer, xvii–xix

    mixed-diet pantry, xi–xiv

    nutrition in mixed-diet menus, xv–xix, xxii, 240

    transitioning to mixed-diet cooking, ix–x

    *See also specific type*

Meatballs, Orecchiette and, *100*, 101–2

meats, sustainably raised, viii, 240

Mexican oregano, 235, 238

milk, xvi, xxi

miso

    buying and cooking with, xvii

    Japanese Eggplant and Halibut with Miso Glaze, 69–70

    Miso Soup with Tofu or Clams, 29–30

mixed-diet cooking, vii–viii, ix–x

mixed-diet menus, nutrition in, xv–xix, xxii, 240

mixed-diet pantry, xi–xiv, xvii–xix, 237

*Mizithra* cheese, 235

monosodium glutamate (MSG), xiii

mushrooms

    Cassoulet for the Whole Crowd, 132–34

    Cedar Plank Salmon and Portobello Mushrooms with Grilled Tomato-Fennel Salad, 93–94

    Creamy Chicken or Portobello Lasagnas with Spinach Noodles, 109–11

    Grilled Vegetable Wedges, 193–95, *194*

    *Haloumi* and Chicken Souvlaki Skewers, 62–63

    mushroom powder, xi, 128, 237

    mushroom stock, cooking with, xii, 237

    mushrooms, dried, xi

    Roasted Mushroom Stock, 226

    Shepherd's Pie, 129–31, *130*

    Stuffed Chicken Breasts and Portobello Mushrooms, 79–81, *80*

    Sweetheart Mushroom Ravioli with Beurre Rouge Sauce, *182*, 183–85

    Tagliatelle Bolognese for All, 127–28

    *Tom Kha Gai* or Tofu (Creamy Coconut-Galangal Soup with Chicken or Tofu), 37–38

    *See also* shiitake mushrooms

## N

nayonaise, xxi

*nigari* tofu

    cooking with, xix, 180

    Kung Pao Chicken or Tofu, *178*, 179–80

    Pulled Pork or Barbecued Tofu Sandwiches with Sweet and Sour Slaw, 121–23

    Thai Satays with Spicy Cucumber Salad, 12–13

noodles

    Creamy Chicken or Portobello Lasagnas with Spinach Noodles, 109–11

    Crunchy Salad Rolls with Coconut Peanut Sauce, *2*, 3–5

    Curry *Laksa* (Malaysian Curry Rice Noodle Soup), 33–36, *34*

    *Fideos* with Chicken or a Poached Egg, 55–56

    Gooey Macaroni and Cheese with Tomatoes and Ham, 141–42

    Lamb and Date Tagine with Seven-Vegetable Tagine and Couscous, 158–60

    Moroccan Vegetables, Fish, and Couscous en Papillote, 95–97, *96*

    Orecchiette and Meatballs, *100*, 101–2

    Pad Thai with Shrimp or Tofu, 150–51

    Quick Tomato Basil Soup with Tortellini, 75–76

    Quickie Cannelloni, 88–89

    Spaghetti Carbonara, *64*, 65–66

    Sweetheart Mushroom Ravioli with Beurre Rouge Sauce, *182*, 183–85

    Tagliatelle Bolognese for All, 127–28

    Two-Way Lo Mein Express, *144*, 145–46

    vegan pasta, xxii

nutrition in mixed-diet menus, xv–xix, xxii, 240

nutritional yeast, xxi, xxii, 235

## O

onions

    Caramelized Onion, Olive, and Ricotta Tart, *200*, 201–2

    French Onion Soup, 31–32

    No-Chicken Stock, 225

    Paella for Everyone, 115–18, *116*

    Provençal Tomato–Fennel Soup with or without Seafood, 39–40

    Roasted Vegetable Stock, 227

    Shepherd's Pie, 129–31, *130*

    Swiss Chard Galettes with Goat Cheese and Soy Nuts, 216–18

    Tagliatelle Bolognese for All, 127–28

    Vegetable and Chicken Korma with Cashews, 171–74, *172*

    Which Came First Curry, 156–57

oregano, Mexican, 235, 238

oyster sauce, vegetarian, 76

## P

Pad Thai with Shrimp or Tofu, 150–51

palm sugar, 235, 238

panko, 108

pantry, mixed-diet, xi–xiv, xvii–xix, 237

paprika, smoked, 17, 236, 238

Parmigiano-Reggiano cheese

    Blender Pesto, 231

    buying and cooking with, xii, 32

    Creamy Chicken or Portobello Lasagnas with Spinach Noodles, 109–11

    French Onion Soup, 31–32

    Fresh Pea and Fennel Risotto with Spice-Crusted Seared Scallops, 135–36

glutamates, xiv

# ABOUT THE AUTHOR

Ivy Manning is the author of *The Farm To Table Cookbook*. Her work has appeared in *Cooking Light*, *Sunset*, and *Fine Cooking* magazines and in *The Oregonian*, among other publications. She lives in Portland, Oregon, with her husband, Gregor Torrence (aka Mr. Tofupants), and her retired greyhound, Mini. Visit her Web site at www.ivymanning.com and her mixed-diet blog at www.ivysfeast .blogspot.com.